From Torah to Paul

The author visits Rome in the summer of 2009

From Torah to Paul

The Prehistory of the Catholic Church

Karl L. Oakes

RESOURCE *Publications* · Eugene, Oregon

FROM TORAH TO PAUL
The Prehistory of the Catholic Church

Resource Publications
An Imprint of Wipf and Stock Publishers
199 W. 8th Ave., Suite 3
Eugene, OR 97401

www.wipfandstock.com

PAPERBACK ISBN: 978-1-4982-9601-4
HARDCOVER ISBN: 978-1-4982-9603-8
EBOOK ISBN: 978-1-4982-9602-1

Manufactured in the U.S.A.   NOVEMBER 14, 2016

This is the second edition of the work previously entitled *From Circumcision to Paul.*

To Denita, my long-suffering wife, the love of my life,
and the most generous human being I have ever known;
for her patience with this twenty-year project,
for cheerfully typing whenever it was needed, and
for feigning interest in what must have seemed a dry
and desolate wasteland.

History is written by the winners

—GEORGE ORWELL

History is written by the victors,
but eventually the truth comes out.

—FORMER SOUTH VIETNAMESE
AMBASSADOR TO THE US

Contents

Contents

Preface

THE EARLIEST STRATUM OF church literature does not contain a single shard of Paul. The Apostle to the Gentiles is curiously missing from all of the Christian documents from the close of the New Testament AD 70 until the emergence of the Catholic Church around AD 150. The theological genius who authored over one half of the New Testament is not mentioned once. This is all the more astounding when you realize how extensive this body of literature is:

- *The Epistle of Clement to James*
- *The Epistle of Peter to James*
- *The Recognitions of Clement*
- *The Homilies of Clement*
- *Second Clement*
- *The Epistle of Barnabas*
- *The Didache*
- *Justin Martyr's Dialogue with Trypho*
- *Justin's Martyr's First Apology*
- *Justin Martyr's Second Apology*
- *The Apology of Quadratus*
- *Papias*
- *Hegisippus*
- *Peri Pashcha*

These books present a picture of the apostolic period that is completely at odds with the New Testament record. There is no Paul and no Acts of the Apostles. Instead of ministering to Jewish believers, as in the canonical Scriptures, Peter travels up the coastline of Lebanon and Syria, preaching to great crowds and debating Simon Magus. He spends the last 25 years of his life in Rome. In this alternate universe it was John, and not Paul, who carried the Gospel of Jesus Christ to Asia Minor and Greece.

From Circumcision to Paul advances a provocative new theory of church history. The biggest controversy of the apostolic age concerned the Gentiles. Did they need to be circumcised and keep Torah, as the Jewish disciples, or was a living faith enough? After avoiding the issue for almost 20 years, the apostles were led to the understanding that we are saved by our faith in Christ.

There was, however, a small clique of believing Pharisees who believed the Law was eternal and binding on all mankind. They followed Paul around on his later journeys, and even won over the babes of western Galatia. This sect split from the New Testament fellowship around AD 60 to form their own church. They embraced circumcision, the purity laws, the liturgical prayer of the synagogues, hand-washing, praying at the third, sixth, and ninth hours, and the Jewish Passover became the Catholic Easter. This obscure sect evolved into the *Katholika Ekklesia*, not emerging from the shadows of history until the middle of the second century.

Abbreviations

Doc of Addaeus	*The Teaching of Addaeus the Apostle*
Antiquities	*Antiquities of the Jews*, Flavius Josephus
Ap Con	*Apostolic Constitutions*
Ap Trad	*Apostolic Traditions*
b.	Babylonian Talmud
Ber	*Berakhot*, a tractate of the *Mishnah* and *Tosephta*
Ep Bar	*Epistle of Barnabas*
Clem to James	*Epistle of Clement to James*
Col	Colossians
1 Cor	1 Corinthians
2 Cor	2 Corinthians
Dan	Daniel
Deut	Deuteronomy
Dial	*Dialogue with Trypho*, Justin Martyr
Did Apos	*Didascalia Apostolorum*
Eph	Ephesians
Ex	Exodus
Gen	Genesis
Gal	Galatians
Heb	Hebrews
Eccl Hist	*History of the Church*, Eusebius
Homilies	*Homilies of Clement*
Ig to Eph	*Epistle of Ignatius to the Ephesians*
Ig to Romans	*Epistle of Ignatius to the Romans*
j.	Jerusalem Talmud
Lev	Leviticus
Life	*Life of Constantine*, Eusebius
Mal	Malachi

Marcion	Harnack, Adolf, *Marcion: The Gospel of the Alien God* (Jamestown, New York: Labyrinth, 1990).
Mish	*Mishnah*
Matt	Matthew
Mur Canon	Muratorian Canon
Num	Numbers
Pan	Epiphanius, *The Panarion*
Peter to James	*Epistle of Peter to James*
Phil	Philippians
Phlm	Philemon
Poly to Phil	*Epistle of Polycarp to the Philippians*
On Prescrip	*Prescription against Heretics*, Tertullian
Mart Poly	*Martyrdom of Polycarp*
Ps	Psalms
Recog	*Recognitions of Clement*
Refut	Hippolytus, *Refutation of all Heresies*
Shape	Dix, Gregory, *The Shape of the Liturgy* (New York: Seabury, 1983).
Shepherd	*The Shepherd of Hermas*
Stromata	Clement of Alexandria, *Stromata*
Ter	Tertullian
1 Thes	1 Thessalonians
2 Thes	2 Thessalonians
Thomas	*The Acts of the Holy Apostle Thomas*
1 Tim	1 Timothy
2 Tim	2 Timothy
Tos	*Tosephta*
Wars	*Wars of the Jews*, Flavius Josephus
Rev	Revelation

Chapter One

The Background of the Schism
AD 30 to AD 60

———————

For in Jesus Christ neither circumcision availeth any thing,
nor uncircumcision; but faith which worketh by love.

—GALATIANS 5:6

THE COMPLETE STORY OF the first century Christian church has never been told. There is an abundance of clues sprinkled through the New Testament and the patristic literature, but they have been overshadowed by counterfeit documents designed to deceive and mislead. And mislead they have. The actual history of the period is dominated by a messy doctrinal dispute, false teachers who rejected the authority of the apostles, and a colossal deception, all culminating in an unrecorded schism. Perhaps we should not be surprised. Heresy, the tendency to mix the teachings of Jesus with the traditions of men, is one of the traits of human nature (flesh) mentioned on Paul's list.[1]

The young Christian movement had to contend with two distinct forms of heresy before the close of the apostolic age. The first to apostatize was a small faction of believing Pharisees. These men had grown up revering the Law of Moses; they stood in awe of its divine origin and believed it was God's will for all men and all time. They simply could not accept the decision of the apostles regarding Gentile believers. The second set of false teachers were the Gnostics. They went to the other extreme, utterly denying the God of Abraham and the covenant He had made with Moses. After

---

1. Galatians 5:19–21 The works of the flesh include conflict, dissension, and heresy. The Greek word hairesis, or heresy, literally means choice, but it is usually defined as an unorthodox or dissenting opinion which often leads to the formation of sects.

1

detaching the gospel of Jesus Christ from its Jewish base, they combined it with elements of Greek philosophy.

The religious tradition that has dominated the western world grew out of a dispute over the Law. God had revealed the Torah, the glory of Israel, to Moses amid the thundering and lightning on Mount Sinai. They were promised wonderful natural blessings and temporal advantages if they lived within its borders.

> If ye walk in my statutes, and keep my commandments, and do them; then I will give you rain in due season, and the land shall yield her increase, and the trees of the field shall yield their fruit. And your threshing shall reach unto the vintage, and the vintage shall reach unto the sowing time: and ye shall eat your bread to the full, and dwell in your land safely. And I will give peace in the land, and ye shall lie down, and none shall make you afraid: and I will rid evil beasts out of the land, neither shall the sword go through your land.

> —Leviticus 26:3–6

This covenant, though, was subject to some limitations. The blessings of Torah were given to a specific people (the Jews), who inhabited a certain land (Israel), and they were restricted to natural life. Eternal life was never part of the bargain and one influential sect, the Sadducees, did not even believe in life after death.[2] Beginning with Moses, the Hebrew prophets wrote with increasing clarity about a Messiah who would usher in an everlasting kingdom of righteousness.

When Christ came, he directed his ministry toward the lost sheep of the house of Israel.[3] Later, of course, he sent them out to the whole world, but the apostles and first disciples were all Jewish. They continued to keep the commandments of Torah and attend synagogue along with their unbelieving neighbors.[4] After the resurrection, however, they withdrew from the synagogues, and the apostles laid the foundation for a Christ-centered fellowship. They established separate gatherings for worship, instituted the breaking of bread to commemorate the risen Savior, and designated Sunday, the day of the resurrection, as the Christian day of fellowship.[5] We are not told when this happened but, according to Acts 2:42, it could not have

2. Matthew 22:23; Acts 23:8

3. Matthew 10:6

4. John 9:22, 12:42, 16:2; Matthew 23:3; Luke 23:56; Acts 11:8

5. Acts 20:7 "And upon the first day of the week, when the disciples came together to break bread, Paul preached unto them. . ."

been too long after the resurrection. "And they continued steadfastly in the apostle's doctrine and fellowship, and in breaking of bread, and in prayers."

The fledgling church grew by leaps and bounds the first few years. Three thousand souls were added on the day of Pentecost, five thousand men on another occasion, and a "multitude" of seekers came to Christ after Ananias was struck dead. The light of the glorious Gospel even penetrated into the temple. "The number of disciples multiplied in Jerusalem greatly, and a great company of the priests were obedient to the faith."[6] This was all happening within the walls of the Holy City, in full view of all Israel.

The apostles had their hands full in those early years. The first Christians broke bread in private homes, and if each one held twenty-five or thirty people, there would have been hundreds of such gatherings in Jerusalem alone. To put this into perspective, Jerusalem, a city of approximately 90,000 inhabitants, had 480 synagogues.[7] The Sadducean establishment initially reacted to the threat of mass apostasy with threats and intimidation. But after several public confrontations in the temple, they stepped it up to beatings and imprisonment. A flashpoint was reached with the trial and stoning of Stephen. Leaving the leadership behind in Jerusalem, many of the disciples fled north up the Mediterranean coastline from Samaria to Syria.

This was when the door of salvation begins to open to the Gentiles. Although they had been given a mandate to "go and teach all nations," the Christian leaders never developed a grand strategy to reach out to the countless millions outside the covenant. Catholic tradition insists that they divided up the known world amongst themselves, and each apostle was given a country to labor in.[8] However, as recorded in the early chapters of Acts, the apostles seemed almost reticent to tackle the complexities of the Gentile issue. This was uncharted territory, with delicate sensibilities to consider and weighty doctrine to decide, and they did not want to get it wrong. We get the distinct impression that God reserved the matter to Himself, taking an active role in shaping events and enlightening minds as needed. The Lord had promised that the Holy Spirit would guide them into all truth and so gradually, step by step, the young apostles were led to an understanding of His will.

The Hebrew church inherited an attitude that did more to hinder the furtherance of the Gospel than the height of the mountains or the vastness of

6. Acts 6:7

7. j. *Megillah* 73d

8. See Syriac *Teaching of the Apostles* on page 147.

the sea. The purity laws, as practiced in the first century, made it impossible for devout Jews to develop personal relationships with non-Jews, and they placed severe limitations on business relationships as well. Gentiles (*Goyim* in Hebrew) were deemed to be like men with running sores, meaning they were ritually unclean in the highest degree.[9] Uncleanness was believed to be transmittable, much like a contagious disease. A conscientious Jew would therefore never set foot in the house of a Gentile for fear of being contaminated, and sitting down at the same table would be unthinkable. The Pharisees, the "separated ones," would not even eat with the common Jewish folk, the *Am Ha'aretz*, much less with the uncircumcised. How would they ever be able to break bread together and drink from the same cup as brothers in Christ?

Peter was the instrument God used to move them beyond such a narrow view of the divine plan. One day, while up on the rooftop praying, Peter fell into a trance and saw a large sheet filled with an assortment of wild animals, reptiles, and birds let down to the ground. "And there came a voice to him, Rise, Peter; kill and eat. But Peter said, Not so, Lord; for I have never eaten anything that is common or unclean. And the voice spoke unto him the second time, What God hath cleansed, that call not thou common."[10] This was done three times, after which three men immediately knocked on the door. Peter and several others were then led to a Roman military officer in Caesaria named Cornelius. As he entered the centurion's house, the meaning of the vision suddenly dawned on Peter. "Ye know how that it is an unlawful thing for a man that is a Jew to keep company, or come unto one of another nation; but God hath shewed me I should not call any man common or unclean."[11] As Peter preached, the Holy Spirit fell upon the assembled men, just as He had on the Jews the day of Pentecost, and it was accompanied with the same miracle of tongues. The implication was not lost on Peter—"What was I, that I could withstand God"—and Cornelius was baptized.

When Peter got back to Jerusalem, he was chastized for eating and mixing with uncircumcised men. So he carefully recounted the whole incident, from beginning to end. The other apostles recognized the hand of God in it, and rejoiced that "God hath also to the Gentiles granted repentance unto life."[12] Thus was the young church delivered from the rigid traditions that had grown up around the purity code.

9. *Tosephta* Zabim 2.1; Sifra on Leviticus 15.2.74d

10. Acts 10:13–15

11. *Ibid* 10:28

12. *Ibid* 11:18

The next phase for the Gentiles involved the qualifications for admission. Were they also required to keep Torah and the traditions, like the Jewish believers, or did God have something different in mind? Because this question is so inextricably bound up with the whole conversion process, we will make a short digression at this point.

Converts to Judaism, or *ger* (meaning strangers) in Hebrew, came in two degrees of commitment. The God-fearers were Gentiles who were loosely attached to the Jewish way of life either through marriage or personal conviction. This ill-defined term is not even used in the Talmud, but it is generally understood to mean they worshipped the God of Abraham as the one true God, observed the moral aspects of the Law, and contributed the annual half-shekel tax toward the maintenance of the temple. They were the "devout" Greeks mentioned so often in the Acts of the Apostles. Cornelius, the centurion of Caesaria, "a devout man who feared God with all his household," was one.[13] Because of their respect for the *Tanakh* (Hebrew scriptures) and acceptance of its moral code, the God-fearers proved to be fertile soil for the gospel. In city after city, Paul formed the nucleus of the Christian church from the Gentile fringe of the synagogues.

The second category of proselytes, the *Ger Tzedek* or proselytes of righteousness, were full converts who entered the covenant through a tripartite ritual. The prospective convert was questioned about his motivation for joining a persecuted people. If he answered, "I know this, and I am not worthy to give my neck to the yoke of him who spake the word and world came into existence,"[14] he was accepted. He was then instructed in some of the "lighter and weightier commandments." If they still were not dissuaded, the men were immediately circumcised. Then, as soon as they had recovered, they were immersed in water or, as we would say, baptized. Finally, they were to bring their first sacrifice, usually a bird offering, to the temple. They were now considered the sons or daughters of Abraham, and bound to observe the 613 commandments of Torah.

The saints who had been persecuted during Stephen's time found safe harbor in what is now Lebanon, Syria, and Cyprus. Although the gospel was still being propagated solely within the Jewish communities, some Greeks at Antioch heard the Word and a "great number" turned to the Lord.[15] Antioch was a sophisticated cosmopolitan city, the third largest in the Roman Empire,

13. Acts 10:2
14. b. *Yev* 47a
15. Acts 11:19

and it contained a sizable Jewish community.[16] Josephus tells us that a large number of Antiochene Greeks had become Jewish proselytes.[17] Barnabas was sent from Jerusalem to shepherd the situation, and he saw the unmistakable evidence of God's favor in their lives. These *Christianoi*, or "followers of Christ" as they were now called, knew nothing of the Law; only faith in Christ Jesus. Antioch thus had the distinction of possessing the first Gentile church. Paul and Barnabas taught there a full year, witnessing the same spiritual miracle in the lives of these people as they had among the believers in Israel.

From this point on, the evangelization of the Gentile world centers on Paul. He and Barnabas left Syria to bring the resurrection message to central Anatolia. Most of the towns in this region had large Jewish populations, and they used the local synagogues as their base of operations. Using messianic passages from the Law and Prophets, they declared that Jesus of Nazareth was the long-awaited hope of Israel. In town after town, the leaders of the synagogues rejected their message and stirred up opposition against them. At Antioch of Pisidia, Paul announced that, from thenceforth, they would direct their preaching to the *Goyim*.[18] On the return trip, Paul and Barnabas separated out those who had believed, formed churches, and ordained elders. They returned to Syria, where they abode "a long time."[19]

During their extended stay in Antioch, probably between AD 46 and AD 48, Peter came up to see the Greek church for himself. He initially embraced the new converts as full brothers in Christ.[20] However, after some conservative believers from Judaea arrived, he stopped sitting at table with them and the younger apostles followed his example. Paul had a face-to-face confrontation with Peter, arguing forcefully for their freedom in Christ. These "false brethren," as Paul called them, told the Antiochene church it was absolutely necessary for them to be circumcised. They were, in effect, saying that *Goyim* had to become full Jewish proselytes and live within the bounds of Torah to be saved. Paul had a heated exchange with these men, and the issue was finally brought before the apostles and elders at Jerusalem.

The Gentile issue had been simmering on the back burner for almost two decades, and it had finally reached the boiling point. The church had to determine the mind of God on the matter. Acts 15 preserves a complete

16. *Wars of the Jews* 7.43

17. *Ibid* 7.45

18. Acts 13:46

19. *Ibid* 14:28

20. Galatians 2:11–14

transcript of the meeting convened by the apostles circa AD 49. After some initial discussion, Peter came out strongly against the yoke of Torah, reminding them that God had given the Holy Spirit to the *Goyim* as well as to them. Paul followed up by rehearsing the manifold blessings that had been showered on the Gentile believers at every turn.

When James rendered his decision, he reached back into their storied past for a precedent. In Leviticus 17 and 18, Moses named four abominations that were prohibited even to the strangers who sojourned among them. They were not allowed to eat meat offered at the alters of demons, consume blood, eat animals which had died or been torn, or engage in the sexual liaisons common among pagans. James co-opts this list, even using the same sequence as the Lawgiver. "For it seemed good to the Holy Ghost, and to us, to lay upon you no greater burden than these necessary things; That ye abstain from meats offered to idols, and from blood, and from things strangled, and from fornication: from which if ye keep yourselves, ye shall do well."[21] These four things were deeply offensive to Jewish sensibilities. James was asking the Gentiles to accept the same minimal courtesies as Moses had so the two peoples could be united into one.

This decision only applied to Gentiles. The Palestinian Christians continued to circumcise their children and live the Jewish lifestyle. As the Jerusalem elders said to Paul on the occasion of his last home visit in AD 58. "Thou seest, brother, how many thousands of Jews there are which believe; and they are all zealous of the law: and they are informed of thee, that thou teachest all the Jews which are among the Gentiles to forsake Moses, saying that they ought not to circumcise their children, neither to walk after the customs."[22] Then, in order to quell rumors he had been teaching Jews to forsake Moses, Paul was told to engage in a purification ritual to demonstrate that he "walked orderly and kept the law."[23] They were not entirely free of the Law until the temple was set ablaze in early August, AD 70.[24] Without the Temple, it was no longer possible for anyone, Jew or Christian, to live by Torah.

What do we know about the opposition party? Paul makes the point in 2 Corinthians that they were Israelites, just as he was.[25] Acts 15:5 tells us

21. Acts 15:28–29; also 21:25

22. *Acts* 21:20–21

23. *Acts* 21:24

24. *Wars of the Jews* 6.4.5

25. 2 Corinthians 11:22

that they were Pharisees, and quite possibly teachers of the law.[26] But Paul, who had sat "at the feet of Gamaliel and been taught according to the perfect manner of the law," was not impressed.[27] To him they were simply "false brethren brought in unawares," nothing more, and he did not even bother to learn their names.[28]

The Pharisees were the largest branch of Judaism. Because they taught and officiated in the local synagogues, they had the backing of the common people. The Pharisees taught that the divine revelation given at Mt. Sinai not only included the written law, the five books of Moses, it also included the oral law. Known as the "traditions of the elders" in the New Testament, this was a body of rabbinical rulings that had built up over the centuries as a kind of case law to interpret the words of Moses.

The second defining characteristic of the Pharisees was a belief in the priestly sanctity of all Israel, citing Exodus 19:5, 6. The purity required of priests and Levites in the temple was extended into the homes of ordinary Israelites, particularly in their mealtime rituals. The food on the table was considered the offerings on the altar and the cleanliness required of priests was made mandatory in the kitchen. The rituals taken from the temple service include the washing of hands, the boiling of pots and pans, the humane method of slaughtering animals, and the various blessings recited over the food. All of these have become staples of Jewish domestic piety.

> **The Oral Law** – As teachers of the Law, the Pharisees were often asked to provide guidance on what was permissible. They tried to keep the people at a safe distance from forbidden ground or, as they put it, to "build a fence around the Torah." The body of legal opinions which resulted is known as the Oral Law, and to the Pharisees, it was just as binding as the Written Law. The followers of Rabbi Hillel were generally more lenient in their rulings, while the house of Shammai was known to be stricter.
>
> Moses forbade work on the Sabbath, but what exactly constitutes work? We are given a definitive answer in the Mishnaic tractate *Shabbat* 7:2. "A. The generative categories of acts of labor [prohibited on the Sabbath] are forty less one: B. (1) he who sews, (2) ploughs, (3) reaps, (4) binds sheaves, (5) threshes, (6) winnows, (7) selects [fit from unfit produce], (8) grinds, (9) sifts, (10) kneads, (11) bakes; C. (12) he who shears wool, (13) washes it, (14) beats it, (15) dyes it; D. (16) spins, (17) weaves, E. (18) makes two loops, (19) weaves two threads, (20) separates two threads..."

---

26. "But there rose up certain of the sect of the Pharisees which believed, saying, that it was needful to circumcise them, and to command them to keep the law of Moses."

27. Acts 22:3

28. Galatians 2:4

The false apostles taught that these laws and traditions were binding on all Christians, including Gentiles, and should have a place in the New Covenant. There was some merit to their position. Did not the Lord keep the law his entire life, and did he not *seem* to tell his disciples it was meant for all time? He even instructed his disciples to follow the temple rites and respect the authority of the rabbis.[29] At the very beginning of his public ministry, in the Sermon on the Mount, Jesus sought to show a continuity between the divinely-inspired Torah and his teachings.

> Think not that I am come to destroy the law, or the prophets: I am not come to destroy, but to fulfill. For verily I say unto you, Till heaven and earth pass, one jot or one tittle shall in no wise pass from the law, till all be fulfilled. Whosoever therefore shall break one of these least commandments, and shall teach men so, he shall be called the least in the kingdom of heaven: but whosoever shall do and teach them, the same shall be called great in the kingdom of heaven.

> —Matthew 5:17–19

The meaning of "fulfill" is admittedly open to interpretation. The Greek word itself means "to become," or "come to pass;" or as we might say, "to complete." Paul's understanding of the term can be found in two of the epistles he wrote to combat the Judaizers. "For all the law is fulfilled in one word, even in this; Thou shalt love thy neighbor as thyself."[30] "Love worketh no ill to his neighbor: therefore love is the fulfilling of the law."[31]

The arguments advanced by the dissenters have been preserved in some of the earliest literature of the church. The so-called *Epistle of Peter to James* has "Peter" warning the flock against a Christian evangelist who is disparaging the Law, an obvious reference to Paul. Directly contradicting the decision reached by the apostles in Acts fifteen, they openly proclaim the "eternal continuance" of the Torah.

> The fraudulent *Epistle of Peter to James* was one of the founding documents of the Catholic Church. It was produced very close to AD 70. The letter was designed to give their converts confidence in the false apostles, and to introduce a new book to their canon of Scripture.

> For some from among the Gentiles have rejected my legal preaching, attaching themselves to certain lawless and trifling preaching of the man who is my enemy. And these things some have

---

29. Matthew 8:4; 23:2, 3, 23:23
30. Galatians 5:14
31. Romans 13:10

attempted while I am still alive, to transform my words by various interpretations, in order to the dissolution of the law; as though I also myself were of such a mind, but did not freely proclaim it, which God forbid! For such a thing were to act in opposition to the law of God which was spoken by Moses, and was borne witness to by our Lord in respect of its eternal continuance; for thus he spoke: 'The heavens and the earth may pass away, but one jot or one tittle shall in no wise pass from the law.'

—Epistle of Peter to James 1

The *Apostolic Constitutions* lists two additional reasons the Torah was meant to be eternal, along with the previous justification from Matthew. This fourth century Syrian document was the great literary storehouse of the ancient church, preserving many old liturgies, church orders, ecclesiastical canons, and miscellaneous material. The following passage takes us back to the days of the founding.

> The *Apostolic Constitutions* was the last of the great church orders, compiled in Syria around AD 380. It has preserved significant material from the earliest days of the church, including much of the first century *Didache* and the third century *Didascalia Apostolorum*. Like the other church orders, it claims to be the words of the apostles.

Remember ye the law of Moses, the man of God, who gave you commandments and ordinances.' Which law is so very holy and righteous, that even our Saviour, when on a certain time He healed one leper, and afterwards nine, said to the first, 'Go show thyself to the high priest, and offer the gift which Moses commanded for a testimony unto them;' and afterwards to the nine, 'Go, show yourselves to the priests.' For nowhere has He dissolved the law, as Simon [i.e., Paul] pretends, but fulfilled it; for He says: 'One iota, or one tittle, shall not pass from the law until all be fulfilled.' For says He, 'I am not come to dissolve the law, but to fulfil it.' For Moses himself, who was at once the lawgiver, and the high priest, and the prophet, and the king, and Elijah, the zealous follower of the prophets, were present at our Lord's transfiguration in the mountain, and witnesses of His incarnation and of His sufferings, as the intimate friends of Christ, but not as enemies and strangers. Whence it is demonstrated that the law is good and holy, as are the prophets.

—Apostolic Constitutions 6.1.19

For reasons that will become clear later, Simon was their code name for Paul.

Paul regarded these misguided men as "false brethren" when he confronted them at Antioch. However, once they began pushing their message in the churches he had founded, he began to view them in a harsher light. In his second letter to the Corinthians, he started to call them "false apostles." "For such are false apostles, deceitful workers, transforming themselves into the apostles of Christ. And no marvel; for Satan himself is transformed into an angel of light. Therefore it is no great thing if his ministers also be transformed as the ministers of righteousness; whose end shall be according to their works."[32]

We may possess the actual identities of these men. The same roster of twelve names appears, with only minor deviations, three times in the pseudo-Clementine literature. "Of whom, next to Peter, Zacchaeus was first, then Sophonius, Joseph and Michaeus, Eleazar, Phineas, Lazarus, and Elisaeus: after these I Clement and Nicodemus; then Niceta and Aquila, who had formerly been disciples of Simon and were converted to the faith of Christ under the teaching of Zacchaeus."[33] The list is probably a blend of truth and fiction, but by embedding the names in their sacred text, they were able to establish a plausible link between the leading apostles and the men they were sending with the alternate gospel.

> **Clementine Literature** – One of the founding books of the 1st century Catholics was the *Preaching of Peter*. It has been lost to history, but two recensions have survived, known as the *Recognitions of Clement* and *the Homilies of Clement*. They are often referred to as the **Clementine literature** or the **pseudo-Clementines**. They are an alternate account of the apostolic period in which Peter plays the prominent role.

The ringleader of the movement may have been the Zacchaeus who, next to Peter in the above statement, was declared to be "first." He is singled out for more attention and honor in the pseudo-Clementines than anyone other than Clement. At Caesaria, the home town of Zacchaeus, "Peter" endows him with all the authority and pretensions of a medieval pope.

> I have ordained Zacchaeus as a bishop for you, knowing that he has the fear of God, and is expert in the scriptures. You therefore ought to honor him as holding the place of Christ, obeying him for your salvation, and knowing that whatever honor and whatever injury is done to him, redounds to Christ, and from Christ to God. Hear him therefore with all attention, and receive from him the doctrine of the faith.
>
> —*Recognitions of Clement* 3.66

---

32. 2 Corinthians 11:13–15
33. *The Recognitions of Clement* 2.1; also *Recognition* 3.68; *Homilies* 2.1

This shadowy figure, remembered in Catholic tradition as the first bishop of Caesaria, may have been the man Paul debated at Antioch."[34]

The false apostles tried every tactic they could to drive a wedge between Paul and the churches he had founded. They challenged his doctrine, cast doubt on his claims of direct revelation, disputed his apostleship, and questioned his standing with the mother church. They made him out to be a renegade and a rogue, preaching on his own without authorization from James. This was their initial approach, which we read about in the pages of the New Testament.

One of their strategies was to follow Paul and win over his converts. As incredible as it sounds, this plan has been preserved in the earliest literature of the Church. They have "Peter" speaking in this fictional account.

> He addressed us to the following effect: 'Let us, my brethren, consider what is right; for it is our duty to bring some help to the nations, which are called to salvation. You have yourselves heard that Simon [i.e., Paul] has set out, wishing to anticipate our journey. Him we should have followed step by step, that whosesoever he tries to subvert any, we might immediately confute him. . . . I wish you the day after tomorrow to proceed to the Gentiles, and to follow in the footsteps of Simon, that you may inform me of all his proceedings.'

> —*Recognitions of Clement* 3.68

They even had a convoluted explanation why Paul came first with the gospel and they followed later. It is found in the *Homilies of Clement*, and we will provide an extended quotation as the last few sentences provide us with a window into their view of Paul:

> As in the beginning God, who is one, like a right hand and a left, made the heavens first and then the earth, so also He constituted all the combinations in order; but upon men He no more does this, but varies all the combinations. For whereas from Him the greater things come first, and the inferior second, we find the opposite in man—the first worse, and the second superior. . . . It is possible, following this order, to perceive to what series Simon belongs, who came before me to the Gentiles, and to which I belong who have come after him, and have come in unto him as light upon darkness, as knowledge upon ignorance, as healing upon disease. And thus, as the true Prophet has told us, a false prophet must first come

---

34. *Apostolic Constitutions* 7.46

from some deceiver; and then, in like manner, after the removal of the holy place, the true Gospel must be secretly sent abroad for the rectification of the heresies that shall be . . . Since then, as I said, some men do not know the rule of combination, thence they do not know who is my precursor Simon. For if he were known, he would not be believed; but now, not being known, he is improperly believed; and though his deeds are those of a hater, he is loved; and though an enemy, he is received as a friend; and though he be death, he is desired as a savior; and though fire, he is esteemed as light; and though a deceiver, he is believed as a speaker of truth.

—The Homilies of Clement 2

The first attempt of the false apostles was also their most successful. When Paul made his third journey through central Anatolia, they followed hard on his heels. All we know about this mission is contained in just one line. "He departed [from Antioch], and went over all the country of Galatia and Phrygia in order, strengthening all the disciples."[35] As Paul passed through Galatia and Phrygia, he led the false apostles straight to these disciples. Some of these unidentified churches were just babes in Christ, and they were won over by the legalists. Paul and Timothy spent the next two years at Ephesus, where Paul wrote to the Galatian churches. "I marvel that ye are *so soon* removed from him that called you into the grace of Christ unto another gospel."[36] The Galatians were, by this time, already observing the Jewish calendar and considering the step of circumcision."[37]

There is much speculation about the location of these churches. They were not the saints in Lystra, Derbe, and Iconium that Paul converted on his first mission and then confirmed with James' letter on his second. No, the Galatian schismatics resided further west, in the western part of the Turkish Lake District. We are told nothing about the origin of these churches, but possibly they had been planted by Epaphras when he preached in nearby Colosse.[38]

They next set their sights on the Corinthians. Paul had planted the gospel at Corinth during his first journey into Greece, in AD 51, and he ended up staying there a year and six months."[39] When he wrote his first

35. Acts 18:23; also 19:1

36. Galatians 1:6, emphasis mine

37. Galatians 4:10, 5:3, 6:12

38. Colossians 1:7

39. Acts 18:11

epistle to the Corinthians in AD 57, there was some talk of circumcision and his rights as an apostle, but by and large he is giving normal pastoral advice. However, when Paul wrote 2 Corinthians less than a year later, he was forced to vigorously defend his doctrine and apostleship.[40] The false apostles had apparently visited the Greek churches that summer and pressed their case.

They told the Corinthians to ask Paul for written proof of his backing by the Christian leaders and, incredibly, a record of this has survived.

> Wherefore observe the greatest caution, that you believe no teacher, unless he bring from Jerusalem the testimonial of James the Lord's brother, or of whosoever may come after him. For no one, unless he has gone up thither, and there has been approved as a fit and faithful teacher for preaching the word of Christ—unless, I say, he brings a testimonial thence, is by any means to be received. But let neither prophet nor apostle be looked for by you at this time, besides us.

> *—Recognitions of Clement* 4.35

> Wherefore, above all, remember to shun apostle or teacher or prophet who does not first accurately compare his preaching with that of James [alternate translation: ". . . unless he come to you with credentials of James . . ."] who was called the brother of my Lord, and to whom was entrusted the administration of the church of the Hebrews in Jerusalem, and that even though he come to you with witnesses.

> *—Homilies of Clement* 11.35

They were deliberately being deceitful. It is true that the Sanhedrin sent their written communiqués to the Jews of the Diaspora by special messengers, the *Selihim*, but in lieu of that, Peter, James, and John had extended the right hand of fellowship to Paul, acknowledging his right to minister to the heathen.[41] The laying on of hands, known as *Semikhah*, was in fact the customary way to convey rabbinical authority.[42] The false apostles pounced on this, and pointed out that Paul could produce no such documentation. We have Paul's reaction in his second epistle to the Corinthians. "Do we begin to commend ourselves? Or need we, as some others, epistles of commendation

---

40. Chapters 3 and 11

41. Galatians 2:9

42. 1 Timothy 4:14; 2 Timothy 1:16; Acts 6:6

to you, or letters of commendation from you?" He pointed out that the ministration of the Spirit in their lives was better evidence of his apostleship than any letter ever written. "Ye are our epistle written in our hearts, known and read of all men. Forasmuch as ye are manifestly declared to be the epistle of Christ ministered by us, written not with ink, but with the Spirit of the living God; not in tables of stones, but in fleshy tables of the heart."[43]

The Torah-observant teachers also attacked his penchant for mystical visions and dreams. To be sure, Paul was vulnerable to these charges. His conversion on the road to Damascus was accompanied by a blinding light from heaven and the audible voice of the Lord.[44] In relating this, he told the Galatians he had not received the gospel from man, but by a direct revelation from the Lord.[45] On another occasion, which Paul related to the Corinthian church, he had been raised up to the third heaven and heard unspeakable things.[46] All of this was fair game with which to discredit him.

Their arguments can be found in the *Homilies of Clement*. It devotes five full chapters to debunking visions as a means of acquiring spiritual insight.

> And Peter said: For your proposition was that one is better able to know more fully when he hears because of an apparition than when he hears with his own ears; but when you set about the matter, you were for persuading us that he who hears through an apparition is surer than he who hears with his own ears. Finally, you alleged that, on this account, you knew more satisfactory the doctrines of Jesus than I do, because you heard His words through an apparition. . . But he who trusts to apparition or vision or dream is insecure. For he does not know to whom he is trusting. For it is possible either that he may be an evil demon or a deceptive spirit, pretending in his speeches to be what he is not.

—*The Homilies* of Clement 17.14

Paul worked tirelessly to contain the heresy and keep it from spreading. Before his last trip into Greece, he left Timothy at Ephesus to guard the flock against "the teachers of the law."[47] On his return, he warned the Ephesian elders against the "grievous wolves" that were coming their way.[48]

43. 2 Corinthians 3:1–3
44. Acts 9:1–9
45. Galatians 1:11–12
46. 2 Corinthians 12:1–4
47. 1 Timothy 1:3–7
48. Acts 20:20

According to the book of Revelation, Paul's efforts in Ephesus were ultimately successful. "Thou hast tried them which say they are apostles, and are not, and hast found them liars."[49]

The crisis could not have come at a worse time. Paul was imprisoned in Caesaria from AD 58 to AD 60 and, after being taken to Rome, remained in military custody until at least AD 62. Although he had extraordinary liberty for a prisoner, even to the extent of having his own rented house, it must have been a very frustrating time.[50] Paul knew exactly what was going on, but he was powerless to help out in person.

The Date of the Schism

The New Testament does not tell us how or when they finally broke communion. Things were definitely coming to a head when Paul wrote to the Galatians AD 56. Although still in fellowship, they had started to observe "days and months and times and years."[51] The problem was uppermost in Paul's mind in all of the epistles he wrote at this time, including Romans, 1 Timothy, Titus, and 2 Corinthians. When he left Timothy at Ephesus in AD 57, he wrote to him contrasting the law-gospel with the true gospel. "Now the end of the commandment is charity out of a pure heart, and of a good conscience, and from faith unfeigned: from which some having swerved have turned aside unto vain jangling, desiring to be teachers of the law; understanding neither what they say, nor whereof they affirm."[52] He also sent Titus to Crete that year to ordain solid elders and purge the churches of legalism. "For there are many unruly and vain talkers and deceivers, specially they of the circumcision: whose mouths must be stopped, who subvert whole houses, teaching things they ought not, for filthy lucre's sake". . . . "Wherefore rebuke them sharply, that they may be sound in the faith; not giving heed to Jewish fables, and commandments of men, that turn men from the truth."[53]

Relying on the limited Biblical evidence at our disposal, we can safely say that the schism did not happen before AD 56. On the other hand, we will adduce several lines of evidence below which show they were on their

49. Revelation 2:2
50. Acts 28:30
51. Galatians 4:10
52. 1 Timothy 1:5–7
53. Titus 1:10–14

own by AD 62. We thus have a set of bookends which bracket the date of the breach. We conclude that, after trying to influence the Christian movement for over a decade from the inside, the false apostles were largely on their own by AD 60.

The first century Catholics did not possess the Gospel of Luke, a fact which will help us date their departure. When Luke was in Rome, he wrote two manuscripts in rapid succession: The Gospel that goes under his name, and the Acts of the Apostles. Acts brings the history of the church up to about AD 62, and the open line tells us that the "former treatise"— the Gospel of Luke—was written sometime before. How much before is an open question, but presumably it was not more than a year or two. This provides us with a *terminus ad quem* for the publication of the third Gospel. We infer that the proto-Catholics were out of fellowship before Luke published his Gospel in the early sixties.

A terminus may also be deduced from the death of James, the Lord's brother. There are two accounts of his martyrdom extant. According to the historian Josephus, Ananus, the high priest, saw an opportunity to get rid of the Christian leader during a vacancy of the procuratorship after the death of Festus in AD 62. Ananus sentenced James and his companions to be stoned "as breakers of the Law" before Festus's replacement arrived.[54] Josephus's testimony in this regard is particularly credible. It appears from the *Life of Flavius Josephus* that he may have lived in Jerusalem at the time, but whether he did or not, he personally knew many of the priests and politicians involved.

The second century version transmitted by the Catholic gadfly Hegesippus is absurd on its face. The priests supposedly ask James, the Lord's brother, to stand on the parapet wall of the temple and tell the Passover crowd that Jesus was not the Messiah. When James declares that Jesus was sitting at the right hand of God, he is pushed from the heights and clubbed to death. The date implied in this tale is just as fallacious as the story line: "And immediately Vespasian besieged them."[55] Vespasian assumed command of the Judean conflict early in AD 67. The

> **Hegisippus** – A converted Jew who visited many of the Catholic congregations in the middle of the second century. He gathered up the oral traditions of the Church and set them down in a now-lost book, *The Memoirs*. Fortunately, Eusebius, the fourth century historian, has preserved many passages in his *History of the Church*.

54. *Antiquities of the Jews* 20.9
55. *History of the Church* 2.23

proto-Catholics were thus outside the camp before AD 62, when James was martyred, or they would not have concocted this story.

The Place of the Schism

There is no doubt where the proto-Catholic teaching first took root and grew. The strongest evidence is Biblical, and it points directly toward central Anatolia. That is where the seeds of Jewish Christianity were first sown, and according to the Galatian epistle, they had been well received. Some of the men had been circumcised or were considering it. They had also started to keep the Sabbath, the new moon ceremonies, and the annual festivals.[56] The most important of these was the Passover, which they observed on the same day as the Jews—the 14th of Nisan.

This assumes importance because, by the end of the second century, it had become standard throughout Christendom to observe Easter on Sunday, except in one or two pockets. One of these was the ancient heartland of the movement. These churches stubbornly continued with the traditional date, the day when Israel partook of the lamb and the bitter herbs. Polycrates, the bishop of Ephesus, wrote a brilliant defense of the ancient date which has been preserved in Eusebius.[57] He provides us with a list of churches which kept the 14th of Nisan Easter: Ephesus, Smyrna, Hierapolis, Laodicea, Sardis, and Eumenia. These six cities all lie within a narrow belt in western Turkey. This region is about fifty miles wide along the Aegean Sea, and it extends easterly up two river valleys, the Meander and the Hermus, about one hundred fifty miles. It lies entirely within the Roman province of Asia, with one notable exception.

> **Quartodecimans** – The first Catholics adopted all of the Jewish holy days, including Passover. They used the same lunar-based formula as Moses, which was the 14th day of the first month Nisan. Early in the second century, the Roman church started to use the Sunday following, which became standard everywhere except in the ancient homeland of Anatolia and parts of Syria. Quartodeciman is simply Latin for "Fourteenthers."

The easterly-most city of the Quartodeciman belt was Eumenia. It lies on the edge of the Turkish Lake District, a place where many geographic and political designations overlap. It could rightfully be called Phrygia, Pisidia, Asia, or Galatia.

56. Galatians 4:10
57. *History of the Church* 5.24

If we continue further east, to Antioch, Iconium, and the other churches of Paul's first mission, the paschal landscape changes dramatically. There is no indication that the churches in that district ever observed the 14th of Nisan Easter. The Christianity which was introduced to central Anatolia in the third century was perfectly orthodox.[58] We have thus gone too far. We conclude that the primary recipients of Paul's epistle to the Galatians resided in the western half of the Lake District, although some of the letter seems to be directed toward the saints of the first mission.[59] Eumenia is located near the modern city of Civril. A quick glance at the map shows that it lies about 75 miles from ancient Philadelphia and the same distance from the Hierapolis/Colosse/Laodicea triangle. Both of these areas had seen the arrival of the false apostles or been influenced by their doctrine in New Testament times.[60] Paul had warned the Colossian saints about the Jewish calendar, dietary laws, and circumcision in the second chapter of his epistle to the Colossians. Hierapolis and Laodicea, less than ten miles from Colosse in the Lycus Valley, were two of the Quartodeciman churches on Polycrate's list. And Papias, the earliest genuine Catholic author whose writings have been preserved, lived above the gleaming white cliffs at Hierapolis.

The ancient city of Apamea, now called Dinar, lies just outside the Quartodeciman belt. Sitting astride the great east-west trade route, and commanding the road to the prosperous Meander valley, it was one of the greatest cities in Asia Minor. Apamea contained a very sizable Jewish population, going back to BC 200 when Antioch the Great transplanted 2,000 Jewish families to Anatolia.[61] They grew so numerous that by BC 62, the Roman consul seized almost 16 lbs. of gold bound for the temple in Jerusalem.[62] The Babylonian Talmud reports disapprovingly just how worldly these Jews had become. "The wines and baths of Phrygia have separated the ten tribes from their brethren in Israel."[63]

---

58. Gregory Thaumaturgis, who had studied under Origen in Palestinian Caesaria, brought Catholicism to Cappadocia in the AD 240s. He was based in Caesaria Mazaca, modern day Kayseri.

59. Galatians 4:13-15

60. Revelation 3:9, Colossians 2:11–17

61. *Antiquities of the Jews* 12.34

62. Cicero, *Pro Flacco* 28.68

63. b. *Shabbat* 147b

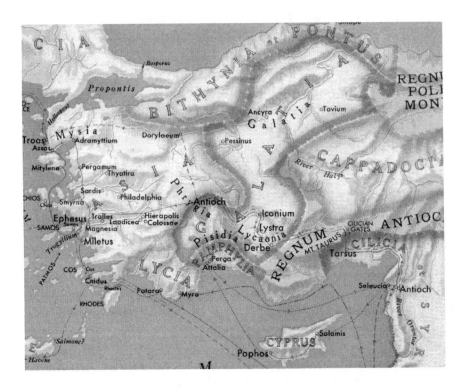

The false apostles broke from the New Testament fellowship to form their own church. This insignificant sect evolved and grew, and 100 years later, gave themselves the grandiose name of *Katholika Ekklesia*, the Universal Church. This book tells the untold story of their early development, which has heretofore been hidden from the prying eyes of history.

The imprint left by the first century founders is still visible in the doctrine, liturgy, and practices of the Great Church. The similarities of the Jewish and Catholic traditions can be readily seen by comparing the second and third columns below. To show just how far this diverges from the New Testament model, the corresponding practice of the apostles is provided in the first column.

	New Testament Christianity	Law of Moses, Jewish Traditions	First Century Catholic congregations
1.	No liturgy; used extemporaneous prayer	Synagogues used the Eighteen Benedictions	Synagogue benedictions were rewritten to become the liturgy of the church
2.	Did not adopt the hand-washing rituals of the Pharisees	Pharisees observed Levitical washings taken from the temple	Washed hands before meals, before prayer, and after sleeping
3.	Sex, menstruation, or childbirth not considered unclean	Observed the Levitical family purity laws	Separated during menstruation, washed after sex, practiced churching of women after childbirth
4.	Gentile believers did not keep the Jewish calendar	Observed annual feasts and holy days	Observe church or liturgical calendar
5.	Passover became the breaking of bread	*Pesah* was the highlight of the religious calendar	Observed Passover, which evolved into Easter
6.	Gentiles were not taught set days of fasting	Pharisees fasted twice/week and Day of Atonement	Fasted twice/week and six days before Pascha
7.	Gentile given no set times for prayer	Prayed daily at the third, sixth, and ninth hours	Taught to pray at the third, sixth, and ninth hours
8.	Baptism consisted solely of immersion	Had three-step conversion ritual	Adopted three-step proselyte ritual
9.	Ministry privately supported by believers	Priests received the first-fruits, dough offering	False apostles received first-fruits, dough offering

Chapter Two

The Founding Charter

AD 70 to AD 75

For we know that Simon and Cleobius, and their followers,
have compiled poisonous books under the name of Christ and
his disciples, and do carry them about in order to deceive you.

— *THE APOSTOLIC CONSTITUTIONS* 6.16

SHORTLY AFTER THE FALL of Jerusalem in AD 70, the false apostles changed
their tactics and embarked upon a new plan. They had not been able to prevail against Paul by persuasion or debate, so they decided to demonize him.
Paul the apostle became Simon the Sorcerer, the blackest of false prophets.
This fictitious character was regarded by the Church as the fountainhead of
all heresy well into the Middle Ages.

They were so certain the apostles had taken a wrong turn in regards to
the Law, one that Christ himself would have opposed, that they felt duty-
bound to rectify the mistake. They truly believed the salvation of the world
rested on their shoulders. "If they should be corrupted by any daring man,
or be perverted by interpretations, as you have heard that some have already done, it will remain for those who really seek the truth to always
wander in error."[1] So they manufactured fictitious letters and books that
interwove Peter and James into a believable historical narrative. The strategy was to clothe their legalistic doctrine with the cloak of apostolic authority, and it succeeded brilliantly. Because their first converts lived in isolated,
remote villages, they did not realize the false apostles were actually apostate

---

1. *Epistle of Peter to James* 5

teachers. They sincerely believed what they were taught, and passed it down to the generations that followed.

In this way the most glorious spiritual movement in history was hijacked by its bitterest opponents. It was perhaps the most successful religious fraud of all time, the grand deception of the ages. All of the surviving documentation of the first centuries tell us just how thoroughly the first generation of proto-Catholics had been deceived. Their descent from the apostles is taken

> **Irenaeus** – The bishop of Lyon, France in the last quarter of the second century. His work *Against Heresies* is a lengthy attack on Gnosticism and a primary source on Valentinus. Irenaeus pointed to the Roman succession list as proof of what is apostolic and true. A native of Asia Minor, he had been acquainted with Polycarp of Smyrna in his youth, supposedly a disciple of John.

for granted by all of the Church Fathers of the second century, including Hegisippus, Irenaeus, and Tertullian.[2] The doctrine of apostolic succession, the ability to trace the lineage back to Peter and the apostles, has become the very cornerstone of the Catholic faith.

Every religious movement must have its authoritative scriptures, and the heresiarchs set about to prepare theirs. The founding charter of the new sect consisted of the following documents:

1. ***The Epistle of Peter to James*** – This work legitimized the false apostles by providing them with the same documentation they told the Corinthians to expect from Paul. One of the pseudo-apostles fabricated a fictional account of Peters' exploits, and this epistle sets the stage to release this book to their flock.

2. ***The Preaching of Peter*** – This was the alternate history of the apostolic period introduced by the *Epistle of Peter to James*. In this tale Peter plays the leading role and Paul, under the pseudonym of Simon Magus, is the villain. Peter travels north up the Levantine coastline, evangelizing and debating Simon Magus at every turn. This lost work underlies two surviving books, the *Recognitions of Clement* and the *Homilies of Clement*.

3. ***The Teaching of the Lord through the Twelve Apostles to the Gentiles*** – This work is known in the patristic literature as the *Didache*, the Greek word for teaching. It was their first manual of church order, and includes sample prayers, baptismal procedures, instructions to the (false) apostles, elders, etc.

---

2. *History of the Church* 4.22; *Against Heresies* 3.3.1; *Prescription against Heretics* 32.1

4. *The Epistle of Clement to James* – This is the source of several key Catholic traditions, including what would become their marquee myth, the papacy of Peter. In the absence of Paul, Peter evangelizes southeastern Europe and travels to Italy, where he becomes the first bishop of Rome. Peter then hand-picks Clement to succeed him to the Roman bishopric.

The Epistle of Peter to James

The Epistle of Peter to James is a two-part work, with "Peter" dictating the first half and "James" issuing instructions in the second. In this extraordinary work, we get to hear the heresiarchs speak in their own voice. It is, in fact, the only text from the hands of the false apostles that has survived the centuries without being sanitized or cleaned up. The epistle provides a fictional backdrop against which the false apostles introduce a major new addition to their canon of scripture. The entire text can be found in the addendum at the back of this book.

The first section of the letter serves as a cover letter for an accompanying volume of Peter's missionary activities. This lost work, known as the *Preaching of Peter*, was their version of the Acts of the Apostles. "Peter" beseeches "James" to exercise extreme caution when he distributes this book to the flock. Peter is also concerned because "the word of truth is being rent" into many factions. "For some from among the Gentiles have rejected my legal preaching, attaching themselves to certain lawless and trifling preaching of the man who is my enemy." He then launches into a broadside against Paul/Simon, his unnamed enemy who is establishing Christianity outside the Law.

> And these things some have attempted while I am still alive, to transform my words by certain various interpretations, *to the dissolution of the law*; as though I also were of such a mind, but did not freely proclaim it, which God forbid! For such a thing would be to act *in opposition to the law of God* which was spoken by Moses, and was borne witness to by our Lord *in respect of its eternal continuance*; for thus he spoke: 'The heavens and the earth shall pass away, but one jot or one tittle shall in no wise pass from the law.' And this He has said, that all things might come to pass. But these men professing, I know not how, to know my mind, undertake to explain my words, which they have heard of me, more intelligently than I who spoke them, telling their catechumens that

this is my meaning, which indeed I never thought of. But if, while I am still alive, they dare thus to misrepresent me, how much more will those who shall come after me dare to do so!

—*Epistle of Peter to James* 2, emphasis mine

This, no doubt, helped the false apostles sell their legalism and Torah-observance to an unsuspecting public.

The second part is James's response. He has received the letter, read it to the elders of the church, and is going about to implement Peter's suggestions on disbursing the book. The elders of the movement were asked to guard the *Preaching of Peter* with a secrecy bordering on paranoia.

> Our Peter has strictly and becomingly charged us concerning the establishment of the truth, that we should not communicate the books of his preachings, which have been sent to us, to any one at random, but to one who is good and religious, and who wishes to teach, and *who is circumcised*, and faithful. And these are not all to be committed to him at once; that, if he be found injudicious in the first, the others may not be entrusted to him. Wherefore let him be proved not less than six years.

The stipulation of circumcision should raise a red flag to anyone familiar with Christian theology. It was the battleground issue between the New Testament apostles and their most vocal opponents. The requirement to be "religious" can, in this context, only mean observant of the Law. The prospective teacher—an actual position in the first and second century church—was then taken to the waters of baptism, where he had to swear an extensive oath not to reveal the books to outsiders. Part of this vow states:

> But even if it should ever seem to me that the books of the preachings given to me are not true, I shall not so communicate them, but shall give them back. And when I go abroad, I shall carry them with me, whatever of them I happen to possess. But if I be not minded to carry them about with me, I shall not suffer them to be in my house, but shall deposit them with my bishop.

This does not sound like the words of an apostle burning with zeal for the truth of the Gospel! It sounds like someone has just written a piece of fiction and is trying everything in his power to keep it from being exposed.

The Homilies/Recognitions of Clement

The second book in the proto-Catholic canon was the *Preaching of Peter*. It was introduced to the church membership shortly after AD 70 by the *Epistle of Peter to James*. We are certain of this because the cessation of the temple sacrifice is mentioned more than once in the heavily-edited forms that have survived. Its early origin is also seen in the fact that the Ebionites, the Palestinian branch of the movement, included the book among their sacred scriptures.[3]

The Preaching of Peter is the Ur-text—the lost literary ancestor—that underlies two extant books called *The Recognitions of Clement* and *The Homilies of Clement*. These books are known variously as the Clementines, the pseudo-Clementine writings, the Clementina, or the Clementine literature. Although they differ in many details, large portions of the two works are almost identical. They have a very complex textual history, comparable in many ways to an old house that has been extensively remodeled, added onto, and repainted over the years. A couple of chronological markers point to a major rewrite around AD 150. The Gospel of John, which was just gaining acceptance in Catholic circles at that time, is cited rather timidly. The same verse, John 3:5, is found in both branches of the Clementina as well as another author of the period, Justin Martyr.

The patriarch of the proto-Catholics, Zacchaeus of Caesaria, may have authored the seminal text. *Homilies* 3.71 sounds suspiciously like a man laying guilt on others in order to feather his own nest.

> Zacchaeus alone having given himself up wholly to labor for you, and needing sustenance, and not being able to attend to his own affairs, how can he procure the necessary support? Is it not reasonable that you are to take thought for his living? Not waiting for his asking you, for this is the part of a beggar. But he will rather die of hunger than submit to do this. And shall you not incur punishment, not considering that the workman is worthy of his hire?

The author, whoever he was, demonstrates a detailed knowledge of the Mediterranean coast, and this would tally with a man from Caesaria.

The saga begins at Rome, where Clement, a philosophically-minded young man, hears a disciple of the Lord, and believes. The two sources agree in placing this event early in Jesus' ministry. (This disciple, Barnabas, is not to be confused with Paul's faithful companion of the same name.) Clement

---

3. *The Panarion* 30.15

follows Barnabas by ship to Caesarea, where he is introduced to Peter. The narrative then tracks Peter as he travels north up the eastern coastline of the Mediterranean, giving private lectures to his followers and engaging in public debates with Simon Magus. As they put words into Peter's mouth, we are treated to the raw, uncensored doctrine of the first century proto-Catholics. At Antioch, Peter hears Clement's family history, meets a beggar lady, recognizes her as Clement's mother—hence the title "Recognitions"—and the family is reunited.

The Preaching of Peter was their counterpart to the Acts of the Apostles. Peter was given roughly the same place in the Clementine world that Paul occupies in the New Testament. The proto-Catholics were taught that Peter, not Paul, carried the Gospel of Jesus Christ to the Gentiles. The Clementina helps us to understand their tenacious attachment to several dogmas which are not found in the canonical Scriptures. Catholics stubbornly insist that Peter was the first bishop of Rome despite the overwhelming witness of Scripture which tells us otherwise. The "Prince of the Apostles" was the heroic figure at the heart of their core myth, created completely independently of the New Testament record.

Another legend created by the Preaching of Peter is that of Simon Magus. He was regarded by the Fathers of the Church as the father of all heresy, a sorcerer and master of black arts. Simon was the proto-Catholic pseudonym for Paul the apostle, although his doctrine and personal history has been distorted beyond all recognition. We find in this caricature what the first generations of Catholics were taught about their great rival and nemesis. Simon was endowed with Superman-like powers. "And they told me that he makes statues walk, and that he rolls himself on the fire and is not burnt; and sometimes he flies; and he makes loaves of stones; he becomes a serpent; he transforms himself into a goat; he becomes two-faced; he changes himself into gold; he opens locked gates; he melts iron; at banquets he produces images of all manner of forms."[4] Simon, like Paul, speaks against the law in numerous places, but the following passage makes the connection virtually undeniable. "Then after three days one of the brethren came to us from Gamaliel, whom we mentioned before, bringing us secret tidings from that enemy [their term for Paul] had received a commission from Caiaphas, the high priest, that he should go arrest all who believed in Jesus, and should go to Damascus with his letters and that there also, he

---

4. Homilies of Clement 2:32, also Recognitions of Clement 2.9

should make havoc among the faithful."[5] This is nothing but a thinly veiled allusion to Paul, prior to his conversion, making his way to Damascus in the ninth chapter of Acts. Clearly, the author was conversant with the Acts of the Apostles, but in order for the deception to work, his intended readers must have been oblivious.

There is nothing new or novel about the identification of Simon the Sorcerer with Saul of Tarsus. It was one of Ferdinand Baur's pet theories in the 1840s. The Tubingen School he founded posited an apostolic schism between Peter and Paul. The Petrine wing of the church became the Ebionites, who remained faithful to their Jewish roots, and Paul was championed in the Gentile churches. According to Baur, the Jewish branch dominated the church for the first one hundred years and produced such literature as the Clementines. The clash between the two branches of Christianity is depicted in the *Recognitions of Clement* as the struggle between Peter and Simon.

The ghost of Clement still roams the halls and corridors of the Vatican after all these years. Even though the *Preaching of Peter* was phased out in the second century, some of its characters have taken up permanent residence in the Great Church. The mass of forgeries under the name of Clement demonstrates the hold he has had on the Catholic mind. And a total of thirteen popes and three anti-popes have chosen the pontifical name of Clement.

The following teachings have absolutely no basis in the New Testament and can be traced back to the *Preaching of Peter* and its offshoots:

- Simon Magus was the father of Christian heresy
- The life of Clement, which was made up out of whole cloth
- Peter founded the church at Rome and served as its first bishop
- It was Peter, not Paul, who evangelized "the west"
- Clement had the direct anointing of Peter to succeed him in Rome
- The Clementine Barnabas, who pops up in a lot of early Catholic works; the *Epistle of Barnabas*, the *Acts of Barnabas*, and the *Gospel of Barnabas*.

There are several warnings in the Clementine literature against "false scriptures" and "false chapters." We shall cite two examples.

---

5. *Recognitions of Clement* 1.71

> Simon, therefore, as I learn, intends to come into public, and to speak of those chapters against God that are added to the Scriptures, for the sake of temptation, that he may seduce as many wretched ones as he can from the love of God. For we do not wish to say in public that these chapters were added to the Bible, since we should thereby perplex the unlearned multitudes, and so accomplish the purpose of this wicked Simon.
>
> —*The Homilies of Clement* 2.39

> If, therefore, some of the Scriptures are true and some are false, with good reason said our Master, 'Be ye good moneychangers,' inasmuch as in the Scriptures there are some true sayings and some spurious.
>
> —*The Homilies of Clement* 2.51

We believe the books they were trying to keep from their converts were the genuine writings of the apostles, what we call the New Testament. The following passage from the *Apostolic Constitutions* basically says as much.

> We have sent all these things to you, that ye may know our opinion; and that ye may not receive those books which obtain in our name, but are written by the ungodly. For ye are not to attend to the names of the apostles, but to the nature of the thing and their settled opinions. For we know that Simon and Cleobius, and their followers, have compiled poisonous books under the name of Christ and of His disciples, and do carry them about in order to deceive you . . .
>
> —*Apostolic Constitutions* 6.16

The Didache

The last major book of the proto-Catholic Bible was lost to the Christian world for hundreds of years. The recovery of this ancient work must rank as the greatest patristic find of all time. In 1873, the Orthodox bishop of Nicomedia, Philotheos Bryennios, discovered a manuscript in a monastery in Istanbul. The codex was dated AD 1056 by the scribe who wrote it. It contained several early Catholics works, which he published, but tucked away inside, unnoticed for a couple of years, was the *Didache*.

The *Didache* was their initial handbook of church order. It provides the clearest window we have to the early days of the movement. The *Didache* sets out regulations for fasting, baptism, and worship; provides them with templates for daily prayer and blessings for the Eucharistic meal; and it gives instructions to apostles and elders. The complete title, The *Teaching of the Lord through the Twelve Apostles to the Nations*, is revealing in itself. It tells us that these teachings were for the "Gentiles," and the use of the term "nations," meaning Gentiles, betrays a Jewish hand behind the document. This little manual thus seeks to establish a form of Christianity among the Gentiles that is completely apart from the Pauline missions.

The *Didache* as presently constituted should be dated around AD 90. We know it was within one generation of their founding, as some of the false apostles were still alive, but enough time had lapsed for them to discard circumcision.

The first five chapters are a moral tract known as the "Two Ways." Many authorities believe this section had its origin in the synagogues as an initiation catechism for Jewish proselytes. It was modified and included in the *Didache* to give their pagan converts an understanding of basic Judaeo-Christian morality. The essence of the teaching is neatly captured in the opening line. "There are two ways, one of life and one of death; but there is a great difference between the two." The way of life consisted of the Great Commandment (love of God and neighbor), the Golden Rule, the Ten Commandments, and extracts from the Sermon on the Mount.

Chapter six jumps right into their obligations under the Law. "If you are able to carry the full yoke of the Lord, you will be perfect; but if you are not able, do whatever you can." The key word here is "yoke," which was a common Hebrew idiom for the Law of Moses. Peter used the same expression at the council which decided on the obligations of *Goyim*: "Now therefore why tempt ye God, to put a *yoke* upon the neck of the disciples, which neither our father nor we were able to bear?"[6] Paul, writing to the Torah-observant Christians in Galatia, also employed it. "Stand fast therefore in the liberty wherewith Christ hath made us free, and be not entangled again with the *yoke* of bondage."[7] It is also found in Jewish literature. "From whoever accepts upon himself the *yoke* of Torah do they remove the yoke of the state and the yoke of hard labor."[8] The sentence about carrying "the full yoke of the Lord" really makes no sense except as a redactor's seam. It sounds to our ear like a block of material has been removed here, perhaps

---

6. Acts 15:10

7. Galatians 5.1

8. Mishnah *Abot* 3.5a

relating to circumcision, and the editor attempted to smooth it over with the bland admonition to "do whatever you can."

The next sentence refers to *kashrut*, the Jewish dietary laws. "And concerning food, bear what thou art able. . ." Behind this brief pronouncement, we see another missing section of text. This lacuna would have set out the distinction between clean and unclean meats, the necessity of separating meat from dairy, and other tips on keeping a kosher kitchen. The food regulations proved too cumbersome and too restrictive to Gentiles not brought up under this kind of discipline, as the exhortation to "bear what thou able" implies. The dietary laws were scrubbed early on, and this reference and one in the *Gospel of Barnabas* are the only evidence we have of their existence in the church.

Chapter seven lays down regulations for baptism. "Baptize in the name of the Father, and of the Son, and of the Holy Spirit, in living water. But if thou have not living water, baptize into other water; and if thou canst not in cold, use warm. But if thou have not either, pour out water thrice upon the head . . ." The charge to use "living water" has a special meaning in rabbinic tradition. The *Mishnah* lists, in ascending order, "six grades among pools of water, each more excellent than the other."[9] Pond water, being stagnant, is at the bottom of the list, and living water, a Hebraism for fresh, flowing water, is at the top. The *Didache* states their preference for living water and then evaluates the suitable alternatives in descending order.

Chapter seven continues: "Before the baptism, let the one who baptizes and the one to be baptized fast, and any others who are able to do so. And you shall require the one being baptized to fast for one or two days." The two-day delay, ostensibly for fasting, was needed to allow the pre-baptismal circumcision to heal. It was totally at odds with the practice of the apostles, who did not waste any time getting believers to the waters of baptism. The Ethiopian eunuch and the Philippian jailor were both baptized within hours of hearing the gospel. A confession of faith was all that was required by the servants of God.[10]

Chapter eight begins with the law of fasting. They openly admit their bi-weekly fasting provisions came from the Pharisees, whom they call hypocrites. "But let not your fasts be with the hypocrites; for they fast on the second and fifth days of the week; but you shall fast on the fourth day

9. Mishnah *Mikvaot 1.1*

10. For examples of the authentic apostolic practice, see Acts 2:41, 8:36–39, 9:18, 10:47–48, 16:33, and 19:5.

and the day of preparation." (The proud Pharisee in Luke 18:12 boasted that he was not as other men because, among other things, he fasted twice a week.) The Eastern Orthodox rites have never deviated from the Wednesday and Friday fasting regulations laid down by their forefathers. The Roman Catholics, on the other hand, treat every Friday as a penitential day, denying themselves the pleasure of meat, but fasting per se is only required on Ash Wednesday and Good Friday.

Didache chapter eight continues with instruction on prayer. The faithful were admonished to say the Lord's Prayer three time a day, the usual number of fixed prayers since the time of David.[11] The Jewish obligation to pray three times daily was, by the end of the first century, fulfilled only by reciting the Eighteen Benedictions. The Lord's Prayer was given the same place in Catholic devotions as the Eighteen Benedictions held in the Hebrew liturgy. It was, as Tertullian put it, the "prescribed and regular" prayer.[12]

Chapters nine and ten contain instructions and sample table blessings for the Thanksgiving, the first century banquet that evolved into the Holy Eucharist. The first two prayers are simply a recasting of the standard Jewish blessings over the bread and wine. The *berakah* pronounced over the cup— "Blessed art thou, O Lord our God, eternal King, Who createst the fruit of the vine"—became "We thank Thee, our Father, for the holy vine of David thy servant, which Thou madest known to us through Jesus Thy Servant; to Thee be the glory forever." Chapter ten warehouses a Christianized version of the *Birkat Hamazon*, the main Jewish table grace, which was—and still is—said after the meal. The *Didache* instructed them to recite this prayer "*after you are filled,*" leaving no doubt that the primitive Eucharist was an actual meal.

In Chapter thirteen, they reworked the Law of First Fruits to provide support for the false apostles. "Every first-fruit, therefore, of the products of the winepress and threshing floor, of oxen and of sheep, thou shalt take and give to the prophets, for they are your high priests. But if ye have not a prophet, give it to the poor. If thou makest a batch of dough, take the first fruit and give according to the commandment." One of the most important duties of the Jewish housewife was the dough offering. They were asked to set aside a small piece of dough every time they baked bread, and this was presented to the priests in due course. God's share, the *challah*, was

11. Psalms 55:17; Daniel 6:10
12. *On Prayer* 10

generally understood to be about 1/24th of the kneaded dough.[13] The first-fruits are still collected by the Catholic Church; not in kind, but in money.

Chapter fifteen deals with matters of administration. "Appoint, therefore, for yourselves, bishops and deacons . . . for they also render to you the service of prophets and teachers. Despise them not, therefore, for they are your honored ones, together with the prophets and teachers." The text of the *Didache* was redacted just as the false apostles were heading off into the sunset and the elders were beginning to assume responsibility. Although the authority of the apostles/prophets had waned, they still commanded considerable respect within the community, especially among older believers. But the actual power was now wielded by the local elder. He could, if necessary, place restrictions on the prophets as to how long they could stay and what they received for sustenance. If we read between the lines, we find there were abuses that had to be curbed. "And when the apostle goeth away, let him take nothing but bread until he lodgeth; but if he ask money, he is a false prophet" . . . "And every prophet who ordereth a meal in the Spirit eateth not from it, except indeed he be a false prophet" . . . "But whoever saith in the Spirit, Give me money, or something else, ye shall not listen to him." The old order was still very much in evidence and honored, but the elders were now calling the shots.

It is often claimed that the *Didache* represents an isolated pocket of Jewish Christians or a minority faction in the backwaters of the primitive church. Not so. There is no doubt whatsoever that it lay directly in the mainstream of historic Catholicism. The "Two Ways" section appears in the *Epistle of Barnabas*, sometimes almost word-for-word. Although unacknowledged citations are difficult to prove, the *Didache* is found in Irenaeus, Origen, Opatatus, and the *Shepherd of Hermas*. Clement of Alexandria referred to it as "Scripture," and the Egyptian church was still using it as an instruction manual in the fourth century.[14] Three of the most influential church orders

> **Clement of Alexandria** – The bishop of Alexandria and author at the end of the second century. Three of his complete works have survived, the most famous being the *Stromata*, meaning miscellanies or patchwork. He was a convert from paganism and Greek philosophy is sprinkled throughout his books. His writings reflect the primitive canon of the Church, citing such works as the *Gospel of the Egyptians*, the *Tradition of Matthias*, the *Didache*, the *Shepherd*, and the *Epistle of Barnabas*.

---

13. *Mishnah* Hallah 2.7

14. *Stromata* 1.20; Athanasius, *39th Festal Letter*

of the first centuries borrowed material from the *Didache*: the *Didascalia Apostolorum*, the *Apostolic Tradition*, and the *Apostolic Constitutions*. The mere fact they all drew water from the same well is proof positive they were from the same tradition.

The *Didache* does not cite Paul or contain even a particle of Pauline theology. This is indeed strange when we consider that it was written to Gentiles, that Paul was the apostle to the Gentiles, and that he gave advice on many of the same matters. This "omission," if we may call it that, has long puzzled scholars, but it is exactly what we would expect. To the false apostles and their followers, Paul was a heretic of the worse sort; indeed, he was "the enemy." They would no more have quoted from Paul than from Satan himself. The *Didache* quotes liberally from the Gospel of Matthew, but never from the other twenty-six books of the New Testament.

> **Didascalia Apostolorum** – Despite the title —Teaching of the Apostles—this work was actually compiled in the middle of the third century. It was an effort to bring the *Didache* up-to-date after the Church accepted the New Testament. This church order lays out the responsibilities of bishops, priests, and deacons, discusses paschal customs, warns against the public baths, and derides those who held to the purity regulations. It recounts the Acts of the Apostles to such an extent that perhaps that book was still controversial. The *Didascalia* quotes extensively from the New Testament, but lacks Revelation, which is consistent with its Syrian origin.

The final member of the founding charter was the *Epistle of Clement to James*. It established the most powerful and enduring myth ever produced by the false apostles; namely, that Peter was the first bishop of Rome. The epistle then proceeds to have Peter hand-pick Clement to be his successor in a carefully staged scene. The Catholic Church still promulgates the Petrine mythology, but Clement has been reassigned to the fourth position in the Roman succession. We will not use much material from this epistle until the last chapter of this book, when we will explore their claims about the Roman bishopric in some depth.

Chapter Three

The Teaching Develops and Spreads

A Reconstruction of the first 100 years

As the true Prophet has told us, a false prophet must first come from
some deceiver; and then, in like manner, after the removal of
the holy place, the true Gospel must be secretly sent abroad
for the rectification of the heresies that shall be.

—PETER, *THE HOMILIES OF CLEMENT* 2.17

OUR FIRST POST-PARTUM GLIMPSE of the new movement comes from the
book of Revelation. It would therefore be extremely useful to know when
John was on the isle of Patmos "for the word of God and the testimony of
Jesus Christ."[1] The issue has never been satisfactorily resolved, but there are
only two serious contenders. John either had the vision shortly after the
death of Nero in AD 69, or it was at the latter end of Domitian's reign in AD
95. After analyzing all of the evidence at the back of the book, we conclude
that the facts are best explained by a provenance in the late sixties.

In John's messages to the seven churches of Asia, he glances twice at
the proto-Catholics. "I know the blasphemy of them which say they are
Jews, but are not, but are the synagogue of Satan."[2] "Behold, I will make
them of the synagogue of Satan, which say they are Jews, and are not, but
lie; behold, I will make them to come and worship before thy feet, and to
know I have loved thee."[3] When the apostle John looked into the camp of

1. Revelation 1:9
2. *Ibid* 2:9
3. *Ibid* 3:9

35

the legalists, this is what he saw: Gentiles who were acting like Jews. It is a very concise but accurate description of the movement.

The proto-Catholics did not amount to much in AD 69. They were just another Christian offshoot, along with the Nicolaitans and the Balaamites, and they did not weigh any heavier on John's mind. He connects them with just two cities, Smyrna and Philadelphia, although there were others further east beyond the provincial border in Galatia. The false apostles had approached the saints at Ephesus, without success. "And thou has tried them which say they are apostles, and are not, and hast found them liars."[4] This leads us to believe that, by AD 69, the sectarians had not yet spread far from their place of incubation at the headwaters of the Maeander River. They had reached the Aegean Sea on the west, but no further.

What were relations like between the Pauline churches and the schismatics? There seems to have been some ill feelings for a while, at least in Smyrna. "I know the blasphemy [the reviling or slander] of them which say they are Jews, and are not, but are the synagogue of Satan."[5] The false apostles initially took a conciliatory stance toward those whom they regarded as deceived. The following passage from the *Apostolic Constitution* is surely from this era. "But whosoever comes to you, let him first be examined, and then received: for ye have understanding, and are able to know the right hand from the left, and to distinguish false teachers from true teachers. But when a teacher comes to you, supply him with what he wants with all readiness. And even when a false teacher comes, you shall give him for his necessity, but shall not receive his error. Nor indeed may ye pray together with him, lest ye be polluted as well as he."[6] The apostle John took a harder line in the churches he was responsible for. "If there come any unto you, and bring not this doctrine, receive him not into your house, neither bid him God speed: For he that biddeth him God speed is partaker of his evil deeds."[7]

So there was some limited contact between the two fellowships for a few years. However, the memory of the "other Christians" did not pass beyond the first generation, and it certainly did not leave Asia Minor. There is no record of anything resembling the New Testament fellowship in any of the pre-Nicene Fathers. The length of time it took for some of the apostolic

---

4. *Ibid* 2:2

5. *Ibid* 2:9

6. *Apostolic Constitutions* 7.28

7. 2 John 10–11

writings to make their way into Catholic hands tells us how little communication there was after the passage of a few decades.

The Early Transformation of Doctrine

The doctrine of the new movement underwent a rapid transformation in the seventh and eighth decades of the first century. There were several contributing factors, all abetted by the fact they were still small enough to change direction easily. The destruction of the temple just ten years after the founding of the sect shook their faith in the sacrificial cult. This was followed by a tsunami of anti-Semitic sentiment that swept through the empire after the Judaean conflict ended in AD 72. The crushing defeat of the Jewish people, the humiliating procession at Rome, and the appearance of Jews as slaves all worked to deprive Judaism of its former mystique and allure. It was not a good time to be promoting anything tainted by Moses.

After the war, the Emperor Vespasian appropriated the former temple tax, which had been voluntarily paid by Jewish men over the age of twenty, as a form of war reparations. A new tax, the *Fiscus Judaicus*, was levied on all Jews; men, women and children.[8] When his son Domitian was elevated to the imperial throne in AD 81, he expanded the tax and ruthlessly enforced payment. "Domitian's agents collected the tax on Jews with a peculiar lack of mercy; and took proceedings not only against those who kept their Jewish origin a secret to avoid the tax, but against those who lived as Jews without professing Judaism."[9] A circumcised and Sabbath-keeping Christian would definitely have been at risk under Domitian.

The changing demographics of the movement also played a role in the reshaping of doctrine. The original band of false apostles were all Jewish, although a couple of names on the Clementine roster appear to be Greek. Within thirty or thirty-five years, however, all of them had settled down or passed on, the founder died, and control of the church passed into the hands of the elders. These men were Gentiles, now on their own without any further influence from the Jewish homeland. Their theology responded, and the more demanding *mitzvahs* (commandments), like circumcision and the dietary laws, were tossed overboard. The proto-Catholic ship did not gain momentum until it was refitted to be more accommodating to Gentiles.

8. *Wars of the Jews* 7.6
9. Suetonius, *Domitian* 12.2

Circumcision was one of the first *mitzvahs* to be dropped. Its quick demise was perhaps inevitable given the spirit of the times and the stiff headwind they ran into. After AD 72, circumcision became the ultimate test to determine who was liable to pay the *Fiscus Judaicus*. (The Nazis of the Third Reich also used this technique to flush out suspected Jews.) The practice thereafter carried a financial penalty with it. Suetonius continues the previous quotation as follows. "As a boy, I remember once attending a crowded court where the procurator had a ninety-year old man stripped to establish whether or not he had been circumcised." Suetonius was born in AD 69, and he would have been a boy in the late seventies.

There were strong cultural biases against circumcision as well. In the Hellenic world, where the beauty of the human body was greatly admired, it was considered aesthetically disfiguring and barbaric. The Greeks, who exercised naked in the gymnasium, looked down with scorn on any form of bodily mutilation. The natural reluctance to undergo such a painful procedure, combined with financial disincentives and cultural disdain, all conspired to doom the practice early on.

The only overt mention of circumcision in the founding documents is in the *Epistle of Peter to James*. Circumcision was one of the criterion for gaining access to the most secret of their Scriptures, the *Preaching of Peter*. They put these words into the mouth of James: "Our Peter has strictly and becomingly charged us concerning the establishing of the truth, that we should not communicate the books of his preaching, which have been sent to us, to anyone at random, but to one who is good, and religious, and who wishes to teach, and who is circumcised, and faithful." Taking the step of circumcision was a huge commitment, but it gave one admission into the inner circle of the sect. Only the select few who were elevated to teacher status were entrusted with a copy of the book.

> **The Gospel of Barnabas** – Barnabas was not only Paul's companion in the Gospel but, in the Catholic literature, he was one of the 12 apostles. In this alternative universe, "Barnabas" was preaching in Rome before the resurrection. The *Gospel of Barnabas* is a Jewish-Christian work of the second century, substantially revised in the 14th century from a Muslim perspective. It is strongly anti-Paul in tone, advocates circumcision and the dietary laws, and denies the divinity of Christ and the triune Godhead.

The only other source touching on circumcision is the *Gospel of Barnabas*. This gospel harmony combines the four Gospels into a single narrative, and it appears to have been compiled in the latter half of the second century as an alternative to the more progressive Diatessaron. Although it bares traces of many revisions, the last one Muslim, it still taps into a genuine vein of proto-Catholic tradition. It is the Barnabas of the Clementines who is telling the tale, not Paul's faithful companion, and this inexorably links the original text to the proto-Catholics.[10] *The Gospel of Barnabas* begins as follows:

> Barnabas, apostle of Jesus the Nazarene, called Christ, to all them that dwell upon the earth, desireth peace and consolation. Dearly beloved, the great and wonderful God hath during these past days visited us by his prophet Jesus Christ in great mercy of teaching and miracles, by reason whereof many, being deceived of Satan, under pretence of piety, are preaching the most impious doctrine, calling Jesus the son of God, *repudiating the circumcision ordained of God for ever*, and permitting every unclean meat: among whom also Paul hath been deceived, whereof I speak not without grief; for which cause I am writing that truth which I have seen and heard, in the intercourse that I have had with Jesus, in order that ye may be saved, and not be deceived of Satan and perish in the judgment of God. Therefore beware of every one that preacheth unto you any new doctrine contrary to that which I write, that ye may be saved eternally. The great God be with you and guard you from Satan and from every evil. Amen.

Later in the book, "Jesus" lays out his uncompromising views on circumcision. They expand the story of the Syrophoenician woman pleading for her demon-possessed daughter by playing off the word dog. The association of uncircumcised with dogs must have been a common saying within the sect as it was invoked both here and in the *Didache*.[11]

> The disciples questioned Jesus on that day, saying: "O master, why didst thou make such answer to the woman, saying that they were dogs?" Jesus answered: "Verily I say unto you, that a dog is better than an uncircumcised man." Then were the disciples sorrowful, saying: "Hard are these words, and who shall be able to receive them?" Jesus answered: "If ye consider, O foolish ones, what the

---

10. The proto-Catholic Barnabas is a completely different personage than the Barnabas of the New Testament. We should remember they did not have the Acts of the Apostles. Thus, in the *Gospel of Barnabas*, Barnabas is an "apostle of Jesus the Nazarene," and in *Recognitions of Clement* 1.7, he is in Rome preaching the gospel during Christ's ministry.

11. *Didache* 9: "But let no one eat or drink of your Eucharist, unless they have been baptized into the name of the Lord; for concerning this also the Lord has said, 'Give not that which is holy to the dogs.'"

dog doth, that hath no reason, for the service of his master, ye will find my saying to be true. Tell me, doth the dog guard the house of his master, and expose his life against the robber? Yea, assuredly. But what receiveth he? Many blows and injuries with little bread, and he always showeth to his master a joyful countenance. Is this true?" "True it is, O master," answered the disciples. Then said Jesus: "Consider now how much God hath given to man, and ye shall see how unrighteous he is in not observing the covenant of God made with Abraham his servant. . . ." Then said the disciples: "Tell us, O master, for what reason man must needs be circumcised?" Jesus answered: "Let it suffice you that God hath commanded it to Abraham, saying: 'Abraham, circumcise thy foreskin, and that of all thy house, for this is a covenant between me and thee forever.'" . . . "Whereupon God told to Abraham the fact concerning circumcision, and made this covenant, saying: 'The soul that shall not have his flesh circumcised, I will scatter him from among my people forever.'" The disciples trembled with fear at these words of Jesus, for with vehemence of spirit he spoke. Then said Jesus: 'Leave fear to him that hath not circumcised his foreskin, for he is deprived of paradise.'

—*The Gospel of Barnabas 23–23*

Although circumcision was phased out in the first century, it still lives on in the vocabulary of the Church. In Judaism, circumcision is known as "the seal," a sign literally written in human flesh to mark the covenant God had made with Abraham. This is implicit in the blessing given at the *Brit Milah* ceremony on the eighth day. "Blessed be He who sanctified His beloved from the womb, and put His ordinance upon his flesh, and His offering with the sign of a holy covenant."[12] Paul also alludes to the connection between circumcision and the seal when he speaks of Abraham. "And he received the sign of circumcision, a seal of the righteousness of the faith which he had yet being uncircumcised: that he might be the father of all them that believe, though they be not circumcised; that righteousness might be imputed unto them also."[13]

When circumcision and sacrifice were discarded, the nomenclature of "the seal" was applied to immersion—the only part of the three-step conversion ritual that remained. This is illustrated in the following passages. "Now God has ordered everyone who worships Him to be sealed by

12. Donin, *To Be a Jew*, p. 275
13. Romans 4:11

baptism."[14] "Before a man bears the name of the Son of God he is dead; but when he receives the seal, he lays aside his deadness, and obtains life. The seal, then, is the water: they descend into the water dead, and they arise alive."[15] "And they entreated him that they might also receive the seal of baptism; and they said to him: As our souls are at ease, and as we are earnest about God, give us the seal; for we have heard thee say that the God whom thou proclaims recognizes his own sheep through his seal."[16] The Pauline Christians were not sealed by circumcision nor any other ritual but by the direct anointing of the Holy Spirit.[17]

The Jewish dietary laws, or *kashrut,* from which the word kosher was derived, were also short-lived. Paul's Epistle to the Colossians was directed toward the saints in the proto-Catholic heartland. "Let no man therefore judge you in meat, or in drink, or in respect of an holyday, or of the new moon, or of the Sabbath day. . . ."[18] Because these Christians were living in such close proximity to the Judaizers, there was some interaction and perhaps even some influence. "Why, as though living in the world, are ye subject to ordinances; touch not; taste not; handle not. . . ."[19] Were some of the saints trying to avoid *touching* unclean carcasses, *tasting* forbidden foods, and *handling* the wine of gentiles? We know from the *Didache* that the food regulations had been completed phased out by AD 90.[20]

How did the sectarians intellectually justify the radical transformation of doctrine? People are generally resistant to change, and they do not like their deepest beliefs and convictions challenged. The answer is provided by the *Epistle of Barnabas,* not to be confused with the *Gospel of Barnabas.* We learn that a literal observance of Torah was allegorized away early in the second century by a highly symbolic method of biblical interpretation.

The *Epistle of Barnabas* was written very close to AD 131. The sixteenth chapter refers to the Temple being pulled down and rebuilt by enemies. In AD 130, the Emperor Hadrian laid the foundations of a temple to Zeus in

---

14. *Recognitions of Clement* 6

15. *Shepherd of Hermas* Similitude 9.16; see also 9.17

16. *Acts of Thomas,* Part 2, 26–27

17. Ephesians 1:13–14, 4:30; 2 Corinthians 1:22

18. Colossians 2:16

19. *Ibid* 2:20–22

20. For a thorough discussion of Paul's views on kashrut, see Romans 14. He sums it up in verse 17: "For the kingdom of heaven is not meat and drink, but righteousness, and peace, and joy in the Holy Ghost."

the holy city, which triggered the Bar Kokhba rebellion. The work is anonymous, despite the attribution in the title to the Clementine Barnabas. The actual author, a self-proclaimed teacher of the sect, stated that his purpose in writing was to "perfect the knowledge" of his brethren. The knowledge he was so anxious to share was an allegorical way of interpreting the Law.

Pseudo-Barnabas delights in deriving simply moral lessons from the Hebrew Scriptures. Circumcision was no mere cutting away of the flesh, but it was a matter of hearing with faith and understanding. What a revelation that would have been to Pauline Christians, see Colossians 2:11![21] The true fast was not sackcloth and ashes, but it was to "loose the bands of iniquity, undo heavy burdens, let the oppressed go free, feeding the hungry with bread, etc, citing Isaiah 58:6. The Sabbath was to be understood in the light of the Psalmist, who proclaimed that a day is as a thousand years. The eighth day is a figure of the new creation and, in the meantime, it is the day on which Jesus rose from the dead. The food laws were also to be understood figuratively. Pork had been forbidden to teach them not to consort with men who forget the Lord in good times but cry out when hungry, like pigs. *The Epistle of Barnabas* was considered quasi-canonical for years, filling the theological niche that the letters of Paul would later provide.

The Spreading of the New Gospel

The movement got off to a slow start. The proto-Catholics were confined to Asia Minor for the first thirty or thirty-five years, with only a minor outlier in Syria and a few disciples in Israel. The churches of proconsular Asia dominated the sect until the middle of the second century. Smyrna on the coast, home to one of the earliest proto-Catholic congregations,[22] served as their initial springboard to the world.

The Torah-observant teachers developed a small following in Palestine. Later called Ebionites, the few Hebrew converts they made did not evolve along with the main branch of the sect but remained faithful to their Jewish roots. Irenaeus sketches out their doctrine in a few broad strokes.

> Those who are called Ebionites agree that the world was made by
> God; but their opinions with respect to the Lord are similar to

21. Colossians 2:11 "In whom also ye are circumcised with the circumcision made without hands, in putting off the body of the sins of the flesh by the circumcision of Christ."

22. Revelation 2:9

those of Cerinthus and Carpocrates [i.e., they were adoptionists]. They use the Gospel according to Matthew only, and repudiate the Apostle Paul, maintaining that he was an apostate from the Law. As to the prophetical writings, they endeavor to expound them in a somewhat singular manner: they practice circumcision, persevere in the observance of those customs which are enjoined by the Law, and are so Judaic in their style of life that they even adore Jerusalem as if it were the house of God.

—Against Heresy 1.26.2

The sect was very much alive in the fourth century, and Epiphanius devoted a long section of the *Panarion* to them. The derivation of *Ebion*, Hebrew for poor, surely hearkens back to the false apostles. "Their boastful claim is that they sold their possessions in the time of the apostles' and laid them at the apostles' feet, and have gone over to poverty and renunciation; and thus, they say, they are called 'poor' by everyone."[23]

> **Hippolytus** – An influential Roman theologian, teacher, and author early in the third century. Hippolytus was a voluminous author, including a primer on heresy called *The Refutation of all Heresies*, possibly the *Apostolic Traditions*, and many other works. He was an ardent supporter of the Gospel and Revelation of John, both still controversial, and championed the Logos Christology found in John's writings.

Hippolytus shines a ray of light into the dark age of church history. He reports that, about the year AD 100, a Syrian holy man named Elchasai received a profound revelation from a gigantic angel.[24] He took the message into Mesopotamia and met with some success. Was Elchasai assuming the mantle of the false apostles, men he had known and respected in his youth? He taught such standard Judeo-Christian fare as circumcision, daily ablutions, the Sabbath, praying toward Jerusalem, an adoptionist Christology, and a reverence for Peter.[25] Elchasai's mission had far-reaching consequences. It is known that the third century prophet Mani was brought up in a strict Jewish-Christian sect in southern Iraq, and the *Cologne Mani Codex* explicitly states that Elchasai was "the founder" of their law.[26]

In AD 112, Pliny the Younger was governor of Bithynia and Pontus, the Roman province which ran easterly from Istanbul along the southern shore of the Black Sea. Among his correspondence to the Emperor Trajan

23. *Panarion* 30

24. *Refutation* 9.8–12

25. *History of the Church* 6.38; *Panarion* 19.3

26. See *On the Origin of His Body*

was a letter seeking council on the legal status of Christians. He paints a picture of an incredible number of believers, although whether they were Catholic or Christian is an open question.

> Others, whose names were given to me by an informer, first admitted the charge and then denied it; they said that they had ceased to be Christians two or more years previous, and some of them even twenty years ago. They all did reverence to your statue and the images of the gods in the same way as the others, and reviled the name of Christ. They also declared that the sum total of their guilt or error amounted to no more than this: they had met regularly before dawn on a fixed day[27] to chant verses alternately amongst themselves in honor of Christ as if to a god, and also to bind themselves by oath, not for any criminal purpose, but to abstain from theft, robbery, and adultery, to commit no breach of trust, and not to deny a deposit when called upon to restore it. After this ceremony it had been their custom to disperse and reassemble later to take food of an ordinary, harmless kind; but they had in fact given up this practice since my edict, issued on your instruction, which banned all political societies. . . . The question seems to me to be worthy of your consideration, especially in view of the number of persons endangered; for a great many individuals of every age and class, both men and women, are being brought to trial, and this is likely to continue. It is not only the towns, but villages and rural districts too which are infected through contact with this wretched cult. I think though that it is still possible for it to be checked and directed to better ends, for there is no doubt that people have begun to throng the temples which had been almost entirely deserted for a long time, the sacred rites which had been allowed to lapse are being performed again, and the flesh of sacrificial victims is on sale everywhere, though up until recently scarcely anyone could be found to buy it.

—Pliny Letter No. 96

Rome was their first venture away from the Asian homeland, a decade or so before the turn of the first century. In their marquee myth, Peter established the bishopric of Rome in the third year of Claudius Caesar, or AD 44. But the New Testament consistently tells a different story. Peter resided at Jerusalem for most of this period, with an occasional foray up to Antioch or over to Caesaria. The next four or five bishops in the Roman succession are equally fraudulent. The names are fictional, their term of office entirely

---

27. Before Constantine, Sunday was just an ordinary work day.

arbitrary, and their accomplishments mere legend. There is not an ounce of historical truth to any of it.

The proto-Catholics may have made a high level convert inside the Roman court. In AD 95, the Emperor Domitian's cousin Flavius Clemens and his wife Domitilla were accused of "atheism, for which offence a number of others also, who had been carried away into Jewish customs, were condemned, some to death, others to confiscation of property."[28] Clemens was executed, and Domitilla was exiled. What is puzzling about this incident is that, if Jewish, they had done nothing wrong under Roman law. Judaism was a legally recognized religion throughout most of the imperial period; indeed, it had been accorded special privileges. The charge of atheism was usually levied against illicit cults like Christianity. It may be, as the historian Suetonius believed, that Domitian used the accusation to cloak his suspicion that members of the ruling family were plotting against him. "The occasion of Domitian's murder was that he had executed, on some trivial pretext, his own extremely stupid cousin, Flavius Clemens."[29] Or it may be that Clemens and Domitilla had embraced a variety of Christianity which practiced "Jewish customs."

If the idea that the cream of Roman society would embrace this "wretched cult" seems far-fetched—and admittedly it does—there is corroborating evidence. The entrance to the oldest Catholic burial ground in Rome, the Cemetery of Domitilla, lies on the ancestral lands of the Flavian family. An inscription bearing Domitilla's name is still visible at the foot of the entrance stairway. The oldest stratum of burial chambers inside the catacomb is pagan, as would be expected, but later in the second century they are surrounded by Christian ones. The emperor Nerva, who succeeded Domitian, "released such as were on trial for treason and restored the exiles."[30] Presumably the proclamation included Domitilla; the noble lady got her property back, and her heirs donated the land to the church.

The origin of the Greek churches has been lost in the mists of time, but they were probably colonized by way of Rome. The Greeks have never observed the traditional fourteenth of Nisan *Pascha*, eliminating a direct lineage from Asia Minor, and the long-winded letter known as *1 Clement* hints at a special and even paternal relationship between Rome and Corinth. The overall tone is that of a parent giving counsel to his children.

---

28. Dio Cassius *History of Rome* 67.14

29. *Domitian* 15

30. Dio Cassius *History of Rome* 68.1

It appears the Corinthians were experiencing a leadership crisis, and the mother church was helping them sort it out. *First Clement* is usually dated AD 95, but we believe it belongs in the middle of the second century. The first solid landmark we come to in the Balkans is the open letter Quadratus addressed to Hadrian, emperor from AD 117 to AD 138.[31] A founding date of AD 120 to AD 125 best fits the meager evidence.

The proto-Catholics did not get established in Palestine until the Bar Kokhba rebellion. After the Romans recaptured Jerusalem in AD 70, the Tenth Legion was permanently garrisoned near the Tower of David, and the Holy City lay in ruins for the next sixty years. The string of fifteen bishops in Jerusalem between the two insurrections, as reported by Eusebius, is thus a historical impossibility.[32]

In AD 130, Hadrian decided to rebuild Jerusalem as a Roman *colonia*, and to compound the blunder, he made circumcision a capital crime. The result was the bloody Bar Kokhba uprising. When it ended in AD 135, Hadrian concluded that Judaism was simply incompatible with Roman civilization. He therefore purged the land of its Jewish inhabitants and re-populated it with foreign settlers. Jews were even banned from the Holy City on pain of death. The first Catholics rode in with the waves of new settlers. A satire by Lucian, *The Death of Peregrinus*, which lampoons the famous Cynic philosopher, tells of his opportunistic conversion to Christianity in Palestine about AD 155.

The Egyptian church was also founded in the years following Bar Kokhba. Justin Martyr relates an incident that took place in Alexandria sometime in the 140s. A young and overly-zealous member of the church petitioned the governor for permission to make himself a eunuch, which was denied.[33] One of the first Catholic teachers on the Nile, Pantae-

> **Justin Martyr** – A prominent teacher and apologist who resided in Rome in the middle of the second century. He taught from his house, which was located "above a man named Martin, near the Timiotinian Bath." Justin wore the philosopher's cloak and extolled Christianity as the "true philosophy." He wrote extensively, but only three works have survived: *1 and 2 Apology*, and the *Dialogue with Trypho*. He was one of the last Catholic Fathers not to acknowledge Paul or cite the Pauline epistles. Details of his death can be found in the *Martyrdom of the Holy Martyrs*, written between AD 162 and AD 168.

31. *History of the Church* 4.3
32. *History of the Church* 4.5
33. *1 Apology* 29

nus, was nicknamed the "Sicilian Bee," which may tell us something of his country of origin.

Catholic missionaries reached France around the middle of the second century. Lugdunum, now known as Lyon, was the administrative center of Roman Gaul and a substantial city of some 50,000 souls. The church at Lyon favored the new Roman theology, an indication that their teachers were part of the Roman occupation, but most of the members came from Asia Minor. The Galatians were the easterly-most branch of the Celts, the same ethnic stock as the Gaul's of France. The *Martyrs of Lyon and Vienne*, a martyrology dated AD 177, provides valuable background on the establishment of Catholicism in Roman Gaul. After a gruesome display of public torture, the survivors sent an account of their sufferings back to their brethren in Anatolia. Several of these martyrs had actually been born in Asia or Phrygia. Their Gallic tormentors were trying to stamp out what they called a "foreign and new religion," which, from their perspective, was certainly the case.[34]

Catholicism was surprisingly slow to reach the northern and eastern reaches of the Fertile Crescent. Edessa was their initial beachhead to the region. It was also the myth-making capital of the east, almost rivaling Rome in the west, and so fact must be separated from fiction. The royal archives of this frontier city were said to contain a two-way correspondence between King Abgar V and Jesus Christ, which Eusebius, gullible as always, passes along without comment.[35] The salient facts are these: The Edessenes were not Quartodecimans, disqualifying neighboring Syria as a port of entry, and the Diatessaron was their first Gospel text.[36]

> **Eusebius** – A prolific writer, Eusebius is best known for his *History of the Church*, the first systematic history of the Christian church. His extensive use of primary sources and citations makes him particularly useful. Eusebius was the bishop of Caesaria from circa AD 315 to AD 335 and, in this capacity, attended the Council of Nicaea AD 325.

Tatian, a student of Justin Martyr, compiled the Diatessaron in Rome, but he was excommunicated for his efforts. In AD 172, the native Assyrian packed his bags and went home. A confidant of the Edessene royal court named Bardaisan connected with Tatian, got a copy of the Syriac-language Gospel, and carried it to Edessa. Among the first to convert was the king himself. King Abgar VIII reigned from AD 177 to AD 212, the last in a long

34. *History of the Church* 5.1
35. *ibid* 1.13
36. *ibid* 5.23

line of rulers bearing that name. Bardaisan's *Book of Laws* states, "In Syria and Edessa, men used to part with their manhood in honor of [the god] Tharatha; but when King Abgar became a believer, he commanded that every one that did so should have his hand cut off. From that day until now, no one does so in the country of Edessa." The sign of the cross replaced the symbol of Baal on his coinage, and in AD 201 the Edessene church, the first Christian chapel known to history, was flooded by the Daisan River.[37]

The northeast corner of the Roman Empire, more or less the eastern half of modern Turkey, was a polyglot of tongues and dialects. This linguistic barrier served as a powerful deterrent to outside missionaries. When Paul and Barnabas reached Lystra, which is still in central Anatolia, the townsmen understood them in Greek but spoke the Lycaonian language among themselves.[38] Peter addressed his first epistle to the saints in Cappadocia, among other places, but it would take Catholicism another 200 years to penetrate this far into the interior. Gregory Thaumaturgis is credited with extending the faith south from Pontus along the Black Sea into Cappadocia around AD 240.[39] An Armenian nobleman, also named Gregory, studied Christianity in Cappadocian Caesaria and introduced it to his homeland late in the third century.[40] Armenia was the first country to make Catholicism the official state religion—some say in AD 301 and others in AD 311—anticipating the conversion of the Roman empire by many decades.

37. See *Chronicle of Edessa*

38. Acts 14:11

39. Tertullian mentions Christians in Cappadocia circa AD 210 but the Roman province included what we now call Pontus (*To Scapula* 3). Under Trajan (AD 98 to AD 117), maritime Pontus was joined with inland Cappadocia to become the imperial province of Cappadocia.

40. Modern Kayseri, Turkey

Chapter Four

Church Polity and the Rites of Worship

===

Elect, therefore, for yourselves, bishops and deacons worthy of the Lord,
men meek, and not lovers of money, and truthful and proved;
for they also render to you the service of prophets and teachers.

—*DIDACHE* 15

THE PRIMITIVE CATHOLIC COMMUNITY was organized along the same lines as the New Testament fellowship. At the top, directing the church, was a class of preachers modeled after the ministry Christ had ordained. They referred to themselves as "apostles" or "prophets." Below them were the local elders—presbyters in Greek—who also served in the role of teachers. The office of the presbytery was created by the twelve apostles to help them care for the flock, and the proto-Catholics found them equally indispensable.

The authority of the new sect was initially vested in the pseudo-apostles. This was a copycat ministry that went forth in much the same way as the Twelve and the Seventy. "But concerning the apostles and prophets, according to the decree of the Gospel, thus do.[1] Their homeless lifestyle is hinted at by the *Recognitions of Clement*. "Be ye constant in hearing the word; that at the end of that time [three months], if any are able and willing to follow us, they may do so, if duty will admit of it. And when I say if duty will admit, I mean that no one by his departure must sadden anyone who ought not to be saddened, as by leaving parents who ought not to be left, or a faithful wife, or any other person to whom he is bound to afford comfort for God's sake."[2] Both the *Homilies* and the *Recognitions of Clement* boast

---

1. *Didache* 11
2. *Recognitions of Clement* 3.72

of recruiting from Paul's ministerial staff. "But whereas we were his fellow-laborers at the first, so long as he did such things without doing wrong to the interests of religion [i.e., the Law]; now that he has madly begun to attempt to deceive those who are religious [observant], we have withdrawn from him."[3] "Then Niceta and Aquila, who had formerly been disciples of Simon [Paul], and were converted to the faith of Christ under the teaching of Zacchaeus."[4]

The *Didache* provides us with a rare glimpse into this rival ministry at the end of its short existence. "Let every apostle who comes to you be received as the Lord. But he shall not remain more than one day. However, if necessary, let him remain a second day. But if he stays for three, he is a false prophet. And when the apostle departs, let him take only enough bread to last until he reaches shelter; if he asks for money, he is a false prophet."[5] Obviously, the aging pseudo-apostles were no longer engaged in mission work. Every provision had been made for them to settle down, and within a single generation, all had done so. "But every true prophet that willeth to abide among you is worthy of his support. So also a true teacher is himself worthy, as the workman, of his support. Every first-fruit, therefore, of the products of wine-press and threshing-floor, of oxen and of sheep, thou shalt take and give to the prophets, for they are your high priests."[6]

The second office was the congregational elders. Their duties and qualifications came partly from the elders of Palestinian Christianity and partly from the rabbis of the synagogues. These men held full time jobs, and it was expected they would marry and bear the responsibility of a family. *The Homilies of Clement* says: "For the sake of chastity, therefore, let not only the elders, but even all, hasten to accomplish marriage."[7] It was, in every respect, a lay ministry.

The first Catholic elders were appointed by the false apostles. However, once all of them had settled down or passed away, the elders were chosen by the congregation. "Elect, therefore, for yourselves, bishops and deacons worthy of the Lord, men meek, and not lovers of money, and truthful and proved; for they also render to you the service of prophets and teachers."[8]

---

3. *Homilies of Clement* 2.75
4. *Recognitions of Clement* 2.1
5. *Didache* 11
6. *Ibid* 13
7. *Homilies of Clement* 3.68
8. *Didache* 15

Paul viewed the unmooring of the eldership from the authority of the apostles as a dangerous step. "For the time will come when they will not endure sound doctrine; but after their own lusts shall they heap to themselves teachers, having itching ears."[9] After the demise of the false apostles, these men were the only authority in the loosely affiliated home-churches for several generations.

The office of the bishop was constituted when they grew numerous enough to have several assemblies in one town. There had to be someone with the authority to settle disputes and coordinate church business, and we deduce from several early sources that this man was known as the Ruler. "Let there be a Ruler over the elders who are in the villages, and let him be recognized as head of them all, at whose hand all of them shall be required . . ."[10] The *Teaching of Simon Cephas* tells us that Peter "served there [Rome] in the rank of Superintendent of Rulers for twenty-five years." This primitive term is obviously pre-Pauline, and it probably derived from the "rulers of the synagogue" mentioned in the Gospels. The same antiquated title is found in many Syrian works of the second and third centuries,[11] although sometimes it was expanded to "Guide and Ruler."[12]

The Catholic deacons (*diakonos*, meaning servant) were, for the first sixty or seventy years, little more than table attendants and waiters. Their primary function was somewhat like Stephen and his fellows who distributed food to the poor widows.[13] The deacons were charged with serving the primitive Eucharistic meal, the sacred banquet that concluded the first century Sunday service. They brought the food to the dining room, set the table, mixed the wine, and cleaned up afterwards. The rise and fall of this institution is the topic of chapter six. After this meal was transformed in the second century into the Holy Eucharist, the office no longer served any real purpose. The deaconate has since become little more than a training ground for the priesthood.

9. 2 Timothy 4:3

10. Syriac *Teaching of the Apostles* 24

11. *Teaching of Simon Cephas; Teaching of Addaeus; Martyrdom of Barsamya*

12. *Teaching of Addaeus, Syriac Teaching of the Apostles*

13. Acts 6:1–6

The Rites of Prayer and Worship

The Christians of the first centuries gathered for prayer and singing twice every day, six days of the week. Although the Jews attended synagogue three times daily in Jesus' time, the evening prayer was ruled optional after the destruction of the temple. The great repository of the ancient church, the *Apostolic Constitutions*, thus says: "Assemble yourselves together every day, morning and evening, singing psalms and praying in the Lord's house; in the morning saying the sixty-second Psalm, and in the evening the hundred and fortieth, but principally on the Sabbath day"[14] *The Apostolic Tradition* (c. AD 215) stresses the morning obligation in numerous passages, but it never speaks of assembling again after work.[15] It appears that the evening service had been dropped at the latter end of the second century.

> **Syriac *Teaching of the Apostles*** – This book purports to be the instructions of the apostles on the day of Pentecost. As each apostle heard in a different tongue, they understood where the Spirit was sending them to preach. It then launches into 27 canons of church law, which Paul and Timothy delivered to the churches, and ends with a list showing where the apostles supposedly labored in the gospel. The work is an odd mosaic of Catholic legend mixed with the canonical Acts, suggesting a composition date between AD 180 and AD 200.

The Psalter was the heart and soul of their weekday prayers. This was a direct carryover of the "Morning Psalms" of the Hebrew liturgy, Psalms 145 to 150, which were recited at morning prayer before the Eighteen Benedictions. The Syriac *Teaching of the Apostles* thus instructs: "In the service of the Church repeat ye the praises of David day by day."[16] The Latin liturgy still concludes the morning office of prayer—known as Lauds—with Psalms 148, 149, and 150. The term springs from the frequent expressions of praise, or "lauds," found in these verses. Psalms 148 begins, "Praise ye the Lord. Praise ye the Lord from the heavens: praise him in the heights. Praise ye him, all his angels: praise ye him, all his hosts . . ."

Their prayer practices came almost exclusively from the Jewish side of the family. The Catholic liturgy was a reformulation of the Eighteen Benedictions, the great liturgical prayer of the synagogue. They prayed standing, a practice that has survived in many of the high churches. They faced toward the east, just as the Eighteen Blessings are directed toward Jerusalem and

---

14. *Apostolic Constitutions* 2.59; also *Didache* 4

15. *Apostolic Tradition* 31.2; 33; 35.2–3

16. Syriac *Teaching of the Apostles* 19

the Temple Mount.[17] They prayed with their arms uplifted, their hands outstretched, and their palms forward. The *orante* position, as it is known, is traceable to the priestly blessing in the temple, and it is widely depicted in early Catholic art.[18] The men prayed with their heads uncovered, the custom of ancient Israel until Talmudic times, while the women veiled themselves.[19] Paul, the ex-Pharisee, taught this as well. "Every man praying or prophesying, having his head covered, dishonored his head . . . For if the woman be not covered, let her also be shorn; but if it be a shame for a woman to be shorn or shaven, let her be covered."[20] And for a few years they even laid on tefillin, a practice which has left a quaint little custom in its wake.

Tefillin, the phylacteries of the New Testament, are worn by all adult men at morning prayers. This *mitzveh* is found in Deuteronomy 6:8. "Thou shalt bind them for a sign upon thine hand, and they shall be as frontlets between thine eyes." Perfectly square black boxes attached to a base, the *tefillin* are bound by thongs onto the inside of the left bicep and the top of the forehead. The two leather cubes contain thin strips of parchment inscribed with four passages of Torah. Devout Jews would often emboss the Hebrew letter *Shin*, meaning *Shaddai* or God, on the case of the head-*tefillin*. The proto-Catholics changed this to the first letter of the word Christ, which is *Chi*, or X, in Greek. When the use of *tefillin* was discontinued, they retained the custom of signing the cross on their foreheads where the head-*tefillin* used to be.

Tertullian, writing around AD 200, tells us what a slavish superstition it developed into. "At every forward step and movement, at every going in or out, when we put on our clothes and shoes, when we bathe, when we sit at table, when we light the lamps, on couch, on seat, in all the ordinary actions of daily life, we trace upon the

> **Tertullian** – The first of the Latin Fathers, and perhaps the most interesting to read. Tertullian hailed from Carthage in North Africa, the country now known as Tunisia. He wrote over thirty extant works on a wide variety of Christian topics. Most of his output can be placed in the period AD 200 to AD 215. Tertullian was the first to use the Latin term Trinity and attempt a rigorous definition.

17. *Ibid* 1 "The apostles therefore appointed: Pray ye towards the east, because 'as the lightning which lighteth from the east and is seen even to the west, so shall the coming of the Son of man be . . .'"

18. *1 Clement* 2; Tertullian *Apology* 30. This was also the practice of the New Testament church. "I will therefore that men pray everywhere, lifting up holy hands, without wrath and doubting" (1 Timothy 2:8).

19. Syriac *Teaching of the Apostles* 130

20. 1 Corinthians 11:4, 6

forehead the sign."[21] The constant signing was believed to protect them from Satan. "And when tempted always reverently seal thy forehead (with the sign of the cross). For this sign of the Passion is displayed and made manifest against the devil if thou makest it in faith, not in order that thou mayest be seen of men, but by thy knowledge putting it forward as a shield. If indeed the adversary, seeing the power of the Spirit outwardly displayed in the image of baptism, he takes to flight trembling, not at thy striking him but at thy breathing [upon him]."[22]

The Liturgy of the Hours (or breviary) was derived from the Hebrew convention of praying at the cardinal points of the day. According to the *Didache*, the first generation Catholics were taught to recite the Lord's Prayer three times daily. This threefold pattern of prayer has been a fixture of Judaism since the time of David.[23] The *Mishnah* gives the range of acceptable times. "The morning prayer [may be recited] until midday. R. Judah says, 'Until the fourth hour.' The afternoon prayer [may be recited] until

> **The Mishnah** – After the loss of the Temple cult, two disastrous wars, and expulsion from their holy city, the leading rabbis felt the need to preserve their oral traditions. So, at the beginning of the third century, they compiled the key legal rulings of the sages. This was done in Galilee, where most of the Jews lived after Bar Kokhba. They organized this voluminous material by dividing it into six orders, which were further subdivided into 63 tractates. The Mishnah is thus cited by name and tractate. This six-part structure became the template for all of the Talmudic literature which followed.

the evening. R. Judah says, 'Until mid-afternoon.' The evening prayer has no fixed [time]."[24] The Jewish disciples continued the practice out of lifelong habit—Peter went up to the housetop to pray "about the sixth hour"—but it was never made incumbent upon Gentile believers.[25] The course of daily prayer prescribed by the Roman Church still includes Terce, Sext, and None, Latin for three, six, and nine, respectively.

The proto-Catholics continued the Jewish custom of *nelilat yadayim*, ritual hand-washing, before prayer and Torah study. The Jesus of the *Gospel of Barnabas* engaged in such. "Tell me, when you wash yourselves for prayer, do you take care that no unclean thing touch you? Yes, assuredly ... And furthermore, I say to you, that no one will make prayer pleasing to

21. *On the Crown* 3
22. *Apostolic Tradition* 37
23. Psalms 55:17; Luke 1:10
24. Mishnah *Berakhot* 4.1
25. Acts 10:9

God if he be not washed, but will burden his soul with sin like idolatry."[26] We have a more reliable witness in Tertullian, who heaps scorn upon the practice and puzzles over its origin. "These are the true purities; not those which most are superstitiously careful about, taking water at every prayer, even when they are coming from a bath of the whole body."[27]

The Lord's Day was the highpoint of the week. All of the major components of this service were taken from the synagogues, perhaps the reason John blasted those assemblies as "the synagogue of Satan."[28] The home where they gathered for worship was known as "the place of instruction," which corresponds to the Hebrew *Beit Midrash*, or "house of instruction." These were the schools where Torah was taught. The proto-Catholics segregated their assemblies, with separate sections for men and women, and this is still the norm in orthodox Judaism.[29] Catholic women covered their heads with a scarf; married Jewish women wear a head covering at synagogue.[30] The elder of each congregation was given the honor of a special high-backed chair known as the "chair of the teacher," or *kathedra* in Greek.[31] It was derived from the chief seat in the synagogue called Moses' seat.[32] A cathedral is now the principal church of each diocese, the one which houses the bishop's throne and acts as the seat of administration.

The *Didascalia Apostolorum* gives us a panoramic snapshot of the seating arrangements in the early house assemblies. We learn they were oriented toward the east, in the manner of synagogues everywhere in the western world. "And for the presbyters let there be assigned a place in the eastern part of the house; and let the bishop's throne be set in their midst, and let the presbyters sit with him. And again, let the laymen sit in another part of the house toward the east. For so it should be, that in the eastern part of the house the presbyters sit with the bishops, and next the laymen, and then the women that when you stand up to pray, the rulers may stand first, and after them the laymen, and then the women also. For it is required that you pray toward the east . . ."[33]

26. *Gospel of Barnabas* 84; also 38

27. *On Prayer* 13

28. Revelation 2:9; 3:9

29. *Apostolic Tradition* 18.2

30. *Ibid* 18.5

31. *Epistle of Clement to James* 19

32. Matthew 23:2

33. *Didascalia Apostolorum* 12

The Sunday service began by reading "the memoirs of the apostles and the writings of the prophets," to use Justin Martyr's memorable phrase.[34] The Christian lection is a direct carryover of the Torah readings on Sabbath and festival days. The entire congregation would rise and stand reverently during the gospel portion. "At the conclusion of the other scriptures let the Gospel be read, as being the seal of all the scriptures; and let the people listen to it standing upon their feet."[35] The Jews also stand respectfully when the Torah scroll is brought up for reading and again when it is returned to the ark. Next, the deacon would stand and ask that quarrelling brethren reconcile.[36] This was done in accordance with Matthew 5:23–24. The congregation would then rise together for common prayer. This, too, came from Jewish precedents. The central liturgy of the synagogue, the Eighteen Benedictions, is recited while standing, and for this reason is often called the *Amidah*, which means "standing."[37] The kiss of peace followed common prayer.[38] This was an affectionate form of greeting in the Middle East, one that was encouraged by the apostles but never incorporated into the *ekklesia*.[39]

At this point, the catechumens were dismissed and the faithful were summoned to the "divine table."[40] The Latin word for dismissed, "missa" or, as we would say, Mass, has become the colloquial name for the entire service. Only the spiritually mature members, those who had been regenerated in the waters of baptism, were invited. The deacons prepared the dining room for the sacred banquet. They would arrange the dining couches around the table; put on a clean tablecloth; and set the plates of bread, wine, and other foodstuffs on the table. The baptized members would then recline together and enjoy "the communion of the table."[41] After the elder said the blessing for the bread and broke the loaf, the meal got underway. The ritual blessings used on this occasion for the bread and cup have been preserved in *Didache* 9, and the meal concluded with the table grace recorded in *Didache* 10.

---

34. *1 Apology* 67

35. Syriac *Teaching of the Apostles* 8

36. *Didache* 14

37. The Lord refers to this custom in Matthew 6:5. "And when thou prayest, thou shalt not be as the hypocrites are: for they love to pray standing in the synagogues and in the corners of the streets, that they may be seen of men."

38. *1 Apology* 65

39. 1 Corinthians 16–20; Romans 16:16

40. *Recognitions of Clement* 10.72

41. *Ibid* 7.36

The Jewish Origin of the Catholic Liturgy

The central prayer of the synagogue liturgy is known as the Eighteen Benedictions, or *Shemoneh Esrei* in Hebrew. It is sometimes called "The Prayer" because the obligation to pray can be fulfilled only by its recitation. The *Shemoneh Esrei* consists of a long, flowing tapestry of nineteen fixed prayers and petitions. Although it did not crystallize into its present form until the end of the first century, most of the material would have been intimately familiar to the false apostles. They took it upon themselves to prepare a Christian liturgy based upon the Blessings but rewritten entirely in terms of the New Covenant. These reformulated prayers became the first Catholic liturgy.

A comparison of the Eighteen Benedictions with the oldest liturgical prayers of the Church leaves little doubt they were the original prototypes. But we must remember that even the earliest of the extant Catholic prayers are generations removed from the *Amidah* of Paul's day, and they had been smoothed, revised, and expanded considerably in the interim. Nevertheless, remarkable similarities in composition, content, and even phraseology are still readily apparent.

- Blessing No. 1 ("Fathers") became *Apostolic Constitutions* 7.33

- Blessing No. 2 ("God's Power") became *Apostolic Constitutions* 7.34 and the first line of 7.35

- Blessing No. 3 ("Holiness of God") became the second part of *Apostolic Constitutions* 7.35

- Blessing No. 4 ("Knowledge") was the kernel for the *Liturgy of Serapion*

- Blessing No. 10 ("Ingathering of the Dispersed") was incorporated into the bread blessing of *Didache* 9

- Blessing No. 15 ("Blessing of David") became the first line of *Apostolic Constitutions* 7.37

- Blessing No. 16 ("Hear Our Prayer") became the balance of *Apostolic Constitutions* 7.37

- Blessing No. 17 ("Worship"), the older version before the petition to restore the temple service was added, became the first line of *Apostolic Constitutions* 7.38

- Blessing No. 18 ("Thanksgiving") became the balance of *Apostolic Constitutions* 7.38

Let us examine the evidence for ourselves. The complete text of the First Benediction and about one-half of the Catholic version from the *Apostolic Constitutions* 7.33 are shown below in parallel columns. This particular blessing is commonly referred to as *Abot*, meaning Fathers.

First Benediction	Apostolic Constitutions 7.33
"Blessed art Thou, O Lord our God and God of our fathers, God of Abraham, God of Isaac, and Jacob. The great, mighty and awesome God, the most high God who extends loving kindness and is Master of all things; who remembers the gracious deeds of our forefathers, and who in love will bring a Redeemer to their children's children for Thy Name's sake. O King, Helper, Savior and Protector, blessed art Thou, O Lord, Shield of Abraham."	"Our eternal Saviour, the King of gods, who alone art almighty, and the Lord, the God of all beings, and the God of our holy and blameless fathers, and of those before us; the God of Abraham, and of Isaac, and of Jacob; who art merciful and compassionate, long suffering, and abundant in mercy . . . For from that truth which was in our forefather Abraham, when he changed his way Thou didst guide him by a vision, and didst teach him what kind of state this world is; and knowledge went before his faith, and faith was the consequence of his knowledge; and the covenant did follow after his faith. For thou saidest: 'I will make thy seed as the stars of heaven, and as the sand which is by the seashore.' Moreover, when thou hast given him Isaac, and knewest him to be like him in his mode of life, Thou wast then called his God, saying: 'I will be a God to thee, and to thy seed after thee.' And when our father Jacob was sent into Mesopotamia, Thou showedst him Christ, and by him speakest, saying: 'Behold, I am with thee, and I will increase thee, and multiply thee exceedingly.' And so spakest Thou to Moses, Thy faithful and holy servant, at the vision of the bush: 'I am He that is; this is my name for ever, and my memorial for generations of generations.' O Thou great protector of the posterity of Abraham, Thou art blessed forever."

The patrimony of the Christian prayer is beyond doubt. We find the exact same themes, with only minor exceptions, in the exact same sequence as the First Benediction.

- The "God of our fathers" vs. the "God of our holy and blameless fathers"

- The God of Abraham, Isaac, and Jacob

- The "Master of all things" vs. the "God of all beings"

- The "gracious deeds of our forefathers" vs. the "truth that was in our forefather Abraham"

- The Hebrew Benediction speaks of bringing a Redeemer to their children's children. The Catholic prayer expands this single line into a recounting of the promises made to the four Patriarchs regarding their seed.

- For "Thy Name's sake" vs. "this is my name forever"

- The "Protector" and "Shield" of Abraham vs. the "great protector of the posterity of Abraham"

- "Blessed art thou, O Lord" vs. "Thou art blessed forever"

A subset of the *Shemoneh Esrei*, known as the Seven Benedictions, provided the template for the Christian liturgies on Saturday and Sunday. On Shabbat, New Moons, and festival days, the *Amidah* is considerably shortened to make room for the Torah lesson. The thirteen middle blessings are dropped and replaced by a prayer that affirms the sanctity of the day, the *Kedushat ha-Yom*. As explained in the Tosephta, "On the Sabbath . . . one recites Seven, with the Sanctification of the Day in the middle."[42] This same collection of seven prayers, all dressed up in Christian terminology, can still be found in the *Apostolic Constitutions*. It is the New Covenant version of the Seven Benedictions. The prayers in *Apostolic Constitutions* 7.33 to 7.38 treat the same topics in the same order as the Seven Benedictions. But most revealing of all, the Christianized *Kedushat ha-Yom* lies between the retooled third and sixteenth blessings, precisely where a knowledgeable and skilled revisionist would place it.

The Lord authorized an absolute minimum of ritual. He adopted the baptismal innovations of John the Baptist and changed the meaning of the ancient Passover Seder into a memorial of Himself. That was it. Ostentatious ceremony and flowery phrases, so beloved of men, did not impress the Man of Galilee. He directed his followers to worship the Father "in

---

42. Tosephta *Berakhot* 3.12

spirit and in truth" and to pray from the heart.[43] "But when ye pray, use not vain repetitions, as the heathen do: for they think that they shall be heard for their much speaking. Be not ye therefore like unto them: for your Father knoweth what things ye have need of, before ye ask him."[44] Surely the apostles would have regarded fixed liturgical forms as "vain repetition." The only description we have been given of the New Testament *ekklesia*, in 1 Corinthians 14, contains nothing of a liturgical nature.

The Rites of Baptism

Baptism was the gateway sacrament of the sectarians. The founders deliberately chose the tripartite conversion ritual of the Jewish proselyte—circumcision, immersion, and sacrifice—over the immersion-baptism of the apostles. The reason, of course, was circumcision. As the rite that symbolized the acceptance and obligation of Torah, circumcision was the doctrinal battleground of the New Testament. The *Apostolic Tradition* (c. AD 215) contains the fullest account extant of the early ritual, and it is still possible to see the outline of the old proselyte initiation under the third century rubrics. The whole schema is based on a baptism at daybreak on Easter Sunday.

The baptismal candidates would wash themselves on Thursday of Holy Week and fast all Friday and Saturday. A pre-baptismal fast of one or two days' duration goes all the way back to the beginning of the sect.[45] The underlying reason for the short delay is found in the tractate *Yebamoth* of the Babylonian Talmud: "He is to be circumcised, and *when healed*, brought immediately to baptism."[46] Assuming there is no infection or hemorrhaging, it takes 36 to 48 hours for the incision to fully heal.[47] Then, on the evening prior to Easter, the Catholic catechumens would kneel in front of the bishop, who exorcised the evil spirits; breathed on their faces; and sealed their foreheads, ears, and noses. The "seal of confirmation" is a living

---

43. John 4:34–24

44. Matthew 6:7–8

45. *Homilies of Clement* 13.9; *Didache* 7

46. b. Talmud *Yebamoth* 47, emphasis mine

47. Genesis 34:24-25 "And unto Hamor and unto Shechem his son hearkened all that went out of the gate of his city; and every male was circumcised, all that went out of the gate of his city. And it came to pass on the third day, *when they were sore*, that two of the sons of Jacob, Simeon and Levi, Dinah's brethren, took each man his sword, and came upon the city boldly, and slew all the males."

linguistic reminder of what used to fit into this time slot. Circumcision was the *seal* of the Abrahamic covenant.

The all-night paschal vigil was then spent "studying the scriptures and instructing them." According to the Babylonian Talmud, Jewish proselytes were to be coached prior to immersion in "some of the lighter and weightier commandments; and to inform him as to the sins regarding the corner of the field, the forgotten sheaf, the gleaning, and the tithe for the poor."[48] They had to be immersed in Torah before they were immersed in water. Thus we read in book seven of the *Apostolic Constitutions*: "Let him, therefore, who is to be taught the truth in regard to piety be instructed before his baptism.[49] In the *Recognitions of Clement*, they have "Peter" making an exception to the rule. "Otherwise she must have been instructed and taught many days before she could have been baptized."[50]

At the water's edge, they were instructed to "put off their clothes" and "stand in the water naked." The Catholics of the first centuries were baptized entirely naked, but we should keep in mind that the ceremony was performed at the break of dawn. The parallel instructions in the Syrian *Didascalia Apostolorum* indicate that the practice was universal and not limited to Rome.[51] The women were even required to take off their jewelry and rings. "And last the women, who shall all have loosed their hair and laid aside the gold ornaments which they were wearing. Let no one go down to the water having an alien object with them." This custom is traceable to the rabbinic ruling that "no separating element shall intervene between the water and the body."[52] Both ribbons and knotted hair, which prevent water from reaching the individual strands, were considered a *chatzitzah*, or barrier.[53] The instruction to "loose the hair" makes perfect sense in this light.

Once in the water, they were asked to face toward the east. The presbyters involved, both the one who anointed their head and the one who went down into the water, turned the candidates toward the east. This eastern orientation is classically Jewish. The People of the Covenant have looked toward Jerusalem since the first temple was built, and the Torah scrolls are

48. *Ibid* 47
49. *Apostolic Constitutions* 7.39
50. *Recognitions of Clement* 7.34
51. *Didascalia Apostolorum* 16
52. b. *Kerithoth* 82a
53. Mishnah *Shabbat* 6.1c, *Mikvaot* 9.1a

still stored in a niche in the eastern walls of their synagogues.[54] The Catholics are also instructed to direct their prayers toward the rising sun and their places of worship are deliberately oriented on an eastward axis.[55]

The baptismal candidates were each required to bring their own offering, usually a loaf of bread. This was a replacement for the first sacrifice made by Jewish converts after immersion.[56] The bread was their contribution to the sacred banquet, which they now join for the first time. We know what happens next from only one source, the *Homilies of Clement*.[57] At the meal, the elder would tear the loaf, sprinkle salt on a piece, and hand it to the newly-baptized member. The salt here is very significant. Salt had to accompany bread or grain offerings in the temple, and the salting of the bread tells us this was intended to be an offering. "And every oblation of thy meat (i.e., meal) offering shalt thou season with salt; neither shall thou suffer the salt of the covenant of thy God to be lacking from thy meat offering: with all thine offerings thou shalt offer salt."[58]

Their baptismal theology was solidly anchored in the sacrificial system of Moses and Aaron. Just as rabbinical Judaism substituted liturgical prayer for the blood of bulls and goats, so the proto-Catholics replaced the temple sacrifices with baptism. This is explicitly stated in the *Recognitions of Clement*.

> But when the time began to draw near that what was wanting in the Mosaic institutions should be supplied, as we have said, and that the Prophet should appear, of whom he had foretold that He should warn them by the mercy of God to cease from sacrificing; lest haply they might suppose that on the cessation of sacrifice there was no remission of sins for them, He instituted baptism by water amongst them, in which they might be absolved from all their sins on the invocation of His name.

—*Recognitions of Clement* 1.39

Nothing could be further from the teaching of the apostles. They unequivocally pointed to Christ as God's complete and perfect provision for sin. "In whom we have redemption through his blood, the forgiveness of

---

54. 1 Kings 8; Mishnah *Berakhot* 4.5
55. *Didascalia Apostolorum* 12; *Stromata* 7
56. b. *Kerithoth* 8b–9a
57. *Homilies of Clement* 14.1
58. Leviticus 2:13

sins, according to the riches of his grace."[59] Peter's expression of this doctrine has been fashioned into one of the most beloved hymns of redemption. "Forasmuch as ye know that ye were not redeemed with corruptible things, as gold and silver. . . . but with the precious blood of Christ, as of a lamb without blemish and without spot. . . ."[60]

Baptism did not blot out man's original sin, as is believed today, but it was intended to banish the evil spirits and demons dwelling within. The baptism of the first centuries was essentially what we would call an exorcism. Indeed, the oil with which they were anointed was called the "oil of exorcism." Exorcism by adjuration was a popular Jewish superstition in those days, playing off the reverence and power accorded to the name of God.[61] This doctrine is clearly spelled out in the *Recognitions of Clement*. "Everyone who has at any time worshiped idols, and has adored those whom the pagans call gods, or has eaten of the things sacrificed to them, is not without an unclean spirit; for he has become the guest of demons, and has been partaker with that demon of which he has formed the image in his mind, either through love or fear. And by these means he is not free from an unclean spirit, and therefore needs the purification of baptism, that the unclean spirit may go out of him."[62]

The pre-baptismal rites focused heavily on releasing the candidate from the power of Satan. In the *Apostolic Tradition*, an exorcism was done daily during the fasting period and again on Easter Sunday, culminating in a formal renunciation at the water's edge. "And when the presbyter takes hold of each one of those who are to be baptized, let him renounce saying, 'I renounce thee, Satan, and all thy service and all thy works.' And when he has said this, let him anoint him with the oil of exorcism, saying: 'Let all evil spirits depart far from thee.'"[63] A three-fold repudiation of Satan, known as the baptismal vows, still lives on in the high Christian churches.

---

59. Ephesians 1:7; also Colossians 1:13–14; 1 John 1:7

60. 1 Peter 1:18–19

61. See Acts 19:13–16; *Antiquities of the Jews* 8.2.5

62. *Recognitions of Clement* 2.71; also 9.19

63. *Apostolic Tradition* 21

Chapter Five

The Fathers of Uncleanness

And put no difference between us and them (Jew and Gentile),
purifying their hearts by faith.

—ACTS 15:9

Now ye are clean through the word which I have spoken unto you

—JOHN 15:3

THE JEWS WERE HEIRS to a curious set of taboos known as the purity laws. This complex set of regulations was tightly woven into the fabric of their daily lives. Some of them were actual *mitzvahs*—commandments of God—and these were honored and respected by the Lord. But others were merely traditions of men, the rulings of prominent rabbis and sages. Jesus strenuously objected to these man-made rules, and we often read of him sparring with the Pharisees over their application. These traditions were not only vain and unprofitable, but they could actually hinder the observance of God's Law.[1]

Moses set down the primary causes of impurity—known as the Fathers of Uncleanness—in the middle chapters of Leviticus and Numbers 19. They are known collectively as the laws of separation because they demarcate the clean from the unclean. It needs to be made clear that ritual impurity is not the same as sin. A menstruant, for example, is considered unclean, even though she has not violated any commandment. In general, sin can only be atoned by blood or sacrifice while uncleanness must be rectified by a process which usually includes washing and the passage of time. The

---

1. See Mark 7:1–23

subject is so vast and complex that an entire division of the Talmud—one out of six—is devoted to purities.

The proto-Catholics, with their reverence for the Law, wholeheartedly embraced the purity code. The agents that trigger cultic uncleanness are listed below. Many are liquids and, in an interesting bit of symmetry, the process that deactivates uncleanness is also a liquid: water. There is an abundance of evidence in the literature that the early Catholics observed the first two, a reference here and there to the second two, and no evidence whatsoever for the last one.

1. Bodily fluids, especially blood, menstrual discharge, or semen – Leviticus 15

2. The birth of a child, with its attendant bleeding – Leviticus 12

3. Contact with a human corpse or graveyard – Numbers 19

4. The bodies of unclean animals, insects, and lizards – Leviticus 11

5. Leprosy and other skin diseases – Leviticus 13–14

Moses implicitly taught that uncleanness was contagious. The *Mishnah* recognizes five gradations in the Fathers of Uncleanness, depending upon how they transmit impurity, how long it lasts, and if it could be passed further.[2] Uncleanness can be spread by direct physical contact, by entering an enclosed space, or in the case of the most virulent—a corpse—merely by overshadowing. In the example of the *Niddah* (menstruant), anyone who touched her or sat on her couch would be unclean in the first remove. He had to wash his clothes, bathe, and he remained impure until the evening. The degree of defilement grew less potent with each step away from the primary generator.

Jesus of Nazareth transcended the purity laws. He touched the leper in Matthew 8:3, the woman with the issue of blood in Matthew 9:20, and the dead maiden in Mark 5:41. All of these acts would normally bring defilement. But instead of transmitting uncleanness to him, healing and virtue were conveyed to the needy. This power was deemed to be a fulfillment of Isaiah 53:4: "He cast out the spirits with his word, and healed all that were sick: That it might be fulfilled which was spoken by Esaias the prophet, saying, 'Himself took our infirmities, and bare our sicknesses.'"[3]

2. Mishnah *Kelim* 1
3. Matthew 8:16, 17

Family purity is the category of Jewish law which deals with menstruation and marital relations. According to Leviticus 15:19, a woman was unclean for seven days following the first appearance of her menses. The sages extended this to seven clean days beyond her period and added a ritual bath to the cleansing process. A *Niddah* would thus immerse herself in a *mikveh* pool on the evening of the twelfth day before she could resume normal life. Marital relations during her separation were strictly forbidden. It was an extremely serious offence, the penalty for which was to be "cut off from the commonwealth of Israel."[4] The *Mishnah* tells us what being "cut off" meant. "On account of three transgressions do women die in childbirth: because they are not meticulous in the laws of (1) menstrual separation, (2) in [those covering] the dough offering, and (3) in [those covering] the kindling of a lamp [for the Shabbath]."[5]

The false apostles and their protégé took this teaching seriously. The importance of menstrual separation is emphasized repeatedly throughout the *Homilies of Clement*.

> However, it is necessary to add something to these things which has not community with man, but is peculiar to the worship of God. I mean purification, not approaching to a man's own wife when she is in separation, for so the Law of God commands.
>
> —*Homilies of Clement* 11.28

> But who is there to whom it is not manifest that it is better not to have intercourse with a woman in her separation, but purified and washed. And also after copulation, it is proper to wash. But if you grudge to do this, recall to mind how you followed after the parts of purity when you served senseless idols; and be ashamed that now, when it is necessary to attain, I say not more, but to attain the one and whole of purity, you are more slothful.
>
> —*Homilies of Clement* 11.30

> But when through carelessness they neglected the observation of the proper times, when the sons in succession cohabiting through ignorance at times when they ought not, place their children under innumerable afflictions . . . and in truth, such afflictions arise

---

4. Leviticus 20:18
5. Mishnah *Shabbat* 2.6

because of ignorance; as, for instance, by not knowing when one ought to cohabit with his wife, as if she be pure from her discharge.

—Homilies of Clement 19.22

To abstain from the table of devils, that is, from food offered to idols, from dead carcasses, from animals which have been suffocated or caught by wild beasts, and from blood; not to live any longer impurely; to wash after intercourse; that the women on their part should keep the law of purification.

—Homilies of Clement 7.8

These practices lingered in the church for many centuries. Even in progressive Rome, the issue of bathing after marital relations was still being discussed in the third century. "He who has used marriage is not defiled; for those who are washed have no need to wash again, for they are pure."[6] In Syria, the old customs may have persisted up until the fourth century. "An husband, therefore, and a wife, when they have company together in lawful marriage, and rise from one another, may pray without any observations, and without washing are clean."[7]

The doctrine of uncleanness manifested itself in a myriad of ways. A woman in her menses was barred from the baptismal font. "And let those who are to be baptized be instructed to wash and cleanse themselves on the fifth day of the week. And if any women be menstruous, she shall be put aside and baptized another day."[8] They were also denied the sacrament of communion. "Concerning menstruous women, whether they ought to enter the temple of God while in such a state, I think it superfluous even to put the question. For, I opine, not even they themselves, being faithful and pious, would dare when in this state either to approach the Holy Table or to touch the body and blood of Christ."[9] The same letter also touches on the uncleanness brought about by a wet dream. "They who have had involuntary nocturnal pollutions are at their own discretion [whether to communicate or not]."[10]

6. *Apostolic Tradition 36.10*

7. *Apostolic Constitutions 6.29*

8. *Apostolic Tradition 20.5, 6*

9. *Dionysius to Basilides 2*

10. *Ibid 4*

The eastern churches have never strayed far from the ancient land-marks. The Russian Orthodox Church reluctantly permits a menstruant to attend Mass, but they are asked not to take communion, touch the communion bread, kiss the icons and crosses, or drink holy water. Presumably a mere touch would defile the holiness of those sacred objects. Greek Orthodox priests also council women not to communicate during their period.

The bleeding brought on by childbirth would also render a woman *niddah*. An Israelite woman was ritually unclean for seven days after the birth of a son and unclean "in the blood of her purification" for an additional thirty-three days.[11] After the forty days had passed, she would bring a lamb to the priests at the door of the temple.[12] This ceremony surfaces in Catholic tradition as the "Purification of Women after Childbirth before the Door of the Church." Forty days after giving birth, a Catholic mother would go to the porch of the church and kneel down in prayer.[13] Being unclean, she had to wait for the blessing of the priest before being allowed back into the church, which blessing is called "The Churching of Women." She was then expected to produce an offering and resume communicating.

The purity regulations also prohibited contact with dead bodies. We know the proto-Catholics believed such, at least for a while, because an entire chapter of the *Apostolic Constitutions* argues that there is nothing wrong with touching a corpse. Reading between the lines, it appears that some were still observing the purity regulations while the church as a whole had moved beyond them. "Do not therefore keep any such observances about legal and natural purgations, as thinking you are defiled by them. Neither do you seek after Jewish separations, or perpetual washings, or purifications upon the touch of a dead body . . . Whence you also, O bishops and the rest, who without such observances touch the departed, ye ought not to think yourselves defiled. Nor abhor the relics of such persons, but avoid the observances, for they are foolish."[14]

Jesus ignored this prohibition when he raised the ruler's daughter from the dead. "But when the people were put forth, he went in, *and took her by the hand*, and the maid arose."[15] The Son of Man was immune from corpse uncleanness.

11. Leviticus 12:2–4

12. *Ibid* 12:6

13. In later years, a special pew was reserved just inside the door.

14. *Apostolic Constitutions* 6.30

15. Matthew 9:25, emphasis mine; also Luke 7:14

The oral law developed its own code of purity. The Pharisees believed that Levitical purity was not just for the priesthood, but it was incumbent upon all Israel. "If ye will obey my voice indeed, and keep my covenant, then ye shall be a peculiar treasure unto me above all people: for all the earth is mine: *and ye shall be unto me a kingdom of priests, and an holy nation*."[16] The "Separated Ones" took these words to heart and sought to live like priests and Levites in the temple. Eating, and everything associated with it, became a sacred act with its own set of regulations. A man's house was viewed as the temple of God, the kitchen table was the holy altar, and ordinary food treated as the priestly portion of the offerings.[17] Therefore, as the priests carefully washed in the brazen laver before approaching the altar, so the Pharisees would cleanse their hands before eating.[18] As the Levites scrubbed the sacred vessels in the sanctuary, so the Pharisees would wash their cups and pots at home.[19]

The Lord did not validate the traditions of hand-washing or pot scrubbing because of their human origin:

> And when they saw some of his disciples eat bread with defiled, that is to say, with unwashen, hands, they found fault. For the Pharisees, and all the Jews, except they wash their hands oft, eat not, holding the traditions of the elders. And when they come from the market, except they wash, they eat not. And many other things there be, which they have received to hold, as the washing of cups, and pots, brasen vessels, and of tables. Then the Pharisees and scribes asked him, 'Why walk not thy disciples according to the tradition of the elders, but eat bread with unwashen hands?' He answered and said unto them. . . 'Howbeit in vain do they worship me, teaching for doctrines the commandments of men. For laying aside the commandment of God, ye hold the tradition of men, such as the washing of pots and cups: and many other such like things ye do.' And he said unto them, 'Full well ye reject the commandment of God, that ye may keep your own tradition.'

—Mark 7:2–9

16. Exodus 19:5–6, emphasis mine
17. Neusner, *Mishnah* xxxiii
18. Exodus 30:17–21; Luke 11:37–39
19. Leviticus 6:28; Mark 7:1–5

This doctrine made it impossible for Pharisees to eat at the same table with Gentiles or even the unwashed masses of Israel.[20] It would be like shaking hands with Typhoid Mary, something to be avoided at all costs. What the Pharisees applied to the uncircumcised and the unclean, the proto-Catholics applied to the unbaptized. Catechumens and hearers were not allowed to join in table fellowship until they had taken the step of baptism.

The Peter of the *Clementina* articulates this fundamental teaching on many occasions.

> But this also we observe, not to have a common table with Gentiles, unless when they believe, and on the reception of the truth, are baptized, and consecrated by a certain threefold invocation of the blessed Name; and then we eat with them.
>
> —*Recognitions of Clement* 7.29

> When he had thus spoken, he [Peter] retired to take food along with his friends; but he ordered me to eat by myself; and after the meal, when he had sung praise to God and given thanks, he rendered to me an account of this proceeding, and added, 'May the Lord grant to thee to be made like us in all things that, receiving baptism, thou mayest be able to meet with us at the same table.'
>
> —*Recognitions of Clement* 1.19

> Let no one of you therefore be saddened at being separated from eating with us, for every one ought to observe that it is for just so long a time as he pleases. For he who wishes soon to be baptized is separated but for a little time, but he for a longer [time] who wishes to be baptized later. Everyone therefore has it in his own power to demand a shorter or a longer time for his repentance; and therefore it lies with you, when you wish it, to come to our table; and not with us, who are not permitted to take food with anyone who has not been baptized.
>
> —*Recognitions of Clement* 2.72

> Nor do we take our food from the same table as Gentiles, inasmuch as we cannot eat along with them, because they live impurely. But when we have persuaded them to have true thoughts, and to follow a right course of action, and have baptized them with a thrice blessed invocation, then we dwell with them. For not even

---

20. *Tosephta* Demai 2.2

if it were our father, or mother, or wife, or child, or brother, or any other one having a claim by nature on our affection, can we venture to take our meals with him; for our religion compels us to make a distinction.

—Homilies of Clement 13.4

The Peter of the New Testament was led to exactly the opposite conclusion, but it did not come about overnight or without a struggle. It was Peter to whom God gave the revelation of the clean and unclean animals. "Ye know how that it is an unlawful thing for a man that is a Jew to keep company, or come unto one of another nation; but God hath showed me that I should not call any man common or unclean."[21] However, when Peter went up to the Gentile church at Antioch a few years later, he still felt the full force and fury of the old tradition. "But when Peter was come to Antioch, I withstood him to the face, because he was to be blamed. For before that certain came from James, he did eat with the Gentiles; but when they were come, he withdrew and separated himself, fearing them which were of the circumcision."[22] But at the end of the day, at the Jerusalem council, Peter helped guide the apostles into accepting Gentiles as equal brothers in Christ.

Jesus had no qualms about eating with sinners and social outcasts. In the fifth chapter of Luke, he answered his critics with the observation that these were the very people who needed help. "But their scribes and Pharisees murmured against his disciples, saying, Why do ye eat and drink with publicans and sinners? And Jesus answering said unto them, They that are whole need not a physician, but they that are sick."[23] He ran into the same contemptuous attitude in the seventh chapter. A Pharisee invited Jesus to his home for supper, and a sinner woman showed up and anointed his feet. The Pharisee thought within himself that a real prophet would know and avoid such an unclean woman. Instead, Jesus reproved him, comparing her love and care for him with his neglect as a host.[24] Finally, in the fifteenth chapter, he responded to their condemnation with the Parables of the Lost Sheep, the Missing Coin, and the Prodigal Son. He was trying to get them to grasp the value of a single repentant soul.[25]

21. Acts 10:28
22. Galatians 2:11–13
23. Luke 5:30
24. *Ibid* 7:36–50
25. See also Matthew 9:10–13; Luke 19:7–10

We have seen how, unlike the Pauline churches, the proto-Catholics embraced the purity code of Moses and the prohibition against table fellowship. We will discover in the next chapter that the doctrine of table separation gave rise to the two-part structure of the Mass.

Chapter Six

The Primitive Eucharistic Meal

When ye come together therefore into one place,
this is *not* to eat the Lord's supper,
for in eating every one taketh before other his own supper:
and one is hungry, and another is drunken.

—1 CORINTHIANS 11:20–21, emphasis mine

THE SPOTLIGHT IN THIS chapter will be on the centerpiece of Catholic religiosity and devotion, the Eucharist. The historical roots of this rite are not as straightforward as it might appear. We are, after all, examining an apostate sect, not the church familiar to us from the New Testament. While the earliest stages of its evolution are concealed by a lack of documentation, there is still enough circumstantial and indirect evidence to allow us to connect the dots.

By the beginning of the Christian era, the common meal had been elevated to a semi-sacred status in Jewish life. The Pharisees had introduced hand-washing and other temple rites to the domestic table, and every mealtime act, no matter how minor, had been invested with religious significance. One of these was a little ritual involving bread that kicked off every group or family meal. The Lord also followed this tradition throughout his ministry. "And he commanded the multitude to sit down on the grass, and took the five loaves, and the two fishes, and looking up to heaven, he blessed, and brake, and gave the loaves to his disciples, and the disciples to the multitude."[1] We find the same sequence at the Last Supper. "And as they were eating, Jesus took bread, and blessed it, and broke it, and gave it to

1. Matthew 14:19, 15:36

73

the disciples, and said, Take, eat; this is my body."[2] Again, on the day of the resurrection, "It came to pass, as he sat at meat with them, he took bread, and blessed it, and brake, and gave to them."[3] It is easy to understand why a common Hebrew idiom for eating or sharing a meal was to "break bread."[4]

This ritual consisted of four consecutive steps performed in rapid succession. The host would:

1. Take the loaf of bread and hold it in his hands

2. Recite the blessing over the bread

3. Break or tear the flatbread into pieces

4. Distribute a piece to each of the guests

The only unchanging constant of the Eucharist down through the ages has been the arrangement of its constituent parts; what we might call its external structure. While the language of the liturgy, the thing which is *said*, has never ceased to evolve, the core of the rite, the thing which is *done*, has remained remarkably stable. A historical analysis of the Eucharist based upon this premise was first proposed by the Anglican liturgist Gregory Dix in the 1940s. In his groundbreaking work, *The Shape of the Liturgy*, he pointed out that the Lord used seven separate acts to institute the New Covenant Breaking of Bread. He (1) took bread, (2) broke it, (3) gave thanks over it, (4) gave it to his disciples, (5) took the cup, (6) gave thanks, and (7) gave it to the disciples.[5] This was the unanimous testimony of all three synoptic evangelists and the apostle Paul. By way of contrast, the ritual used by the Catholic Church, from ancient times to modern, from the Euphrates River to the Atlantic Ocean, has uniformly consisted of only four steps. These are:

1. The offertory,

2. The prayer,

3. The fraction, and

4. Communion.

---

2. Matthew 26:26

3. Luke 24:30

4. Acts 2:46, 20:11, 27:35

5. Dix, *Shape of the Liturgy* page 48

Why does Catholic tradition ignore the clear teachings of the Gospel? We must understand that the Eucharist was not the result of obeying the Lord's instructions at the Last Supper. It was instead the vestige of a sacred banquet that the pseudo-apostles placed at the end of their Sunday prayer service. It was known in the first century as the "Thanksgiving," but we will call it the Primitive Eucharistic Meal—PEM for short—to differentiate it from the sacramental Eucharist.

Feasting, with the special joy and personal bonding it brings, played a large role in all of the Jewish holy days. Even an ordinary Sabbath had its *Oneg*, an informal time of socializing with refreshments after the service. The proto-Catholics felt a commemoration of the Lord's death deserved no less, and so they ended the reading of Scripture and prayer with a ritualized meal. It is astounding to think that the nucleus of the present Mass was born of a simple Jewish supper, but this fact explains much of the terminology and structure of the rite.

The Thanksgiving meal goes back to the founding of the sect. *The Didache* 14 contains instructions that point us in the direction of a meal, but it requires some knowledge of Jewish table customs to decipher. "But every Lord's day do ye gather yourselves together, and break bread, and give thanksgiving after having confessed your transgressions, that your sacrifice may be pure." Let's pull this sentence apart line by line. They "broke bread," meaning they shared a meal together, and then they "gave thanksgiving," meaning they recited the customary blessing after the meal. The "sacrifice" in this context was the food on the table. The Pharisees viewed food as an offering to God, and because it had been accompanied by thanksgiving and confession, they hoped it would be acceptable.

The table blessings for the sacred meal have been warehoused in the *Didache*. Chapter nine contains the proto-Catholic version of the two most common mealtime blessings; those for the bread and the wine. The first *berakah* was for the cup. As a symbol of joy and good cheer, the rabbis made extensive use of wine in their rituals. Each person at the table would recite this blessing for his or herself before the meal began. The second blessing was for the bread, and it was delivered by the host on behalf of the whole company. If this blessing is recited at the beginning of the meal, it blesses all of the food which follows, except wine and fresh fruit, which have their own separate blessings.

Chapter ten contains the reformulated Grace after Meal, the main Jewish table blessing. This prayer is required if bread or cereal grains in any form are consumed. A meal—as opposed to a mere snack—is defined by the presence of bread. Known as the *Birkat Hamazon*, this blessing is recited after everyone is finished eating. The specific language of the *Didache* leaves little doubt this was an actual meal and not a symbolic sacrament. "But after ye are *filled*, thus give thanks." Peter gives the same blessings over the food followed by a thanksgiving in the *Homilies of Clement*. "And having blessed the food, and having given thanks *after being satisfied* . . ."[6] Again, as in the *Didache*, the main table grace was delivered *after* they had eaten the bounty of the table.

The summons to recite the *Birkat Hamazon* was also incorporated into the PEM. When three or more adults have dined together and all must say grace, the host issues a formal invitation to pray and those at the table give their assent. Known as the *Birkat Zimun*, the summons is phrased in a slightly different manner according to the number of people at the table. According to the *Mishnah*, they had a standard formulation for three, ten, 100, 1,000, and 10,000 people.[7] This shows up in the Mass as the pre-Eucharistic dialogue between the priest and the congregants. The declaration of the priest, "Let us give thanks unto the Lord our God," is phrased in precisely the same language employed by the rabbis when one hundred persons are present, except the *Birkat Zimun* has "bless" in the Jewish manner instead of the Christianized "give thanks." The Hebrew invitation simply says, "Let us bless the Lord our God."

The dining furniture of the classic Mediterranean civilizations are as foreign to us as their table manners. The dining room of the upper-class Roman family was called the *triclinium*, named for the three couches that filled the room. These couches faced inward upon three sides of a square, leaving the front open for serving. In the middle stood an elevated, round table upon which household slaves would place the food and beverages. Each couch supported a large, stuffed cushion, wide enough to accommodate three recumbent diners. In polite society, diners would recline on their left elbow, which rested on a pillow, and eat with their right hand. The host reclined on the left couch, and in the place of greatest access and proximity, the guest of honor faced him on the middle couch. The *Tosefta* explains the protocol: "When there are three couches, the greatest [in importance] reclines at the head of the middle [couch]."[8] The guests were arranged

---

6. *Homilies of Clement* 1.22, emphasis mine

7. Mishnah *Berakhot* 7.3

8. Tosephta *Berakhot* 5.5

further to the right by decreasing rank and social status, while the family members lounged behind the host on the left couch. At the Last Supper, Jesus served as host, and John, who was "leaning on Jesus' bosom," was reclining next to him on the left cushion.[9]

A formal Jewish feast was preceded by an extensive bout of preliminary rituals, and some of these made it into the Primitive Eucharistic Meal. They washed their hands by pouring water over one hand and then the other. The wine was mixed with water. Normally these duties were the responsibility of the household servants, but at the sacred banquet, they were done by the church deacons.

One of the duties of the deacon was to mix the cup. The wines of ancient times were not the quality of modern vintages, and they were diluted with water to make them less potent and more palatable. (The Greeks and Romans added honey to improve the flavor.) The Jews incorporated the act of mixing the cup into their mealtime rituals, and the *Mishnah* recounts several rabbinical disputes over matters of procedure. "They do not recite the blessing over wine until one puts water into it—the words of R. Eliezer. But (other sages) say, They even recite the blessing (beforehand)."[10] "The House of Shammai say, They wash the hands and then mix the cup. But the House of Hillel say, They mix the cup and then wash the hands."[11] The Hillelites and the Shammaites were the two principal schools of the Pharisees.

After the preliminaries were over, the meal began with the breaking of bread. The host would hold the bread in his hands, recite the blessing, tear off a piece, and one by one hand it to each person at the table. This ritual in its entirety was incorporated into the primitive Eucharistic Meal and from there it passed to the sacramental Eucharist. *The four actions of the Catholic Eucharist—the offertory, the prayer, the fraction, and communion—are nothing more than the four steps of the Hebrew bread blessing ritual.*

The Four Steps of the Primitive Eucharistic Meal

The sacred meal—and later the Holy Eucharist—began with the offertory. The original offerings, those of the first and early second centuries, were the bread, wine, cheese, olives, fruit, and fish which the congregants brought for the potluck-style meal. This food was deemed to be an *offering* to God, in

9. John 13:23–25
10. Mishnah *Berakhot* 7.5d, e
11. *Ibid Berakhot* 8.2

the Jewish manner, like the sacrifices made by the priesthood in the Temple. They probably carried the food in the same type of woven baskets we see depicted in banqueting scenes on catacomb walls. These baskets were deposited on a special table at the back of the assembly room until they were needed.

Two different customs developed to get the food offerings—later the sacraments—from the back of the room to the banqueting table or altar. In the east, the laity brought their oblation to a designated table before the service began. Then, after the Gospel portion was read, the offerings were taken up to the front in a resplendent ceremony known as the Great Entrance. In a solemn procession, beginning with torches and candles, a deacon held the sacred bread high above his head, followed by a priest with the chalice. In the west, the laity has always made the offerings themselves at the chancel rail, laying the bread on a linen cloth and pouring the wine into a silver cup. Gregory Dix threw down the gauntlet to some aspiring liturgist to explain what lay behind the divergence in custom.[12] It may be no more complicated than this: in the Levant, the first century deacons were assigned the task of bringing the baskets of food to the table, while in Rome, the congregants brought their own basket of food up to the front themselves.

A passage from the *Didascalia Apostolorum* brings us back tantalizingly close to those days. "But of the deacons, let one stand continually by the oblations of the Eucharist and let another stand without by the door and observe them that come in. And afterwards, when you offer, let them minister together in the church."[13] It has been customary since ancient times to collect alms at this time, and consequently the offertory has become a euphemism for the collection of money.

The second act of the bread-breaking ritual was the blessing. After all of the guests were seated at the table, the Jewish head of household would recite the blessing over the bread, which is known as the *Hamotzi*. "Blessed art Thou, Lord our God, King of the universe, who brings forth bread from the earth."[14] While they had still the Primitive Eucharistic Meal, the proto-Catholics would recite the much longer Christianized version. We know the exact wording from the *Didache*:

> We thank Thee, our Father, for the life and knowledge which Thou made known to us through Jesus Thy Servant; to Thee be the glory forever. Even as this broken bread was scattered over the hills,

12. Dix, *Shape of the Liturgy* p. 121
13. *Didascalia Apostolorum* 12
14. Donin, *To be a Jew* p. 168

and was gathered together and became one, so let Thy Church be gathered together from the ends of the earth into Thy kingdom; for Thine is the glory and the power through Jesus Christ forever.

—Didache 9

The third step in the bread ritual was the fraction. This was the physical tearing or breaking of the loaf. This act marked the beginning of the meal proper. "R. Simeon b. Gamaliel says, Pieces [of bread] serve as an important sign for the guests. Whenever the guests see the pieces [being brought out], they know that something else [some other course] is to follow them."[15] It was an expected courtesy for each diner to take the piece of bread from the host. This rubric was incorporated into the sacred banquet and from there made its way into the liturgical Eucharist. Tertullian, writing around AD 200, drives the point home. "We take also, in congregations before daybreak, and from the hand of none but the presidents, the sacrament of the Eucharist . . ."[16] We observe the continuance of this practice today when the officiating priest places the wafer in the hand or on the tongue of the communicants.

Communion, the culmination of the four-step ritual, was the sacred meal itself. The *Recognitions of Clement* speaks explicitly of the baptized enjoying "the communion of the table."[17] The parallel passage in the *Homilies* describes the scene in greater detail, beginning with the breaking of bread, the blessing, the distribution, and finally the meal. "Peter came several hours after, and breaking the bread after thanksgiving, and putting salt upon it, he gave it first to our mother and, after her, to us her sons. And thus we took food along with her and blessed God."[18]

It was their first food of the day and, indeed, of the week: "The faithful shall be careful to partake of the Eucharist before eating anything else."[19] Pious Jews, on the Sabbath, are careful not to eat before morning prayers, and the proto-Catholics transferred this rule to the first day of the week. The Eastern Orthodox still refrain from eating or drinking on Sundays before receiving the sacraments.

15. Mishnah *Berakhot* 7

16. *On the Crown* 3

17. *Recognitions of Clement* 7.36

18. *Homilies of Clement* 14

19. *Apostolic Tradition* 36

The Thanksgiving Meal becomes the Liturgical Eucharist

The Primitive Eucharistic Meal gave rise to two institutions: the Holy Eucharist of the Mass and the *agape*, or love feast. Gregory Dix believed the sacramental Eucharist was detached from the sacred supper by the first generation of Jewish apostles, but the same chain of evidence leads us into the early years of the second century.[20] The *Didache* unquestionably refers to a meal of some kind, as we have seen. Then, as we move into the second century, the writers of the period have almost nothing to say about the subject. The literary record is a blank slate. Pliny's Letter to Trajan dated AD 112 may be the smoking gun we are looking for. "After this ceremony [the Sunday morning service] it had been their custom to disperse and reassemble later to take food of an ordinary, harmless kind."[21] We have to ask ourselves: if some of them had just eaten the Primitive Eucharistic Meal, would they be inclined to get together for another fellowship meal? It is more likely the Bithynian Catholics had just participated in a sacramental Eucharist, and the potluck of "ordinary" food was a replacement for their customary PEM. The first definite Eucharist we come across in the literature is found in Justin Martyr's *First Apology*, and it can be dated very close to AD 150. We can thus tentatively place the beginning of the liturgical Eucharist around AD 110 in Asia Minor and perhaps a bit later in Rome.

The new Eucharistic rite took the old four-action shape of the bread ritual and reassembled the component parts. The summons to say grace became the dialogue before the Eucharistic prayer. The offertory was now restricted to just bread and wine. The blessing over the bread was jettisoned and replaced by the Thanksgiving prayer, heretofore recited after the meal. The fraction remained the breaking of the loaf, and communion became the reception of the bread and cup from the hand of the presbyter.

The Source of the Eucharistic Prayer

The invocation over the sacramental Eucharist was taken from the last of the Hebrew table blessings, the one given after the meal. The *Birkat Hamazon* is by far the longest of the mealtime blessings, taking two or three minutes to recite. The outline of this prayer was framed by the words of Moses.

20. Dix, *The Shape of the Liturgy* p. 101
21. *Pliny to Trajan* No. 96

"When thou has eaten and art full, then thou shalt bless the Lord thy God for the good land which he hath given thee."[22] It is the only benediction expressly commanded by Torah and therefore occupies a special place of honor in Jewish ritual. This obligation is discharged by reciting a blessing 1) for the food, and 2) for the land, and 3) for Jerusalem and the Sanctuary. A fourth benediction was added after the Great Jewish War.

The primitive Eucharistic prayer of the church contained the same series of three thanksgivings as the original "Three Blessings," as it is called in the Talmud, but the material was recast in a Christian mold. The revised table grace has passed into Catholic usage as the "Eucharist," which is simply the Greek word for thanksgiving (*Eucharistia*). Let us view the text of the first century Catholic Thanksgiving after Meal, as preserved in *Didache* 10, alongside the modern Jewish Grace after Meal. The *Birkat Hamazon* has been taken from Hayim Donin's authoritative *To Pray as a Jew*.[23] We have underscored, italicized, and bolded the portions of the two prayers that show the closest correspondence.

The Birkat Hamazon	The Didache 10
First Blessing: "Blessed art Thou, Lord our God, King of the universe, who in His goodness, grace, loving kindness, and mercy, nourishes the whole world. He gives food to all flesh, for His loving kindness is everlasting. In His great goodness, we have never lacked for food; may we never lack for food <u>for the sake of His great Name</u>. For He nourishes and sustains all, He does good to all, and prepares food **for all his creatures that He created**. *Blessed art Thou, Lord, who provides food for all.*"	"We thank thee, holy father, for thy holy name which Thou didst cause to tabernacle in our hearts, and for the knowledge and faith and immortality which Thou madest known to us through Jesus Thy Servant; to Thee be the glory for ever. **Thou, Master almighty, didst create all things** <u>for Thy</u> Name's sake; *Thou gavest food and drink to men for enjoyment,*
Second Blessing: <u>"We thank Thee, Lord our God, for the desirable, good and spacious land</u> that Thou gave our forefathers as a heritage; for having brought us out of the land of Egypt and redeemed us from slavery; for Thy covenant that Thou sealed in our flesh; for Thy Torah which Thou taught us and Thy statues which Thou made known to us; for the life, the grace and loving kindness that Thou has bestowed on us; and for the food with which	<u>That they might give thanks to Thee; but to us Thou didst freely give spiritual food and drink and eternal life through Thy Servant.</u>

22. Deuteronomy 8:10

23. Page 289

Thou constantly feed and sustain us every day, at all times and in every hour. **For everything, Lord our God, we thank Thee and bless Thee;** may Thy name be blessed in the mouth of every living creature at all times and for all time; as it is written: 'When you have eaten and are satisfied, you shall bless the Lord your God for the good land that He has given you.' Blessed art Thou, Lord, for the land and the food."

Before all things we thank Thee that Thou art mighty; to Thee be the glory forever.

Third Blessing: "Be merciful, Lord our God, to Thy people Israel, to Thy city, Jerusalem, and to Zion, the dwelling place of Thy glory, *to the Royal House of David*, Thine anointed, and to the great and holy Temple that was called by Thy name. Our God, our Father, tend us, feed us, sustain us, maintain us, and comfort us. Grant us speedy relief, Lord our God, from all our troubles. And please, Lord our God, let us not need other people's gifts or loans, but only Thy filled and open hand, holy and bountiful. So that we may not ever be shamed or humiliated. **Rebuild Jerusalem, the holy city,** soon in our days. Blessed art Thou, Lord, who in His mercy builds Jerusalem. Amen."

Remember, Lord, Thy Church,

to deliver it from all evil and to make it perfect in Thy love, and to **gather it from the four winds,** sanctified for Thy kingdom which Thou has prepared for it; for Thine is the power and glory for ever. Let grace come, and let this world pass away. *Hosanna to the God of David."*

There are marked similarities, both in subject matter and actual verbiage, between the two prayers. In the first benediction, we find that the proto-Catholics were not as profuse in praising God for feeding the world as the rabbis. Instead, they focused on the spiritual blessings of the indwelling Name, knowledge, and faith, contrasting the "everlasting" kindness of God in providing for his creation with the "immortality" they had received in Jesus. Both prayers touch on the themes of creation and the Name, and the "food for all His creatures that He created" becomes "food and drink to men for enjoyment."

In the second blessing, gratitude for giving their forefathers the land of Israel, Torah, and circumcision becomes appreciation for the "spiritual food and drink and eternal life" freely given to them through Jesus. Both prayers go on to offer an explicit expression of gratitude: "For everything, Lord our God, we thank Thee," becoming, "Before all things we thank Thee."

In the third blessing, the lengthy petition to be merciful to Israel, Jerusalem, Zion, and the holy temple becomes a simple request to remember the church. Both benedictions refer to David, but the emphasis has shifted from a restoration of the Davidic Kingdom to the purification of the Kingdom of God. The request to rebuild the Holy City was converted into a petition for the ingathering of the sanctified (holy) church. "Grant us speedy relief from all our troubles" was transformed into "deliver us from all evil," a line taken from the Lord's Prayer.

We have provided six legs of support for the theory that a sacred meal, now discontinued, underlies the Eucharist of the Mass. Let us recap the evidence:

- The technical term Eucharist has no basis whatsoever in Scripture. It is clearly derived from the Jewish Grace after Meal, which is usually called the Blessing or Thanksgiving. The apostles almost always referred to the New Covenant rite as the "Breaking of Bread," while the word "thanksgiving" is connected with mealtime prayers, see 1 Tim 4:3–5.[24]

- The four-step structure of the Catholic rite also has no foundation in Scripture, where Jesus used seven steps. Instead, it represents the normal progression of the Hebrew bread blessing ritual.

- The Pharisaic prohibition against table fellowship with the uncircumcised became the Catholic rule forbidding the unbaptized to eat with the baptized. The catechumens were therefore dismissed before the Primitive Eucharistic Meal and later before the liturgical Eucharist.

- The dialogue preceding the Eucharist is clearly derived from the Hebrew invitation to say grace. It cannot be a coincidence that this dialogue is framed in almost exactly the same language as the *Birkat Zimun*. As Gregory Dix observed, this fact alone would be enough to identify the Christian Eucharistic prayer with the *Birkat Hamazon*.[25]

- The Catholic Eucharistic prayer was patterned after the *Birkat Hamazon*. Why use this particular benediction if it was not an actual meal? A different template would have been used for a

---

24. "Forbidding to marry, and commanding to abstain from meats, which God hath created to be received with thanksgiving of them which believe and know the truth. For every creature of God is good, and nothing to be refused, if it is received with thanksgiving, for it is sanctified by the word of God and prayer."

25. Dix, *Shape of the Liturgy* p. 127

ceremonial Eucharist, perhaps something from the passion narratives of the Gospels.

- The *Didache* supplies separate blessings for bread and wine, in accordance with Jewish mealtime customs, and instructs them to say the main prayer after they are satiated, also the normal custom. The word "filled" indicates it was an actual meal and not mere ceremony.

The Lord's Supper

The *agape* or, as it was usually called, the Lord's Supper, was not the love-feast celebrated by Peter and Jude.[26] It was, instead, what remained of the Primitive Eucharistic Meal after the Eucharistic elements had been extracted. The bread ritual at the beginning of the PEM was combined with the cup of blessing and the Grace after Meal to form the sacramental Eucharist. Everything that lay between, which was basically the meal, became the *agape*.

The Lord's Supper remained a corporate affair of the church. They were held under the auspices of the bishop or elder, and the old rule that prohibited catechumens from eating with the baptized was strictly observed. It was a solemn occasion, eaten in silence unless the presbyter decided to expound on the Scriptures or asked someone to sing.[27] Everyone at the table received bread from the elder, as they had at the Primitive Eucharistic Meal, but this was "blessed bread," carefully distinguished in their minds from the bread of the Eucharist. *The Apostolic Tradition* explains the difference. "And they shall take from the hand of the bishop one piece of a loaf before each takes his own bread, for this is 'blessed' bread, but it is not the Eucharist as is the Body of the Lord."[28]

We can hardly do better than to quote Tertullian at this point. He is taking great pains in this passage to explain that the Lord's Supper is a religious gathering, not an occasion for debauchery.

> The participants, before reclining, first taste of prayer to God. As much is eaten as satisfies the cravings of hunger; as much is drunk as befits the chaste. They say it is enough, as those who remember that even during the night they have to worship God; they talk

26. 2 Peter 2:13; Jude 12

27. The tractate *Derekh Eretz* gives the rules governing formal Jewish meals. "It is forbidden to talk during the meal, lest the food be swallowed the wrong way."

28. *Apostolic Tradition* 26

as those who know that the Lord is one of their auditors. After manual ablution, and the bringing in of lights, each [or perhaps "one"] is asked to stand forth and sing, as he can, a hymn to God— either one from the holy scriptures or one of his own composing— a proof of the measure of our drinking. As the feast commenced with pray, so with prayer it is closed.

—*First Apology* 39

We know the exact wording of the concluding prayer. It is an abridgement of the Grace after Meal. "Thou art blessed, O Lord, who nourished me from my youth, who givest food to all flesh. Fill our hearts with joy and gladness, that having always what is sufficient for us, we may abound unto every good work, in Christ Jesus our Lord, through whom glory, honor, and power be to Thee forever. Amen."[29]

A painting of the Lord's Supper or the PEM, known as the Breaking of Bread, has been preserved in the Catacomb of Priscilla. It lies directly above a *triclinium* chamber carved out of the rock, couches and all. This is one of the oldest catacombs in Rome, and the so-called Greek chapel, where the *Fractio Panis* fresco was found, belongs to its earliest phase. Even the fact that the inscriptions are in Greek attest to its high antiquity. The mural, which dates from the middle of the second century, was miraculously preserved by a thick crust of stalactites until it was uncovered in 1893.

The fresco shows six men and a veiled woman behind a table, reclining on sloped couches. The diners rest on their left arms and reach for food with their right. The presiding elder, a bearded man, is sitting upright in the place of the host on the left. His arms are stretched out straight, holding a small loaf, and his head is thrown back, depicting the recitation of the blessing over the bread.[30] There is a round table in the foreground set with a two-handled cup, which was used in the hand-washing ritual, a plate with five loaves, and another with two fishes. The five loaves and two fishes connect the supper with the Miracle of the Loaves.[31] Several large wicker baskets of bread are sitting on both sides of the table.

29. *Apostolic Constitutions* 7.49

30. The elevation of the bread, an act that regained significance in medieval times, derived from the raising of the *matzah* at the Passover supper.

31. Matthew 14:19

The Breaking of Bread fresco with the elder on the left,
caught in the act of blessing the bread.

Chapter Seven

The Dawning of the Pauline Day

AD 144 to AD 155

For Christ is the end of the law for righteousness
to everyone that believeth.

—ROMANS 10:4

Love worketh no ill to his neighbor:
Therefore love is the fulfilling of the law.

—ROMANS 13:10

THE *KATHOLIKA EKKLESIA* BEGAN as a curious blend of Palestinian
Christianity and Pharisaic Judaism. The false apostles kept to the founding
creed for a decade or two before moving away from the Law. The more
burdensome obligations, like circumcision and the dietary laws, were
among the first *mitzvahs* to go. They justified the shift in doctrine by taking
refuge in symbolism and allegory. All of this was bringing them closer to
the theological position blazed by the apostle Paul, but he had not yet been
accepted. The catalyst that finally put them over the top was a reformer
named Marcion.

Marcion was born and raised in Sinope, a thriving Greek settlement
on the southern shores of the Black Sea. The town has a beautiful natural
harbor and, in antiquity, it was the foremost port on the *Pontus Euxinus*.
Marcion became a ship owner and, by all accounts, a wealthy merchant. His
father was the elder of the local Catholic congregation, and it is safe to assume they gathered for worship in his home. He was thus brought up in the

sect and thoroughly versed in its Scriptures, ceremonies, and tenets. The leading authority on Marcion, Adolf von Harnack, believed that Marcion and his family must have come out of Judaism, so thoroughly Jewish were his expositions of the Old Testament.[1] Harnack did not realize that Marcion was simply reflective of the Catholicism of his day.

Sometime in the 130s, Marcion came across a collection of Paul's epistles in his hometown. We can only speculate where he stumbled onto them, but there is no compelling reason to look elsewhere. If there was any place where Pauline Christians were thick on the ground, it was western Anatolia. Peter had addressed his first epistle to "the strangers scattered throughout Pontus, Galatia. . . ." clear back in the sixth decade of the first century, and the Roman administrator Pliny tells us how numerous Christians had become by AD 112.[2] Reading Paul was, for Marcion, a life-altering experience, and he began to see the Gospel in an entirely new light. Martin Luther had the same epiphany some 1400 years later. Marcion journeyed to Ephesus, the Vatican of that era; he was rebuffed, and then sailed on to Rome around AD 140.

The key that unlocked the puzzle was Paul's epistle to the Galatians. After reading Galatians and comparing it with the church he grew up in, Marcion correctly guessed at the history of the apostolic period. The true message of Jesus Christ had been corrupted by "false apostles and Jewish evangelists,"[3] and only Paul, who had received a direct revelation from God, had grasped the spiritual essence of the Gospel. Even the twelve apostles had not completely made the break with Judaism that was needed. As Irenaeus wrote, "For [they maintain] that the apostles intermingled the things of the law with the words of the Savior."[4] This makes little sense until you realize that Marcion had been raised on the legalism of the *Preaching of Peter* and not the Acts of the Apostles. Marcion saw himself as a reformer, attempting to restore Christianity to the purity of its original Pauline foundation. "For they allege that Marcion did not so much innovate on the rule [of faith] by his separation of the law and gospel, as restore it after it had been previously adulterated."[5]

---

1. Harnack, *Marcion* chapter 2
2. 1 Peter 1:1; *Pliny Letter No. 96*
3. Harnack, *Marcion* p. 36–37
4. *Against Heresies* 3.2.2
5. Tertullian, *Against Marcion* 1.20

Marcion set down his theology in a little work Tertullian styled the *Antitheses* ("Contradictions").[6] The book contrasted, in a point-by-point fashion, the commandments of the Law with the precepts of the Gospel. The following examples are typical of his exegesis. While Moses had legislated "an eye for an eye;" Christ advocated unconditional forgiveness. Joshua had conquered Canaan with violence and cruelty; Christ stressed mercy and compassion. Elisha had children eaten by bears; Christ said, "Let the little children come unto me." Marcion rejected the orthodox tendency to allegorize the Old Testament, insisting what was written must stand on its own merits. One need only read Papias, *The Epistle of Barnabas, The Shepherd of Hermas*, or even Justin Martyr to see why he took this position. The use of allegory had reached utterly preposterous proportions by the second quarter of the second century. Marcion could not reconcile the two covenants and, insisting that the God of Israel could not possibly be the Father of Jesus Christ, fell into dualism. He therefore rejected the entire Hebrew canon.

> **Papias** – The bishop of Hierapolis, the holy city across the Lycus Valley from Colosse, in the early decades of the second century. Papias was the author of a five-part work entitled *The Exposition of the Sayings of the Lord*, fragments of which survive in Irenaeus and Eusebius. The work was probably a compilation of the oral traditions of the sectarians. Eusebius, who had read the book, judged Papias to have been "a man of low intelligence."

Marcion's Bible consisted of two parts: The Gospel and the Apostle. The *Apostolikon* was a collection of the ten Pauline epistles he considered authentic: Galatians, Romans, 1 and 2 Corinthians, 1 and 2 Thessalonians, Colossians, Philippians, Philemon, and Ephesians. Marcion carefully went through the letters and culled any material that pertained to the old covenant. He then turned his attention to the Gospel, and sought to re-establish the original text by means of excision and emendation. He chose to start with the Gospel of Luke, probably because Luke was a Gentile and the evangelist most closely associated with Paul. The Gospel of John, arguably the most spiritual of the four and the least friendly to the Jews, would have been the logical choice, but it was probably unknown to him. Matthew, the traditional Gospel of the proto-Catholics, the one he grew up with, would have been irredeemably tainted. He removed the opening chapters relating to the birth and infancy of Jesus, references to the Hebrew prophets, and all the passages where Jesus participated in the Passover or showed respect to the Law.

---

6. *Ibid* 4.1

Marcion spent his first few years in Rome writing the *Antitheses* and preparing the *Evangelicon* and the *Apostolikon*. He made large financial contributions to the church, and gained respect by the force of his intellect and personal piety. He then asked Pius, the bishop of Rome, for a formal hearing. In AD 144, Marcion stood before a gathering of the Roman presbyters and took as his point of departure the Parable of the Good and Corrupt Tree. "For a good tree bringeth forth not corrupt fruit; neither doth a corrupt tree bring forth good fruit."[7] By his analysis, the Old Law was the corrupt tree and the Gospel of Jesus Christ the good tree. His listeners must have been in shock; he was attacking the very foundation of their faith, and using an unauthorized Gospel to do so. Marcion was sharply rebuked, expelled from fellowship, and all of his money returned. The year of his excommunication is unusually secure for this nebulous period of church history. It was burned into the memory of the Marcionites as the beginning of their reformed church.

This was the first time Paul had been openly debated in Catholic circles. We have no record of their initial response, but we can guess. Justin Martyr, an orthodox teacher living in Rome, wrote about the extraordinary success of the Marcionites just a few years after the excommunication. "And he, by the aid of the devils, has caused many of every nation to speak blasphemies."[8] Tertullian confirmed the phenomenal growth of the sect 50 years later: "Marcion's heretical teaching has filled the whole world."[9] Such was the power of the Pauline corpus. The Roman presbyters themselves saw the passion aroused in their own congregations by the Apostle. After reading the *Didache*, the *Epistle of Barnabas*, and the other literature of the second century Catholics, it is not difficult to see why. They are dry and lifeless compared to the brilliant insights and magnificent language of Paul.

The grassroots enthusiasm generated by Paul is vividly seen in an incident that happened in Asia Minor around AD 170. An unidentified Catholic presbyter got so carried away with passion for Paul that he composed an apocryphal tale about the apostle. *The Acts of Paul and Thecla*, as it is known, embellishes the Iconium mission with details of a beautiful virgin, her conversion, and her steadfastness. After being removed from office, the man admitted he did it "out of love for Paul" and to "augment Paul's fame."[10] The Asian presbyter provided the Catholic world with a physical

7. Luke 6:43

8. *1st Apology* 26

9. *Against Marcion* 5.19

10. Tertullian, *On Baptism* 17

description of their new celebrity. "And he saw Paul coming, a man small in size, baldheaded, bandy-legged, well-built, with eyebrows meeting, rather long-nosed, full of grace."

How do we know Marcion was the source of the Pauline corpus? It turns out that he left his literary fingerprints all over the letters in the form of a distinctive prologue. These introductions are known as the Marcionite or Old Latin prologues because they were still attached to the epistles in the fourth century Latin translation, the Vulgate. They all follow the same basic outline. The prologues begin by giving the nationality of the recipients, notes they had received the gospel from Paul, declares they had been led astray by false apostles, and concludes by giving the place of composition. The preface to the Galatian letter is representative of them all.

> The Galatians are Greeks. They accepted the word of truth first from the apostle, but after his departure were tempted by false apostles to turn to the law and circumcision. These the apostle recalls to the faith of the truth, writing to them from Ephesus.

The first generation of Catholics to handle these letters, not being familiar with the material, did not recognize the headings for what they were. Consequently, when they made copies for neighboring congregations, they carefully duplicated them exactly as they had received them, headings and all. The prologues thus tell us not only *where* they got the epistles, but also *when* they entered the Catholic canon.

The prologues are widely held to be Marcionite in origin because of their anti-Jewish message, but there is another powerful reason. The internal chronology presupposed by the headings makes it almost a dead certainty. The historical order of the letters as understood by the author is the same order they are listed in Marcion's *Apostolikon*. Statistically speaking, the odds of this being a coincidence are close to zero.

Marcion was not the only one to possess the riches of Paul. The Egyptian Gnostics also had their own hoard of his epistles. Hippolytus, in his *Refutation of all Heresies*, has preserved excerpts from the writings of Basilides, a renowned Alexandrian theologian who taught "in the time of Hadrian," AD 117 to

Basilides – One of the earliest Christian teachers of record, Basilides was an Egyptian Gnostic who taught in the 120s and 130s. He wrote a commentary on the Gospel called the *Exegetica*, fragments of which survive in the works of his detractors. Basilides claimed he had heard the gospel from Glaucias, Peter's interpreter, another assertion of apostolic succession.

AD 138.[11] We find partial but recognizable citations from 1 Corinthians, 2 Corinthians, Romans, and Ephesians.[12]

One passage in particular, 1 Corinthians 2:9, shows up in an astonishing number of Catholic and Gnostic manuscripts. "But as it is written, eye hath not seen, nor ear heard, neither have entered into the heart of man, the things which God hath prepared for them that love him." In 1945, fifty-two scrolls were discovered in an earthenware jar near the village of Nag Hammadi in Upper Egypt. They were written in Coptic, the language of Egyptian Christianity. The texts included the *Gospel of Thomas*, the *Acts of Peter*, the *Dialogue of the Saviour*, and the *Prayer of the Apostle Paul*, all of which contain variants of this saying. It is also cited in the *Book of Baruch*,[13] the *Acts of the Holy Apostle Thomas*, and the Manichaen Fragment M 789 from Turfan.

The Catholic Fathers of the 140s and 150s were also partial to this passage. It is cited in the *Memoirs* of Hegisippus, *1 Clement*, *2 Clement*, the *Martyrdom of Polycarp*, and the prefix to the Ethiopic version of the *Epistle of the Apostles*. Not one of them credits Paul as the source. The *Clementine Homilies* was redacted during this time into something like its present form. The editor includes the following statement in a debate between Clement and Appion. "For it has been well said *by someone*, 'Evil communications corrupt good manners.'"[14] That someone, of course, was Paul, see 1 Corinthians 15:33. The author, though, does not attribute the quotation to the blessed apostle. No, it was cited anonymously.

> **1 Clement** - An anonymous letter sent from the Roman Catholics to their Greek compatriots at Corinth. It was occasioned by a leadership crisis, and the mother church, called "ancient," was offering advice to the young congregation at Corinth. It is usually dated from a mention of "sudden and repeated calamities," taken to mean a persecution under Domitian, but it should be placed in the middle of the second century. 1 Clement was read in churches and considered nearly canonical for centuries.

This perfectly illustrates how Paul was treated between the expulsion of Marcion AD 144 and his admittance to the canon circa AD 155. He was *persona non grata* for the entire decade. The literature written during this period shows a reoccurring pattern of citing Paul's epistles and appropriating his theology but without acknowledging

11. *Stromata* 7.17, *1 Apology* 1.26

12. *Refutation* 7.13–15

13. *ibid* 5.19

14. *Homilies of Clement* 4.24

his authorship. You could say that Paul had made it to the door, but he had not yet been invited into the church.

The First Epistle of Clement to the Corinthians belongs at the end of the transitional period. Paul is twice mentioned by name, but only one of his epistles, 1 Corinthians, is cited as Scripture. Nevertheless, the author uses Pauline imagery, metaphors and language at least half a dozen times without naming the source. In chapter 34, we find the familiar citation from 1 Corinthians 2:9: "Eye hath not seen, nor ear heard. . . ." In chapter 47, they are admonished to "Take up *the* epistle of the blessed apostle Paul," undoubtedly referring to 1 Corinthians but leading us to believe the author did not know 2 Corinthians. He was familiar with the Roman epistle as well.

The seven Ignatian letters were also fabricated in that uneasy decade after Marcion. The author's command of the Pauline corpus was astonishingly thin. Pseudo-Ignatius was very familiar with 1 Corinthians and quotes from it liberally, but he never gives Paul the credit. A good case can be made that he knew the Epistle to the Ephesians, and possibly even Romans. But that's it. Paul is mentioned by name in just two passages of Ignatius. In the *Epistle of Ignatius to the Ephesians*, he writes: "You are initiates of the same mysteries as our saintly and renowned Paul of blessed memory (may I be found to have walked in his footsteps when I come to God!), who has remembered you in Christ Jesus in every one of his letters."[15] The statement about Paul remembering them "in every letter" is obviously not true, but it might make sense if Paul had only written a couple of letters.

> **Ignatius and his Epistles** – The most controversial figure in the entire field of patristics is Ignatius. He was allegedly the bishop of Antioch around the turn of the first century, but his seven letters do not appear in the literature until AD 150. The storyline is that he was arrested by the Romans, is being taken to Rome for trial, and along the way he manages to write to six churches and one fellow bishop. The letters are a steady stream of cliches, mixed metaphors, and silly symbolism. Pseudo-Ignatius tries to mimic Paul and sound profound, but he lacks the intellect to pull it off. The letters are plagued with anachronisms, which betray their mid-second century origin.

Not everyone in Rome got on board the Pauline Express. Certainly Pius, the bishop who presided over Marcion's hearing, did not favor the questionable new books, and acceptance of Paul was never going to happen on his watch. Pius held the reins of power until his death in AD 155, which turns out to be a key date in the whole transition. His brother wrote the *Shepherd of Hermas* slightly before AD 150, and it does not display the slightest knowledge of

15. *Ignatius to the Ephesians* 12

Paul. Even Justin Martyr, surely one of the more progressive Catholics of that era, does not explicitly quote from the Apostle to the Gentiles. Living at Rome, he would have seen the whole drama play out before his very eyes.

We may also count Hegesippus among the literati who did not join the Roman reformers. The sixth century writer Stephanus Gobarus has preserved a fragment of the second century historian.

> **The Shepherd of Hermas** – A picturesque religious allegory, the *Shepherd* was written at Rome between AD 145 to AD 150. It follows Hermas, a freed slave, as he is led through five visions and given 12 mandates of conduct. The book is a call to repentance and emphasizes morality over theology, although it does manifest the old Christology known as adoptionism. Deemed to be almost canonical and read in some of the churches, it was one of the most popular books in Christendom for centuries.

> The good things prepared for the righteous, eye has not seen nor ear has heard nor have they entered into the human heart. Hegisippus, an ancient writer who belonged to the apostolic age, says in the fifth book of his *Memoirs*, on what basis I do not know: "This is said in a twisted manner, and those who use this saying are liars, since both the Holy Scriptures and the Lord said, 'Blessed are your eyes, which see, and your ears, which hear.'"

> —Photius, *Library*, codex 232

The passage he had trouble with is our old friend 1 Corinthians 2:9, although the first and third sentences have been transposed. Hegesippus strenuously objects to those who accept this verse—and by extension its author—because it seems to contradict the irrefutable words of Jesus from the trusty old Gospel of Matthew. He had some harsh words for Paul's supporters, whom he called "liars."

The Final Step of Paul's Acceptance

The leading Christian in the middle of the second century was Polycarp of Smyrna. There is no exact modern equivalent of his spiritual position inasmuch as ecclesiastical authority was more personal and less institutional in AD 150. Nevertheless, the eighty-year old Polycarp commanded great respect in the Catholic world, and his words carried enormous weight. Polycarp derived his preeminence from great age, his eldership of Smyrna—the historical hub of the movement—and from his alleged relationship with the apostle John. He was martyred in AD 156, and the mob looking on was heard to shout: "This is the teacher of Asia, the father of the Christians."[16]

This background is necessary to an understanding of the epistle he sent to the Philippian church around AD 155. This letter— *Polycarp's Epistle to the Philippians*— has no discernable purpose except to signal his endorsement of Paul. Twice he calls him "blessed." All of Marcion's *Apostolikon* is represented in this little missive ex-

> **Polycarp** – Polycarp was the Catholic bishop of Smyrna in the middle years of the second century. He is one of the few links in the alleged Catholic chain of apostolic succession. Only one of his writings have survived along with an account of his martyrdom in AD 156. His epistle to the Philippians is a confusing jumble of short citations, including extracts from almost all Paul's letters. As the *de facto* leader of the church, Polycarp was signaling his endorsement of the new apostle and, sure enough, after AD 155, Paul is ubiquitous.

cept Colossians and Philemon, and it contains the first patristic references to 1 and 2 Timothy as well. He quotes or alludes to the Pauline corpus no less than twenty times, and many of the citations are clumsy, hardly fitting the context. He finally comes out toward the end of the letter and flatly declares one of Paul's sayings to be Scripture. "For I trust that ye are well versed in the sacred scriptures, and that nothing is hid from you; but to me this privilege is not yet granted. It is declared then in these scriptures, 'Be ye angry, and sin not,' and 'Let not the sun go down upon your wrath.'"[17]

What Polycarp designates as "Scripture" are the two parts of Ephesians 4:26. In the first half of the verse, Paul is loosely paraphrasing the Septuagint version of Psalms 4:4. When Polycarp said that they were "well versed in the Scriptures" and "nothing was hid from them," he was making sure they got the subtle message. The new Epistle to the Ephesians was just as much Scripture as the old, venerated book of Psalms.

That same year, AD 155, Polycarp traveled to Rome to meet with his counterpart in the capital. We cannot help but wonder if the aged Polycarp did not offer some guidance and council to Anicetus, the young man who had just been installed as bishop. We know they discussed the differences in their Easter observances, and it is easy to speculate that Polycarp put his weight behind the growing chorus of Paulinists. Possibly Polycarp had been waiting for new, like-minded leadership in Rome before publicly voicing his support. The Roman church had inspected the letters for a full decade by then, and many of her brightest minds had cited them anonymously.

16. *Martyrdom of Polycarp* 12

17. *Polycarp to the Philippians* 12

Polycarp now validates them with his stamp of approval. We could say that the official acceptance of Paul in the *Katholika Ekklesia* began that year.

Polycarp also began the task of connecting the Catholic communities in Greece and Asia Minor to the apostolic churches planted by Paul. Enough time had lapsed since the Catholics had established a church at Philippi—a couple of generations—that he could make the following assertion without raising any eyebrows. "But I have neither seen nor heard of any such thing among you, in the midst of whom the blessed Paul labored, and who are commended in the beginning of his epistle."[18] Although Polycarp pretends they were the fruit of Paul's labor and acquainted with his letter to the Philippians, he unwittingly lets the cat out of the bag. "He, when among you, accurately and steadfastly taught the word of truth in the presence of those who were then alive. And when absent from you, he wrote you a letter, which, if you carefully study, you will find to be the means of building you up in that faith which has been given you." This is terribly awkward language for those who, if they actually were the planting of Paul, should have known that letter from beginning to end.

The only anti-Pauline faction in the historical record is the Severians, named after one of their leaders. The later Fathers confused them with other sectarians, but we have a contemporaneous account in Irenaeus. "But again, we allege the same against those who do not recognize Paul as an apostle: that they should either reject the other words of the Gospel which we have come to know through Luke alone, and not make use of them, or else, if they do receive all these, they must necessarily admit also that testimony concerning Paul."[19] Eusebius tells us a little more about them in his *History of the Church*. "They, indeed, use the Law and Prophets and Gospels, but interpret in their own way the utterances of the Sacred Scriptures. And they abuse Paul the apostle and reject his epistles, and do not accept even the Acts of the Apostles."[20] The Severians may have been the last keepers of the old proto-Catholic flame.

Is it realistic—or even possible—for a group that started out so virulently opposed to Paul to reverse itself so quickly? An example pulled from more recent times proves that it is. Joseph Smith, the Mormon Prophet, secretly began to take "celestial wives" early in the 1840s, but it was not pronounced an official doctrine of the new movement until 1852. It was greatly

18. *Ibid* 3
19. *Against Heresies* 3.15
20. *History of the Church* 4.29

resisted at first, and many Latter Day Saints left the church. Nevertheless, a plurality of wives quickly became one of the distinctive tenets of the American sect. Just a few decades later, because of continual troubles with the law and a desire for statehood, they began to back away from the practice. In 1890, President Wilford Woodruff published a manifesto repudiating plural marriage, and the Latter Day Saints began to censure members who did not fall in line. They have been outspoken in their opposition ever since, even providing legal assistance to prosecute fundamentalists still living the Principle, as they call it. The Mormons thus managed to move into and out of a very controversial teaching within a span of only 50 years.

Chapter Eight

The Evolution of the Canon

AD 60 to AD 200

———————————————

All scripture is given by inspiration of God, and is profitable for
doctrine, for reproof, for correction, for instruction in righteousness:
that the man of God may be perfect, thoroughly furnished
unto all good works.

—2 TIMOTHY 3:16, 17

THIS CHAPTER WILL BE devoted to the ever-changing canon of the first centuries. The Bible of the proto-Catholics was nothing like any current Bible.
When the pseudo-apostles left the fold, only a handful of New Testament
books were even in existence, and the few Pauline letters beginning to cir-
culate were automatically rejected. The Gospel according to Matthew was
the only genuine apostolic artifact they carried out with them. The *Didache*
thus refers to Matthew as "the Gospel," "the Gospel of our Lord," and "His
Gospel."[1] For sixty to seventy years, it was the only written account they had
of the life and teachings of Jesus Christ.

The Old Testament made up the bulk of the Catholic canon until the
middle of the second century. The proto-Catholic teachers took over and
used the Hebrew writings the same way as the first disciples. They were
the "holy scriptures" that Timothy had known from his youth.[2] The sectarians were very familiar with all the major books of the Old Testament, and
quotations from the Law, the Prophets, and the Writings abound in all the

1. *Didache* 8, 11, 15
2. 2 Timothy 3:15

early Church Fathers. It was thus entirely natural for the second century Hegesippus to refer to his canon as "the Law, the Prophets, and the Lord."[3]

A third class of books cited with the full weight of canonical authority was the apocrypha. This is somewhat of a surprise as neither the Jewish rabbis nor the Christian apostles regarded them as Scripture. The Greek translation of the Old Testament, the Septuagint, contained these fifteen books and additions, and they were very popular in Palestine at the beginning of the Christian era. When the rabbinical authorities closed the Hebrew canon around AD 90, these biblical embellishments were not given a place.[4] They limited the sacred writings to only 24 books; essentially the same as our Old Testament.[5] Bucking the consensus of both rabbinic and apostolic tradition, the false apostles brought these books into the church they founded.

Once these books were banished from the synagogues and the scribes ceased production, the Aramaic texts were lost. It is a historical fact that this collection of Jewish fables and legends has been preserved almost entirely by Christian sources. When Jerome was commissioned by Pope Damascus I to produce a definitive Latin translation of the Bible, he started with the Greek Septuagint, which included the extra books. In this way, the apocrypha were transmitted *en bloc* to the Latin Bible, the Vulgate, and forever enshrined in the Catholic canon. The following books still find a place in the authorized Douay-Rheims Bible: 1 and 2 Maccabees, Tobit, Judith, the Wisdom of Solomon, Ecclesiasticus, Baruch (including the Letter of Jeremiah), the several additions to the Book of Daniel (Prayer of Azariah, Susanna, Bel and the Dragon), and several additional chapters to the Book of Esther. Only three have been rejected by the Roman church: 1 and 2 Esdras, and the Prayer of Manasseh.

The eastern rites are more inclusive. The Bible of the Greek Orthodox Church includes everything used by the Roman Catholics, plus they accept 1 Esdras, 3 Maccabees, the Prayer of Manasseh, and Psalm 151. The Russian Orthodox Church recognizes both 1 Esdras and 2 Esdras (which they call 2 and 3 Esdras); the Ethiopian Orthodox admit 2 Esdras, Jubilees, and Enoch; and the Syrian Peshitta includes 2 Baruch.

---

3. *History of the Church* 4.22

4. Mishnah *Sanhedrin* 10.1e; b. *Sanhedrin* 100b

5. The Jews combine some of the books differently. For example, the twelve minor prophets are all considered as one book.

The false apostles not only appropriated the Scriptures of both Jews and Christians, but they also produced their own sacred writings. This included a volume of administrative procedures and devotional practices (*The Didache*), an alternate history of the apostolic period (*The Preaching of Peter*), interpretational guidelines for the Old Law (*The Epistle of Barnabas*), and their own apocalypse (*The Shepherd of Hermas*). The Two Ways section of the *Didache* served as their first catechism, and when the *Didache* fell into disuse, the *Epistle of Barnabas* reproduced it.

The Scriptures employed in the *Epistle of Barnabas* are a fair representation of the Catholic canon in the first half of the second century. The eminent authority Adolf von Harnack dated this work to AD 131. Although there are almost one hundred citations in this little homily, the author does not display any knowledge of the New Testament beyond the Gospel of Matthew. He cites the Hebrew canon extensively. He treats the author of the intertestamental Wisdom of Solomon as a prophet. He quotes 2 Esdras and 2 Baruch, both written during the early Christian period, and prefaces a passage from 1 Enoch with the formula, "For the Scripture says." Finally, the *Epistle of Barnabas* is full of the strange-sounding "quotations" known as agrapha.

> *Agrapha* or *Logion* – Catholic authors of the first two centuries often cite passages attributed to the Lord which are not found in the canonical Gospels. These are called agrapha, meaning "non-written." The *Clementine Homilies* has 6 of them, the *Epistle of Barnabas* has 8, and both *1* and *2 Clement* have 5. They disappear once the Church adopts the New Testament. There is even an agraphon in the New Testament itself: Acts 20:35.

Agrapha—also known as logion—are the pithy little proverbs attributed to the Lord but not found in the canonical Gospels. *The Epistle of Barnabas* 12 is a typical specimen of this species. "In like manner He points to the cross of Christ in another prophet who saith, 'And when shall these things be accomplished?' And the Lord saith, 'When a tree shall be bent down, and rise again, and when blood shall flow out of wood.'" Genuine agrapha tend to have this same enigmatic, paradoxical quality. By the middle of the second century, the proto-Catholics had amassed a considerable body of these sayings.

Papias, the presbyter of Hierapolis circa AD 130, collected the agrapha and oral traditions that were circulating among the churches of Asia Minor and set them down in a book called the *Expositions of the Sayings of the*

Lord. The preface to this work underscores the great weight that he put on the oral tradition.

> But I shall not be unwilling to put down, along with my interpretations, whatsoever instructions I received with care at any time from the presbyters, and stored up with care in my memory, assuring you at the same time of their truth. For I did not, like the multitude, take pleasure in those who spoke much, but in those who taught the truth; nor in those who related strange commandments, but in those who related the commandments given by the Lord to the faith, and which are derived from Truth itself. If ever anyone came who had been a follower of the presbyters, I inquired into the words of the presbyters, what Andrew or Peter or Philip or Thomas or James or John or Matthew or any other of the Lord's disciples had said, and what Aristion and the presbyter John, the Lord's disciples, were saying. For I did not think that information from books would help me so much as the utterances of a living and surviving voice.

—History of the Church 3.39

Unfortunately, the full text of the *Expositions* has not survived the ages. However, we have the testimony of Eusebius, who had read it, and he was not impressed. "He [Papias] seems to have been a man of very small intelligence, to judge from his book."[6]

There is a notable—indeed, glaring—omission in Papias' gallery of illustrious predecessors and presbyters. Paul, the apostle who had brought the gospel to the region in the first place, does not even rate a mention. In reality, Papias had never heard of Paul other than in his guise as Simon Magus. The Hierapolitan elder is, however, our first witness to the Gospel of Mark.[7] Perhaps Mark was one of the books which did not "help him" as much as listening to the old Catholic presbyters spinning their tales.

The presbyters who cite agrapha are, with only a couple exceptions, not familiar with the apostle Paul. And once Paul is accepted by the Catholic community, these uncanonical proverbs dry up and disappear. It is almost an either/or proposition. This gives us a crude mechanism to arrange the early writings ordinally, if not absolutely, in time.

The earliest stratum of Catholic writings does not contain the slightest trace of Paul, his theology or his epistles. It is a perfect reflection of this phase in their history. The following list is not meant to be complete, but it

6. *Ibid* 3.9

7. *History of the Church* 3.39

does illustrate the astonishing number of first and second century church documents which lack Paul.

- *The Epistle of Peter to James*
- *The Epistle of Clement to James*
- *The Didache*
- *The Recognitions of Clement*
- *The Homilies of Clement*
- *The Epistle of Barnabas*
- *The Apology of Aristides*
- *Peri Pascha*
- The fragments of Papias
- *The Shepherd of Hermas*
- *The Teaching of Simon Cephas*
- Justin Martyr's *First Apology*
- Justin Martyr's *Second Apology*
- *The Dialogue with Trypho the Jew*

Only a couple of these writings can be dated with any degree of precision, but it is enough to establish a benchmark. *The Shepherd of Hermas* was, according to the almost contemporaneous *Muratorian Canon*, written between AD 140 and AD 154, and the *Apologies* of Justin Martyr and his *Dialogue with Trypho* may be placed within a few years of AD 150. Therefore, using nothing but the literary evidence at hand, we could say that Paul was accepted by the *Katholika Ekklesia* around AD 150.

The letters of Paul had been in circulation for almost 90 years by this time. The New Testament Christians, who also began with just the Hebrew Bible, eagerly embraced the solid Christian teachings and wisdom of Paul. They shared his epistles by passing them around, a practice that Paul encouraged. "And when this epistle is read among you, cause that it be read also in the church of the Laodiceans; and that ye likewise read the letter from Laodicea."[8] The inspired quality of his handiwork was quickly recognized by the church, and we have the testimony of Peter that they were considered Scripture before the close of the apostolic age. "Even as

---

8. Colossians 4:16

our beloved brother Paul, also according to the wisdom given unto him hath written unto you; as also in all his epistles, speaking in them of these things; in which are some things hard to be understood, which they that are unlearned and unstable wrest [twist], as they do also the *other* scriptures, unto their own destruction."[9]

The Roman heresiologist Hippolytus (c. AD 215) is a rich gold mine for early Pauline texts. He takes us back into the early years of the second century. Hippolytus had read many of the Gnostic tracts and preserved little snippets in his work *The Refutation of all Heresies*. We learn that one sect, the Naassenes, possessed the epistles to the Ephesians, Romans, and 1 and 2 Corinthians.[10] A lesser known Gnostic sect, the Peratae, considered 1 Corinthians to be "Scripture."[11] It is difficult to position these sectarians either in time or place.

We are on firmer ground when it comes to the two great Egyptian theologians, Basilides and Valentinus. They were at the peak of their influence in the second quarter of the second century. Hippolytus cites several passages from the *Exegetics* of Basilides, which includes paraphrases from Ephesians, Romans, and 1 and 2 Corinthians.[12] The epistles of Paul were *bona fide* Scripture to Basilides and his followers. The other Alexandrian Gnostic, Valentinus, boasted that his instructor, a man named Theudas, had been a disciple of Paul.[13] Valentinus was familiar with the same universe of Pauline epistles as the Naassenes and Basilides, and he had read Colossians as well.[14] Decades before anyone in the Catholic Church had ever heard of Paul, the Egyptian

> **Valentinus** – The most influential Gnostic of the second century left a huge mark on the *Katholika Ekklesia*. Valentinus grew up in cosmopolitan Alexandria before the Catholics had gained a foothold in Egypt. He was thus exposed to a wide range of Christian doctrine and apostolic writings which were not available in Catholic circles. Valentinus moved to Rome in the late 140's and was welcomed as a brother in Christ by the Catholic community. He even ran, unsuccessfully, for the office of the bishop, what we would call the pope. Valentinus introduced the Gospel of John to the Roman church and many exotic doctrines including a primitive Trinity, the Logos Christology, and the real presence in the Eucharist.

9. 2 Peter 3:15–6, emphasis mine

10. *Refutation of all Heresies* 5.1–3

11. *Ibid* 5.7

12. *Ibid* 5.13–15

13. *Stromata* 7

14. *Refutation of all Heresies* 6.29, 30; Irenaeus, *Against Heresies* 1.3, 1.8

Gnostics were quietly discussing the finer points of Pauline theology every Sunday morning.

The epistles of Paul cannot be traced back further than AD 120 in the literature. Save some startling new discovery in the field of patristics, we will never know how the Pauline corpus was transmitted prior to Basilides and Marcion. The literary trail dies with them. For the previous sixty or seventy years, it is not just cold; it is nonexistent.

The Canon Modernizes and Expands

The Catholic Bible was in a continual state of flux throughout the third quarter of the second century. Never before or since has there been such a reshuffling of the deck. They sorted through the historic documents of the church; discarded the *Didache*, the *Epistle of Peter to James*, and the *Preaching of Peter*; brought in three new Gospels, most of the epistolary output of Paul and John; and gave their blessing to the Acts of the Apostles. Their efforts are documented in the first surviving canon of the church, the *Muratorian Fragment*. Although damaged and incomplete, beginning in the middle of a sentence and ending just as abruptly, it gives us the tentative consensus of the Roman church around AD 180. We find they were using all of the current New Testament with the exception of 1 and 2 Peter, Hebrews, James, and 3 John.

The omission of 1 and 2 Peter almost leaps off the page. How could the "home church" of Simon Peter have failed to include his correspondence in their Bible? Under what scenario would that even be possible? It would make more sense if the Romans had *more* of his letters than anyone else; perhaps a personal note or two. It tends to blow the whole mythology about St. Peter and the Apostolic See right out of the water.

> **Muratorian Canon** – This was the Catholic Church's first attempt at defining a New Testament canon. It is the product of Rome, where reformers had been collecting the apostolic writings since Valentinus and Marcion gave them Paul's letters. The Greek–language fragment lists 22 of the 27 New Testament books. The dating is a bit tricky, but Pius, the bishop until about AD 154, "recently sat on the *cathedra*." A date around AD 180 cannot be far off the mark.

The compiler of the *Muratorian Canon* was not even familiar enough with the new material to get the chronology right. He maintains that John, who wrote to the seven churches of Asia, was the "predecessor" of Paul, who also wrote to seven apostolic congregations. The truth, of course, is exactly the opposite. John received the vision on Patmos and passed the messages along to the Asian churches *after* Paul had gone on to his reward. The Canonist then asserts that Paul wrote his general epistles in the following order which, as can be seen, is completely at odds with the Book of Acts.

Muratorian Chronology	New Testament Sequence
Corinthians	Thessalonians
Ephesians	Galatians
Philippians	Corinthians
Colossians	Romans
Galatians	Philippians
Thessalonians	Colossians
Romans	Ephesians

The author of the *Muratorian Fragment* had to resort to a ruse to justify including the Gospel of John. The Fourth Gospel was still such a novelty, and its standing in the church so shaky, that he had to endow it with additional authority.

> When John's fellow disciples and bishops urged him to write, he said, 'Fast with me from today for three days, and let us tell one another whatever will be revealed to each of us.' In the same night it was revealed to Andrew, one of his apostles, that John should write down everything in his own name, while all of them should review it.

We are asked to believe that John, who was counted among Jesus' inner circle, privileged to go up with him to the Mount of Transfiguration, and rested on his bosom at the Last Supper, had to have his work approved by a committee of his peers? Is that not laughable? John himself wrote of his unquestioned authority. "This is the disciple which testifieth of these things, and wrote these things: and we *know* that his testimony is true."[15]

The Gospel of John was not known to the proto-Catholics until the middle of the second century. The oldest Johannine codex in existence is the tiny fragment known as the Rylands papyrus—just a few precious verses

15. John 21:24, emphasis mine

of John 18—and it has been dated on paleographic grounds from AD 125 to AD 150. Found in the sands of Egypt, it is almost certainly Gnostic. The physical evidence meshes perfectly with the patristic record. In the *Refutation of all Heresies*, the Egyptian teacher Basilides quotes John 1:9 almost verbatim and attributes it to "the Gospels."[16] His fellow countryman, Valentinus, moved to Rome "in the time of Hyginus" (c. AD 138) and attached himself to the Roman community. Shortly thereafter, Catholic authors in Rome begin to cite phrases and passages from the Fourth Gospel. The first crossover of John into Catholic literature occurs with Justin Martyr around AD 150. Justin's pupil Tatian compiled his harmony of the four Gospels, the *Diatessaron*, in the early 170s, and Church Fathers subsequent to him quote freely from John.

The books of John raised more of a firestorm than the epistles of Paul. There were entire churches in the ancient proto-Catholic heartland which flatly rejected the Gospel of John and the book of Revelation. Epiphanius christened this sect the *Alogi*, meaning "Deniers of the Word,"[17] but they were simply traditional Catholics who resisted the changes coming out of Rome. Irenaeus, a contemporary, tells us they "held themselves aloof from the communion of the brethren."[18] In truth, Catholics everywhere had reservations about the Johannine works. The Gospel of John had been used in Gnostic circles for decades, it had been brought to Rome by Valentinus, and for these reasons alone it was suspect. The *Alogi* went even further and concluded it had been written by Gnostics.[19] The controversy smoldered for years, and even as late as the third century, Hippolytus felt compelled to write a tract, now lost, called *Defense of the Revelation and Gospel of John*.

There are real chronological disparities between the Gospel of John and the other three, which further fueled their doubts and suspicions. The synoptic evangelists depict the Last Supper as the evening Passover meal, with the crucifixion following the next morning. John seems to place the crucifixion in the afternoon before Passover, at the time when the paschal lambs were slaughtered.[20] The length of his public ministry also differed. There was a persistent belief in the early church that the ministry of Jesus

---

16. *Refutation* 7.10
17. *Panarion* 51.3
18. *Against Heresies* 3.11.9
19. *Panarion* 51.3
20. John 19:14, 31

only lasted one year, an impression left by the Gospel of Matthew.[21] The Fourth Gospel follows his travels over the course of three years, punctuated every Passover by the annual pilgrimage to Jerusalem.[22] Finally, the *Alogi* were appalled by the Christology presented in John's writings—the "Word made Flesh" doctrine. The second century Catholics understood Jesus to be a prophet *extraordinaire* whom God had poured His Spirit into; not the divine Son of God.

The Gospel of John went on to become accepted throughout all Christendom. Not so with the Revelation. Ambivalence about the book remained until the fourth or fifth century in the western church, and it has never been granted canonical status in Syria.

The *Diatessaron* was a mixed or composite Gospel. Tatian, a native of Adiabene, a border state east of the Euphrates River, had studied under Justin Martyr in Rome. He thus had witnessed first-hand the lively debate over the new Gospels and letters that were added to the canon. He decided that the format of a single harmonizing Gospel was less confusing than the emerging consensus of four separate accounts.[23] Using the Johannine chronology as the basic framework, he wove details from the four Gospels together into a single seamless narrative. He used over 95% of the Gospel of John, lesser percentages of the three synoptic Gospels, and some material from an unknown Judeo-Christian Gospel. He compiled the book in Rome and brought it to Syria in AD 172, where it became the standard Gospel text until the fifth century. We have to ask ourselves: Would the Syrian Christians have even considered using the mixed Gospel if they had been hearing the four canonical Gospels read from the pulpit every Sunday? The *Diatessaron* reached them just as the new Gospels and their place were being debated within the Catholic community.

The book of Acts is intertwined with, and necessarily follows, their acceptance of Paul. Our first glimpse of the genuine history of the New Testament comes, ironically, from the bogus proto-Catholic account of the period. The *Recognitions of Clement* has, at the end of Book One, several recognizable incidents from the book of Acts placed in a completely different setting. Would they have so blatantly plagiarized this material if it was well known? The present text of the *Recognitions* is pre-Pauline, but there

---

21. *Homilies* 19; *Stromata* 1.21

22. John 2:23, 6:4, 11:55, 12:1

23. The term *Diatessaron* comes from the music world, and it signifies a series of four harmonic notes.

are indications it had been substantially revised around AD 150. There is a single citation of Acts 1:9, without attribution, in what must be the last work of Justin Martyr,[24] and one of Acts 2:24 in *Polycarp's Epistle to the Philippians.*[25] They can both be dated around AD 155.

Acts was then put on the shelf and disappears from the patristic record for the next 20 years, the very time Paul marches triumphantly through the churches. It then appears simultaneously in several writings at the end of the 170s: *The Epistle of the Apostles,* the *Muratorian Canon,* and the *Martyrdom of Vienne and Lyon.* Thereafter, the Acts of the Apostles joins their embryonic New Testament and was included in their first attempt at defining a canon of Scripture, the *Muratorian Fragment.*

The author of the *Muratorian Canon* makes the following observations about the book of Acts. "Moreover, the acts of all the apostles were written in one book. For 'Most excellent Theophilus' Luke compiled the individual events that took place in his presence, as he plainly shows by omitting the martyrdom of Peter as well as the departure of Paul from the city when he journeyed to Spain." It would be hard to pack more misleading and factually challenged comments into just a couple of sentences.

- The book does not exclusively cover the events that Luke experienced firsthand, as is stated. Luke does not begin to use the first-person pronouns until chapter sixteen.

- Paul did not go to Spain, as the Canonist claimed. After conveying this desire to the Roman church, he was imprisoned and his plans thwarted.

- The Canonist clearly believes the legends about Peter's death, which were part and parcel of the *Preaching of Peter.*

Reading between the lines, we learn that the Acts of the Apostles neither verified their expectations of Paul's exploits, built up after thirty years of reading the Roman epistle, nor did it affirm the received tradition concerning Peter's death. The Canonist mollified his audience by saying that these things happened in Luke's absence.

Irenaeus wrote his massive tome *Against Heresies* from Lyon, France around AD 185. He was an immigrant from Asia Minor and the second elder of Lugdunum, the Roman capital of Gaul. The five books that comprise

---

24. *On the Resurrection* 9

25. *Polycarp to the Philippians* 1.2

this work are principally concerned with refuting the intricate theology of the Gnostics. Irenaeus uses all of the New Testament except 1 Peter, 2 Peter, and 3 John. The fourfold Gospel was now solidly embraced by the western churches. "It is not possible that the Gospels can be either more or fewer in number than they are, since there are four directions of the world in which we live, and four principal winds."[26] Irenaeus deems the *Shepherd of Hermes* to be Scripture and quotes uncritically from the apocryphal *Wisdom of Solomon*. Although well acquainted with the Acts of the Apostles, he still clung to the old Simon Magus myth.

Alexandria on the Nile was a backwater of the church until Origen took the helm in the third century. It also retained the primitive canon far longer, as is amply demonstrated by the *Stromata* ("Patchwork), written by Clement around AD 195. Clement of Alexandria recognizes the authority of the four Gospels, but he has no qualms using the *Gospel of the Egyptians*, the *Gospel of the Hebrews*, and the *Traditions of Matthias*.[27] He cites the *Preaching of Peter* with every confidence it came from the hand of the apostle.[28] Agrapha are considered legitimate Scripture long after they disappear everywhere else.[29] And Clement places the *Didache*, *1 Clement*, the *Epistle of Barnabas*, the *Shepherd of Hermes*, and the *Apocalypse of Peter* in the same league as the genuine writings of the apostles.

The eastern churches did not blindly follow the lead of the Roman reformers. This can be seen by comparing the unorthodox Scriptures employed by the Egyptian church with the modernity and maturity of Irenaeus's canon. The elasticity of the eastern canon is further illustrated by an incident that happened in Rhossus, a coastal village north of Antioch, around the year AD 200. Bishop Serapion made a visit to the flock, discovered they were reading the *Gospel according to Peter*, and thought nothing of it. But later, after doing a little research, he felt alarmed enough to warn them of the dangers which were lurking within.[30] According to the spurious *Doctrine of Addai*, the first New Testament of the Syriac-speaking church in the Euphrates Valley consisted of just the *Diatessaron*, the letters of Paul, and the Acts of the Apostles. Even to this day, the Bible of the Syrian

---

26. *Against Heresies* 3.11.8

27. *Stromata* 3.6, 3.9, 3.13, 2.9, 5.14, 7.13, 7.17

28. *ibid* 1.29, 6.5, 6.6, 6.15

29. *ibid* 1.17, 5.6, 3.7

30. *History of the Church* 6.12

Orthodox and Maronite churches, the *Peshitta*, does not contain 2 Peter, 2 and 3 John, Jude, or Revelation.

The designation of a "New Testament" did not enter the Catholic lexicon until late in the second century. Irenaeus, circa AD 185, was the first of the Fathers to recognize a two-fold collection of Scripture. He refers to "both" testaments, the "new" testament, and even to the "two" testaments.[31] The nomenclature for an authoritative collection of apostolic writings appears to be brand new. Tertullian, just fifteen years later, protests against Marcion dividing the Deity into two gods, "one for each Instrument, or Testament, as it is more usual to call it."[32] This language suggests that the delineation of Scripture into two parts was well on its way to universal acceptance.

The Fathers of the church had considerable trouble winnowing and separating the divinely-inspired wheat of Scripture from the man-made chaff. Eusebius of Caesaria gives us a fair assessment of the state of the canon AD 325. He divides the sacred books into three categories: the accepted writings, the disputed writings, and the rejected or spurious writings.

> At this point it seems appropriate to summarize the writings of the New Testament. In the first place is the holy quartet of the Gospels, followed by the Acts of the Apostles. After this must be reckoned the epistles of Paul, then the epistle of John and that of Peter. After them should be placed, if it is really proper, the Revelation of John, concerning which we shall give the differing opinions at the proper time. These are the accepted writings. Those that are disputed, yet familiar to most, include the epistles known as James, Jude, and 2 Peter, and those called 2 and 3 John, either the work of the evangelist or of someone else with the same name. Among the rejected writings must be reckoned the Acts of Paul, and the *Shepherd*, as it is called, the *Epistle of Barnabas*, the *Teaching of the Apostles* [ie, *Didache*], and the Revelation of John, which some reject and others class with the accepted books.

—History of the Church 3.25

It was not until AD 367 that the 27 books of the Protestant New Testament were all assembled in one place, no more and no less.[33]

The books that caused the most difficulty were placed at the end of the New Testament: James, Jude, 2 Peter, 2 and 3 John, and Revelation.

31. *Against Heresies* 4.28, 4.32

32. *Against Marcion* 4.1, also 4.6

33. Athanasius *39th Festal Letter*

Allusions from the epistle of James can be detected as early as the *Shepherd of Hermas* and *1 Clement*, but the genuine letter was probably tossed out along with the fraudulent *Epistle of Peter to James* and *Epistle of Clement to James*. Second Peter and 3 John were not even discovered by the Great Church until the third century, so it is not surprising their legitimacy would be suspect. Most of the *Katholika Ekklesia* went on to absorb the disputed books into their canon, while the Syrian, Maronite, and Nestorian rites, not convinced of their apostolicity, still do not recognize 2 Peter, 2 and 3 John, Jude, or the Revelation.

Chapter Nine

The Meaning of the Eucharist

AD 100 to AD 200

━━━━━━━━━━━━━━━━━━━━━━━━━

The cup of blessing which we bless, is it not the communion
of the blood of Christ? The bread which we break,
is it not the communion of the body of Christ?

—1 CORINTHIANS 10:16

WE LEARNED IN CHAPTER six that the Eucharist is the vestige of a first century church banquet. How, though, did it get from a minor mealtime ritual
to the highly symbolic drama at the heart of the Mass? The steps leading to
transubstantiation, the doctrine that the bread and wine are the literal body
and blood of Christ, is the subject of this chapter.

The Primitive Eucharistic Meal had none of the symbolism that has
come to be associated with Holy Mass. The loaf was considered blessed
bread, a notch up from common bread, but certainly nothing as mystical or
metaphysical as the body of Christ. A fragment of Theodotus (c. AD 160),
cited by Clement of Alexandria, expresses the idea. "The bread and the oil
are sanctified by the power of the Name, and they are not the same as they
appeared to be when they were received, but they have been transformed
by power into spiritual power."[1] Invoking the name of God is a very Jewish
concept, elevating what would otherwise be just ordinary food into something hallowed.

---

1. *Excerpts of Theodotus 82*

Matthew, the only Gospel known to the proto-Catholics for many years, articulates the new significance Jesus attached to the Passover *matzah* and cup of blessing.

> And as they were eating, Jesus took bread, and blessed it, and brake it, and gave it to the disciples, and said, Take, eat; *this is my body.* And he took the cup, and gave thanks, and gave it to them, saying, Drink ye all of it. *For this is my blood of the new testament,* which is shed for many for the remission of sins.
>
> —Matthew 26:26–28, emphasis mine

As long as they had the cultic meal, these words lay dormant on the page. They were not invested with any special significance. And even for a few years after the separation into *agape* and sacrament, the Eucharist was still an empty symbol, a ritual in search of a meaning.

They found it in magic. For the first couple of centuries, the bread which had been blessed by prayer was believed to possess talismanic powers. It was, as pseudo-Ignatius told his mythical friends circa AD 155, "the medicine of immortality and the antidote against death."[2] We would normally construe this kind of language to be mere hyperbole, but it was confirmed by Hippolytus a couple of generations later. "The faithful shall be careful to partake of the eucharist before eating anything else. For if they eat with faith, even though some deadly poison is given to them, after this it will not be able to harm them."[3]

A more powerful symbol fell into their lap when they acquired the Gospel of John. Valentinus, the freethinking Egyptian theologian who straddled the fence between Gnostics and Catholics, moved to Rome around AD 138. He brought his Bible with him, which included the Gospel of John. Valentinus was orthodox enough at the time to be a serious candidate for bishop and, as Tertullian tells the story, he barely lost. Tertullian credits him as "an able man, both in intelligence and eloquence."[4] It was the first time the Roman presbyters had seen the Fourth Gospel, and they were dumbstruck with the language of John six.

> I am the living bread which came down from heaven: if any man eat of this bread, he shall live forever: and the bread that I will give is my flesh, which I will give for the life of the world. The Jews

2. *Ignatius to the Ephesians* 20
3. *Apostolic Tradition* 36
4. *Against the Valentinians* 4

therefore strove among themselves, saying, How can this man give us his flesh to eat? Then Jesus said unto them, Verily, verily, I say unto you, except ye eat the flesh of the Son of man, and drink his blood, ye have no life in you. Whoso eateth my flesh, and drinketh my blood, hath eternal life; and I will raise him up at the last day.

—John 6:51–54

To their carnal minds, the bread to which he referred must be the bread of the Eucharist.

The Egyptian Gnostics had their own Eucharist. Like all Gnostics, Valentinus rejected the physical incarnation, insisting that Jesus only *seemed* to take on a physical body. In a colorful turn of phrase, they taught that the Son of man "passed through Mary like water flows through a tube.[5] The Jesus of the Gospels only *seemed* to get hungry, to thirst, to sweat, and to bleed. By Gnostic dogma, matter was intrinsically evil, so the Lord's body could not possibly be flesh and bone. Instead, his human form was ethereal and incorporeal, the curious doctrine known as docetism.

Irenaeus, the bishop of Lyon late in the second century, takes us inside the Gnostic Eucharist. "The bread over which thanks have been given is the body of their Lord, and the cup his blood.[6] What could a docetist possibly mean by the "body of the Lord" and "his blood" when they believed in neither? Irenaeus explains: Jesus had been "begotten by a [special] dispensation with a body endowed with an animal nature, yet constructed with unspeakable skill, so that it might be visible and tangible, and capable of enduring suffering. At the same time, they deny that He assumed anything material, since matter is incapable of salvation."[7] It was not that big of a stretch for them to believe that the spiritual body of Christ was infused into the bread by invocation and prayer.

The Gnostics believed in a bloodless Christ, yet the wine represented his blood. How exactly did that work? According to the Valentinian *Gospel of Philip*, the blood of his non-physical body was the Holy Spirit.

Flesh and blood shall not inherit the kingdom of God. What is it which will not inherit? This which is on us. But what is it which will inherit? It is that which belongs to Jesus and his blood. Because of this, he said, 'He who shall not eat my flesh and drink my

5. Irenaeus, *Against Heresies* 1.7.2

6. *Ibid* 4.18.4

7. *Ibid* 1.6.1

blood has no life in him.' What is it? His flesh is the word, and his blood is the Holy Spirit."

—*Gospel of Philip* 25

The cup of prayer contains wine and water, since it is appointed as the type of the blood for which thanks is given. And it is full of the Holy Spirit, and it belongs to the wholly perfect man. When we drink this, we shall receive for ourselves the perfect man.

—*Gospel of Philip* 106

The wine was also altered by the word of prayer. "Pretending to consecrate cups mixed with wine, and protracting to great length the word of invocation, he contrives to give them a purple and reddish color, so that Charis, who is one of those who are superior to all things, should be thought to drop her own blood into that cup through means of his invocation, that thus those who are present should be led to rejoice to taste of that cup, in order that, by so doing, the Charis, who is set forth by this magician, may also flow into them."[8] So, after being consecrated by prayer (and trickery), the wine was presented as the blood of Charis, the feminine side of the Gnostic deity. The infused blood of Charis became, for the Catholics, the literal blood of Christ.

The doctrine of the real presence in the sacraments bursts very suddenly over the Catholic sky in the 140s. After being blessed by the priest, the bread and wine now becomes the literal body and blood of Christ. Justin Martyr, writing around AD 150, was one of the first spokesmen. "For not as common bread and common drink do we receive these; but in like manner as Christ Jesus our Savior, having been made flesh by the Word of God, had both flesh and blood for our salvation, so likewise have we been taught that the food which is blessed by the prayer of His word, and from which our blood and flesh by transmutation are nourished, is the flesh and blood of that Jesus who was made flesh."[9] Pseudo-Ignatius also delights in the new and mysterious doctrine. "I desire the bread of God, the heavenly bread, which is the flesh of Jesus Christ, the Son of God, who became afterwards of the seed of David and Abraham; and I desire the drink of God, namely

8. *Ibid* 1.13.2
9. *1 Apology* 66

his flesh. The Eucharist is the flesh of our Savior Jesus Christ, which flesh suffered for our sins and which God the Father raised."[10]

We are led in almost a straight line to a startling conclusion: The Catholic Church obtained its peculiar Eucharistic theology from Valentinus. Certainly the timing was right (early 140s), the place was right (Rome), the means was there (Valentinus brought the Gospel of John), and the theology was half-right. The Catholics plagiarized the sacramental symbolism of the Gnostic mysteries, disassociated it from the docetism that made it plausible, and then justified it with passages from the new Johannine Gospel. The doctrine of the Real Presence, which made perfect sense within the contours of Gnostic theology, makes no sense whatsoever outside of it.

It was a profound misunderstanding of Christian spirituality. The abundant new life promised in the gospel flows from the words of Jesus, not from any ritual act. The Word of God contains within itself the germ of spiritual life when it is received with faith. As Peter defiantly told the temple priests, "God gives His Spirit to those who obey Him."[11] The Holy Spirit, the third person of the Godhead, accompanies and quickens the Word of God, the second member.

Jesus made this point many times during his ministry. In the parable that explains all parables—the Sower and the Seed—the word is specifically identified as the seed of the Kingdom.[12] It is our response to his words that determines our spiritual fruitfulness and eternal destiny. At the conclusion of the Sermon on the Mount, the Lord summed it up by saying that they who heard his sayings and applied them would be saved.[13] Again in John 14: "If a man love me, he will keep my *words*: and my Father will love him, and we will come unto him, and make our abode with him."[14]

The passage at the heart of transubstantiation is found in John six. This chapter is entirely about bread, from the miracle of the loaves at the beginning to the revelation of Peter at the end. In verse 27, Jesus chastises them for being content with natural food instead of seeking bread for their soul. They ask him how to do this, and Jesus tells them the work of God begins when they believe on His Son. They ask for a sign, pointing out that Moses had given them manna from heaven. Jesus declares that he is the

10. *Ignatius to the Romans 7*

11. Acts 5:32

12. Matthew 13:19–23

13. Matthew 7:24, 25

14. John 14:23

bread of life, and like the manna, he also came down from heaven. They murmur, knowing his natural parents, and he repeats it in the strongest possible terms. "Then said Jesus unto them, Verily, verily, I say unto you, Except ye eat the flesh of the Son of Man, and drink his blood, ye have no life in you. Whoso eateth my flesh, and drinketh my blood, hath eternal life; and I will raise him up at the last day."[15] This was years before he instituted the memorial of the bread and cup, and in a completely different context. Some of his disciples were confused—and understandably so—so he clarified it in verse 63. "It is the spirit that quickeneth; the flesh profiteth nothing: the *words* that I speak unto you, they are spirit, and they are life." Peter got the message loud and clear. "Then said Simon Peter unto him, Lord, to whom shall we go? Thou hast the *words* of eternal life."[16]

15. John 6:53–54
16. *Ibid* 6:68, emphasis mine

Chapter Ten

The Roman Reformation

AD 144 to AD 200

All truth passes through three stages.
First, it is ridiculed. Second, it is violently opposed.
Third, it is accepted as self-evident.

—ARTHUR SCHOPENHAUER

FOR THE CATHOLIC INTELLIGENTSIA living in the 140s and 150s, all roads led to Rome. They streamed in from every corner of the empire. Marcion came from Pontus, Valentinus from Egypt, Cerdo from Syria, Justin Martyr from Samaria, Tatian from Assyria, and Hegesippus from Palestine. As the Roman Empire reached the pinnacle of its power, they were drawn to the City on the Tiber like iron filings to a magnet. All of their learning and erudition combined was not nearly as transformative as the books they carried in their luggage.

The modern *Katholika Ekklesia* was forged at Rome. The remnants of the apostolic writings were brought together in one place for the first time, and the Catholic New Testament went from a single Gospel to twenty-plus books within two decades. The enlargement of their canon ushered in the most dynamic era of reform the Church has ever known. It was responsible for sweeping changes in their understanding of apostolic history, the nature of the Godhead, the person of Jesus Christ, and the Eucharistic formula.

The leadership of the Church passed from Asia Minor to Rome in the third quarter of the second century. For the first hundred years, the proto-Catholics were little more than a loosely-knit confederation of autonomous congregations. However, during that time they spread far and wide across the Roman Empire. A concerted effort to consolidate and to centralize appears, and the impulse springs entirely from Rome. There is nothing quite as unifying as a name, and they grandly began referring to themselves as the Universal Church, or *Katholika Ekklesia* in Greek. It is not a coincidence that the first documents to apply the new name were all of Roman origin.[1] Prior to this time, they were simply "Christians" who belonged to the "church of God."[2]

The Roman reformers laid the foundation for the top-down hierarchy that has characterized the Church though the ages. They saw with great clarity that the key to unity and uniformity of doctrine was a strong bishopric. Admonitions to obey the bishop are sprinkled throughout the documents of the period, both the genuine and the fictitious. *First Clement*, a letter from the Roman congregation to their fellow travelers at Corinth, touches on this theme at least half a dozen times. The bundle of letters attributed to Ignatius never misses an opportunity to exhort the laity to obedience. In every letter, there are admonitions to "love" (Ephesians), "reverence" (Magnesians), "do nothing apart from" (Trallians), "give heed to" (Philadelphians), or "to follow" (Smyrneans) their respective bishops.

The Acts of the Apostles

The reformers had to update their history library; not just once but twice. The *Preaching of Peter* was taken off the shelf, rewritten as the *Homilies/Recognitions of Clement*, and replaced 25 or 30 years later with the Acts of the Apostles. Justin Martyr, a highly regarded instructor in the Roman church, authored several long books on the cusp of the Pauline Revolution. It is crystal clear that, even at this late date (AD 150), his trusted source for church history was the *Preaching of Peter* and not the Acts. He wrote about Simon Magus as an actual person who had hoodwinked the Roman authorities and whom they honored as a god.

> There was a Samaritan, Simon, a native of the village called Gitto, who in the reign of Claudius Caesar, and in your royal city of Rome, did mighty works of magic, by virtue of the devils operating in him. He was considered a god, and as a god was honored by you with a statue, which statue was erected on the Tiber River,

---

1. *Ignatius to Smyrneans*; *Martyrdom of Polycarp*; Muratorian Canon
2. *1 Clement* 1; *Polycarp to Philippians* 1; *Shepherd of Hermas* Sim 9.18

between the two bridges, and bore this inscription, in the language of Rome: To Simon the holy God. . . .

—1 Apology 26

. . . . they again, as was said above, put forth other men, the Samaritans Simon and Menander, who did many mighty works by magic, and deceived many, and still keep them deceived. For even among yourselves, as we said before, Simon was in the royal city Rome in the reign of Claudius Caesar, and so greatly astonished the sacred senate and people of the Romans, that he was considered a god, and honored, like the others you honor, with a statue.

—1 Apology 56

When the Acts of the Apostles was added to their New Testament, the Catholics had to revise their history of the apostolic period. The pioneering work of Paul was now acknowledged, although not in the purely biblical sense. Dionysius of Corinth, circa AD 175, shares the new perspective in the post-Acts environment. "You have thus by such an admonition bound together the planting of Peter and Paul at Rome and Corinth. For both of them planted and taught us at Corinth. And they taught together in like manner in Italy, and suffered martyrdom at the same time."[3] Irenaeus (c. 185) held the same opinion about the foundation of the Roman church. "The blessed apostles [Peter and Paul], then, having founded and built up the church (of Rome), committed into the hands of Linus the office of the episcopate. Of this Linus, Paul makes mention in the epistles to Timothy."[4] We see in these statements the two streams of tradition, the old *Preaching of Peter* and the new Acts of the Apostles, mixing and merging together.

There is an entire book devoted to reconciling the two streams of apostolic history, and it is the Syriac *Teaching of the Apostles*. This little-known church order starts out with the apostles on the day of Pentecost—obviously modeled on Acts 1—wondering how they were going to reach out to the Gentiles. They see tongues of fire, which alight and sit on them, and each one hears in a different tongue. They perceive the language is a sign telling them where they should preach, and so they divide up the world accordingly. We are then treated to 27 ecclesiastical canons, where we learn they prayed facing the east, kept the Sabbath on Friday evenings, and read the Law, the Prophets, the Gospel, and the Acts from the altar. The apostles

3. *History of the Church* 2.25
4. *Against Heresies* 3.3.3

then send Paul and Timothy to deliver these 27 canons to the churches of Syria and Cilicia, when in reality it was Paul and Barnabas who took the apostolic decision of Acts 15 to Syria and later to Anatolia, where they met up with Timothy.[5] It concludes with a long list of countries where the apostles spent their days laboring for souls, all bogus, of course.

What are we to make of this? The author had a very limited familiarity with Paul and his exploits. He uses the early chapters of Acts as a framework on which to hang the old proto-Catholic legends. He pretends the apostles composed these 27 "ordinances and laws" on the day of Pentecost and sent them to the churches instead of the letter of James. And in spite of all this, the Acts of the Apostles was read from the altar. It was an unsuccessful— and amateurish—attempt at reconciliation, and the book never gained any traction in the Great Church. It must have been composed after AD 160, because of the Pauline material and Acts, but not much later because the Church quickly went on to embrace the Lucan version of events.

From Prophet to Deity: Christology

Their theology department also received a substantial upgrade in the third quarter of the second century. The pre-Pauline Catholics held very simplistic views of both the Godhead and Person of Jesus Christ. Their conception of the Supreme Deity was the uncompromising monotheism one would expect of a Jewish sect. Their Christology was the natural outgrowth of a long tradition of Hebrew prophets, ordinary men

> **Christology** – Christology is the branch of theology which deals with the person and nature of Jesus Christ. How did his two natures, the human and the divine, interact? Was he really tempted in all points like us? Could he sin? How did he do the miracles? The false apostles embraced an adoptionist Christology. To them, Jesus was just another prophet—an exceptionally virtuous one—who was "adopted" by the Father at the River Jordan. The apostles taught that Jesus was the pre-existent Son of God, a higher Christology known as the Logos from John's writings.

filled with the Holy Spirit who spoke as God gave them utterance.

The false apostles and their followers were adoptionists. They taught that Jesus was a mere mortal who, because of his purity and righteousness in keeping the Law, God chose or "adopted" as his Son. The celestial adoption occurred when the Holy Spirit descended upon him at the Jordan River. "And Jesus, when he was baptized, went up straightway out of the

5. Acts 15:22–27,16:1–4

water: and lo, the heavens were opened unto him, and he saw the Spirit of God descending like a dove, and lighting upon him. And lo a voice from heaven saying, This is my beloved Son, in whom I am well pleased."[6] In adoptionist theology, there is a special relationship between the Holy Spirit and the Son of God. The Holy Spirit was an offspring of the Father and, after He was poured into Jesus bar Joseph at the River Jordan, Jesus became the Son of God.

Matthew, the sole Gospel of the sectarians, does not breathe a word about the pre-existence of Christ. You would think the miracle of the virgin birth would spoil the theory, but according to Hippolytus, it did not.[7] *The Clementine Homilies* and *Recognitions of Clement* both speak repeatedly of Jesus as the "Prophet" or the "True Prophet"—a man who was filled with the Holy Spirit but, nevertheless, just a man.

The *Shepherd of Hermas* was one of the last outposts of adoptionism in Catholic literature. It was written at Rome around AD 145, and quickly became one of the most popular books in the Christian world. It was so venerated that, for a few centuries, it was sometimes bound along with the Holy Scriptures. The following passages from the *Shepherd* give us the flavor of the unfamiliar Christology.

> I wish to explain to you what the Holy Spirit that spake with you in the form of the Church showed you, for that Spirit is the Son of God.

> —Book 3, Similitude 9.1

> The Holy Spirit, who created all things, God made to dwell in flesh as He desired. This flesh [i.e., body] therefore, in which the Holy Spirit dwelt, was subject unto the Spirit, walking honorably in holiness and purity, without in any way defiling the Spirit. When it [i.e., Jesus] had lived honorably in chastity, and had labored with the Spirit, and had cooperated with it in everything, behaving itself boldly and bravely, He chose it as a partner with the Holy Spirit; for the career of this flesh pleased [the Lord], seeing that, as possessing the Holy Spirit, it was not defiled upon the earth.

> —Book 3, Similitude 5.6

---

6. Matthew 3:16–17

7. *Refutation of all Heresies* 7.23

As they walked the dusty roads of Galilee at his side, the twelve apostles perceived that Jesus was more than just a prophet. One day, while trekking up to Caesaria Philippi, he asked his disciples, "Whom do men say that I, the Son of man, am? And they said, Some say that thou art John the Baptist; some, Elijah; and others, Jeremiah, or one of the prophets."[8] Jesus then utters the words that have been the cause of so much contention between Catholics and Protestants. "He said unto them, but whom say ye that I am? And Simon Peter answered and said, Thou art the Christ, the Son of the living God. And Jesus answered and said unto him, Blessed art thou, Simon Bar-jona: for flesh and blood hath not *revealed* it unto thee, but my Father which is in heaven. And I say also unto thee, That thou art Peter, and upon this rock I will build my church; and the gates of hell shall not prevail against it. And I will give unto thee the keys of the kingdom of heaven. . . ."[9] Jesus was not just another prophet, like Elijah or Jeremiah, but he was the promised Messiah, the actual Son of God. This revelation is the great rock foundation of the Christian faith.

The doctrine of the pre-existent Son entered the *Katholika Ekklesia* by way of the Fourth Gospel. It is often called the Logos (or "Word") Christology because Jesus is equated with the Word of God. The Johannine Gospel begins with a glorious declaration of his divinity. "In the beginning was the Word, and the Word was with God, and the Word was God. The same was in the beginning with God. All things were made by him, and without him was not anything made that was made." In the eighth chapter, Jesus affirms his divine origin. "If God were your Father, ye would love me: for I proceeded forth and came from God; neither came I of myself, but he sent me."[10]

Irenaeus of Lyon (c. 185), who had all of the Pauline and Johannine texts at his disposal, was one of the first proponents of the higher Christology. He is a reflection of the liberal reforms coming out of Rome. A showdown between the old believers and the reformers occurred in the 190s, pitting the bishop of Rome, Victor, against Theodotus the Leathermaker. The adoptionists strenuously defended their turf, insisting, quite correctly, that their theology was the traditional teaching of the church.

> For they say that all the early teachers and the apostles received
> and taught what they now declare, and that the truth of the Gos-
> pel was preserved until the time of Victor, who was the thirteenth

8. Matthew 16:13–14

9. Matthew 16:16–19, emphasis mine

10. John 8:42

bishop of Rome from Peter, but that from his successor, Zephyrinus, the truth had been corrupted.

—*History of the Church* 5.28

What a difference fifty years makes! Theodotus was put outside the camp and barred from communion. What was perfectly orthodox and almost canonized in the *Shepherd of Hermas* was now a dangerous heresy.

The adoptionists did not go down without a fight. The *Gospel of Barnabas* was a product of this period, and it is decidedly adoptionist; almost militantly so. This work has since been exploited by anti-Trinitarian Muslims for their own purposes.

Dearly Beloved, the great and wonderful God hath during these past days visited us by his prophet Jesus Christ in great mercy of teaching and miracles, by reason whereof many, being deceived of Satan, under the pretense of piety, are preaching the most impious doctrine, calling Jesus the son of God. . . .

—*Gospel of Barnabas Preamble*

They said, 'Some say that thou art Elijah, others Jeremiah, and others one of the old prophets.' Jesus answered, 'And ye; whom say ye that I am?' Peter answered, 'Thou art the Christ, the son of God.' Then was Jesus angry, and with anger rebuked him, saying, 'Begone and depart from me, because thou art the devil and seekest to cause me offence!'

—*Gospel of Barnabas 70*

Then Jesus, having lifted his hand in a gesture of silence, said, 'Verily ye have greatly erred, O Israelites, in calling me, a man, your God. And I fear that God may send a heavy plague upon the holy city for this, handing it over in servitude to strangers. . . . Whereupon when God shall come to judge, my words like a sword shall pierce each one that believe me to be more than a man. . . .

—*Gospel of Barnabas 93*

The Holy Trinity

The false apostles grew up reciting the Shema Yisraʾel prayer every morning and evening. It starts out with an affirmation of God's sovereignty and unity: "Hear, O Israel, the Lord is our God, the Lord is One. . . ."[11] They brought this strict, uncompromising monotheism into the church they founded. The Peter of the *Clementines* gives voice to a theology that would have sent the Nicean Fathers spinning in their graves.

> Our Lord neither asserted that there were gods except the Creator of all, nor did He proclaim Himself to be God, but He with reason pronounced him blessed who called Him the Son of that God who has arranged the universe. And Simon [Magus] answered: "Does it not seem to you, then, that he who comes from God is God?" And Peter said: "Tell us how this is possible; for we cannot affirm this, because we did not hear it from Him. In addition to this, it is the peculiarity of the Father not to have been begotten, but of the Son to have been begotten; but what is begotten, cannot be compared with that which is unbegotten or self-begotten." And Simon said: "Is it not the same on account of its origin?" [Or, Is not that which is begotten identical with that which begets it?] And Peter said: "He who is not the same in all respects as someone cannot have all the same appellations applied to him as that person." And Simon said: "This is to assert, not to prove." And Peter said: "Why, do you not see that if the one happens to be self-begotten or unbegotten, they cannot be called the same; nor can it be asserted of him who has been begotten that he is of the same substance as he is who has begotten him?

—*Homilies of Clement 16.15–16*

The doctrine of the Trinity was hammered out in the last quarter of the second century. As was so often the case, they got the raw material from Valentinus. According to Marcellus of Ancyra, Valentinus was "the first to devise the notion of three subsistent entities in a work that he entitled *On the Three Natures*."[12] Valentinus' book has been lost to history, but the *Apocryphon of John*, a second century Gnostic work of Egyptian provenance, may shed some light on the identity of the three entities. It speaks of the "Father, the Mother, and the Son."[13]

The first Catholic writer to reference the *Triados* was Theophilus of Antioch around AD 180. The terminology he uses is right out of a Gnostic handbook.

11. Deuteronomy 6:4

12. Valentinus, Fragment B

13. *Apocryphon of John* 9

And as the sun remains ever full, never becoming less, so does God always abide perfect, being full of all power, and understanding, and wisdom, and immortality, and all good. But the moon wanes monthly, and in a manner dies, being a type of man; then it is born again, and is a crescent, for a pattern of the future resurrection. In like manner, the three days which were before the luminaries are also types of the *Triados; of God, and His Word, and His Wisdom.* And the fourth is a type of man, who needs light, so that there may be God, the Word, Wisdom, and man.

—*To Autolycus* 2.15, emphasis mine

The Word, a minor member of the Gnostic Godhead, is identified with the Son elsewhere in this letter, but the identity of Wisdom is left somewhat nebulous and indeterminate.[14] There may be a good reason. In Valentinian cosmology, Wisdom was the emanation of the unknowable Father that gave birth to a formless substance and brought about the creation of the universe. Wisdom—Sophia in Greek—still occupies a central place in Eastern Orthodox mysticism. Indeed, the largest and most magnificent cathedral in the world for over a millennia was the Hagia Sophia in Constantinople.

The good bishop of Antioch lays out his understanding of the Godhead earlier in the letter. The God-Word-Wisdom Triad is unfamiliar territory to Christians schooled in the classic Trinity.

For if I say He [God] is Light, I name but His own work; if I call Him Word, I name but His sovereignty; if I call Him mind, I speak but of His wisdom; if I say He is Spirit, I speak of His breath; if I call Him Wisdom, I speak of His offspring.

—*To Autolycus* 1.3

God, then, having His own word internal within His bowels, begat Him, emitting Him along with His own wisdom before all things. He had this Word as a helper in the things that were created by Him, and by Him He made all things.

—*To Autolycus* 2.10

It's not as polished as the Nicene Creed, but you have to start somewhere.

Tertullian, a Carthaginian lawyer at the turn of the third century, was the first to try defining in precise language what the human mind cannot even comprehend. We learn that Catholic theologians had made

14. *To Autolycus* 2.22

tremendous strides in the two decades from AD 180 to AD 200. The Trinity is now the familiar threesome of Father, Son, and Holy Ghost.

> As if in this way also one were not All, in that All are of One, by unity (that is) of substance; while the mystery of the dispensation is still guarded, which distributes the Unity into a Trinity, placing in their order the three Persons—the Father, the Son, and the Holy Ghost: three, however, not in condition but in degree; not in substance but in form; not in power but in aspect; yet of one substance, and of one condition, and of one power, inasmuch as He is one God, from whom these degrees and forms and aspects are reckoned, under the name of the Father, and of the Son, and of the Holy Ghost.
>
> —*Against Praxeas* 2

The Completion of the Eucharistic Prayer

The flood of new books—with their wealth of new information— also changed the Eucharistic formula. The primitive Eucharistic prayer was a Christianized version of the *Birkat Hamazon*, with the same framework of three thanksgivings followed by a glorification of the Name. It was the universal prayer over the elements from apostolic times until the Pauline Revolution. The *Didache* is our earliest witness to the Table Grace, and it is nothing but the *berakah* rewritten in terms of the New Covenant. The patristic record is then blank until the time of Justin Martyr, who, as luck would have it, wrote just before the enlargement of the canon. He mentions the prayer of consecration in several passages and, although the language is vague, it abounds with thanksgivings.[15]

The primitive Thanksgiving prayer did not include the words of consecration. Considered mandatory today, these are the Lord's instructions at the Last Supper which dramatically changed the meaning of the ancient Passover. The bread and wine are no longer about bitter slavery and deliverance, but are symbols of his body and blood. Justin was the first of the Fathers to report on the institution narrative.

> For the apostles, in the memoirs composed by them, which are called Gospels, have thus delivered unto us what was enjoined upon them; that Jesus took bread, and when He had given thanks,

15. *1 Apology* 65

said, 'This do ye in remembrance of Me, this is My body'; and that, after the same manner, having taken the cup and given thanks, He said, 'This is My blood'; and gave it to them alone.

—*First Apology* 66

Although these directives are mentioned in all three of the synoptic Gospels, the *anamnesis*, the command to "to this in remembrance of me," is only found in Luke and 1 Corinthians. Justin specifically tells us the directive came from the "Gospels," which in this context can only mean the Gospel of Luke. The Third Gospel was thus beginning to broaden their understanding of the Eucharistic ritual, but they had not yet altered the accompanying liturgy.

That happened in the generation which followed. A second set of prayers was appended to the primitive nucleus of the Thanksgiving which links the taking of the bread and cup with the command to "do this in remembrance of me." We find a fully developed Eucharistic prayer incorporating the *anamnesis* in the *Apostolic Tradition*, written around AD 215.[16] Sometime between the days of Justin Martyr and Hippolytus, both of them from Rome, the second half of the anaphora (Eucharistic prayer) took shape and was fused to the mealtime Grace.

We can narrow it down even further. The *Epistle of the Apostles* is a little-known Catholic work which conveniently dates itself. "We said unto him, Lord: after how many years shall this come to pass? He said unto us: When the hundredth part and the twentieth part is fulfilled, between the Pentecost and the feast of unleavened bread, then shall the coming of my Father be."[17] The Coptic version reads: "When an hundred and fifty years are past. . . ." The epistle was thus first written 120 years after the resurrection—or around AD 150—and then substantially revised thirty years later.

The passage that touches on the Eucharistic question is in paragraph fifteen. "And we said unto him: Lord, is it then needful that we should again take the cup and drink? [The Ethiopic version has: "Lord, didst not thou thyself fulfill the drinking of the Passover? Is it then needful that we should accomplish it again?"] He said unto us: Yea, it is needful, until the day when I come again with them that have been put to death for my sake." The tenor of this exchange strongly suggests that the words of institution had not yet been added to the anaphora by AD 180.

16. *Apostolic Tradition* 4
17. *Epistle of the Apostles* 17

Gregory Dix explored the liturgical boundaries of Irenaeus, a key figure of the period, and reaches the same conclusion. The bishop of Lyon believed in the Real Presence but, as late as AD 185, he did not do it "in remembrance" of the Lord's death.

> Unmistakably, Irenaeus regards the eucharist as an 'oblation' offered to God, but it is as well to note the particular sense in which he emphasizes its sacrificial character. Primarily it is for him a sacrifice of 'first-fruits,' acknowledging the Creator's bounty in providing our earthly food, rather than as 'recalling' the sacrifice of Calvary in the Pauline fashion. It is true that Irenaeus has not the least hesitation in saying that 'The mingled cup and the manufactured bread receives the Word of God and becomes the eucharist of the Body and Blood of Christ,' and similar teaching is to be found in the passage above. . . .but when all is said and done, he never quite puts these two ideas together or calls the eucharist outright the offering or the 'recalling' of Christ's sacrifice."
>
> —*The Shape of the Liturgy* p. 114

The oldest surviving Eucharistic prayer is that of Addai and Mari. Still in regular use by the Chaldean Syrian Church, the anaphora of Addai and Mari has *never* had an explicit institution narrative. It represents a living time capsule of the primitive church. In fact, many of the East Syrian liturgies do not even have a proper epiclesis, the petition directed toward the Holy Spirit to transform the offerings into the body and blood of Christ. They originated in Edessa, which was cut off from the main body of Byzantine Christianity when the Sassanian Persians swept across Syria in the AD 240s.

The new, enlarged Bible fueled an unprecedented period of growth for the *Katholika Ekklesia*. The rich spirituality of Peter, Paul, and John had far more appeal to the Greco-Roman mind than the dry legalism of Torah and the *Clementina*. Eusebius marks their progress in his *History of the Church*. "About the same time, in the reign of Commodus (AD 180 to AD 192), our condition became more favorable, and through the grace of God the churches throughout the entire world enjoyed peace, and the word of salvation was leading every soul from every race of man to the devout worship of the God of the universe. So that now at Rome many who were highly distinguished for wealth and family turned with all their household and relatives unto their salvation."[18] The Roman historian Dio Cassius tells us that Christianity even reached into the inner sanctum of the palace.

---

18. *History of the Church* 5.21

"The tradition is that she [Marcia, the mistress of Commodus] very much favored Christians and did them many kindnesses, which she was able to do by possessing all influence with Commodus."[19]

19. Dio Cassius, *Roman History* 73.4

Chapter Eleven

The Great Feast: Easter

In the fourteenth day of the first month at even is the Lord's Passover.
And on the fifteenth day of the same month is the feast of unleavened
bread unto the Lord: seven days ye must eat unleavened bread.

—LEVITICUS 23:5–6

IF THE CATHOLIC CHURCH descended from the false apostles, as we have
asserted, there ought to be a remnant of the Hebrew holy days in their liturgical calendar. In fact, there is. Easter, the most hallowed season of historic
Christendom, came straight out of Judaism. It is a vestige of the Feast of
the Passover (*Pesah* in Hebrew), which, along with the Feast of Unleavened
Bread, formed the foremost national festival of Israel. The connection is
seen in the Greek word *pascha*, which can mean either Passover or Easter,
depending upon the context.

For Pauline Christians, the Old Testament Feast of Unleavened Bread
was completely fulfilled in the New Testament breaking of bread. The
proto-Catholics also broke bread at the Sunday banquet, but they began
to keep Christianized versions of the major Jewish festivals as well. Our
first glimpse of this comes from the Epistle to the Galatians, written just
a year or two before the schism. Paul chided the faltering saints who had
started to observe "days, and months, and times, and years."[1] This would
have definitely included *Pesah*, the most popular of the annual feasts. Five
or six years later, he advised the Christians in the upper Meander Valley

---

1. Galatians 4:10

131

not to let the neighboring Judaizers judge them "in meat, or in drink, or in respect of an holyday, or of the new moon, or of the Sabbath days."[2]

The false apostles completely revamped the Great Feast at the onset. Instead of a week-long feast *after* the 14th of Nisan, as Moses taught, they placed a week-long fast *before* the Passover. However, they were not allowed to fast on Sunday, as the old rabbinical rule against fasting on the Sabbath was transferred to Sunday.[3] The resulting six days were considered a full week of fasting.[4] The instructional rubrics for this fast have been preserved in two passages, both ultimately going back to the same document. *The Didascalia Apostolorum* 21 has a slightly more primitive cast, beginning the fast on the tenth day after the paschal new moon.

> Therefore shall you fast in the days of the Pascha from the tenth, which is the second day of the week; and you shall sustain yourselves with bread and salt and water only, at the ninth hour, until the fifth day of the week. But on the Friday and on the Sabbath fast wholly, and taste nothing.
>
> —*Didascalia Apostolorum* 21

From such humble beginnings were the extravaganza of Holy Week and Lent born.[5]

The proto-Catholics thus turned the Great Feast of the Jews on its head. Why did they do this? Epiphanius has preserved a passage from the *Apostolic Constitution*, no longer found in the extant version, which may explain their motivation. "And when the Jews are feasting, do you fast and wail over them, because on the day of their feast they crucified Christ; and while they are lamenting and eating unleavened bread in bitterness, do you feast."[6] The final drama of Jesus' life, played out against the backdrop of the Passover, was filled with sorrow and suffering. He went from the Last Supper to Gethsemane, endured the betrayal in the garden, the midnight trial, the scourging and mocking, and finally, to a humiliating and painful death. The joyous atmosphere of the old feast no longer made sense.

---

2. Colossians 2:16

3. *Panarion* 6.70.11: "Who so afflicted his soul on the Lord's Day is under God's curse."

4. *Didascalia Apostolorum* 21: "Fast then. . . . six days, and it shall be reckoned to you as a week."

5. See *Apostolic Constitutions* 5.3.18 for the other version of this passage.

6. *Panarion* 6.70.11: see also *Apostolic Constitutions* 5.3.15

The primitive Passover/Easter of the proto-Catholics was an all-night affair. Like the Hebrew *Pesah*, it began at eventide on the fourteen of Nisan, the night of the full moon. The faithful gathered at the home of their presbyter, where they went for Sunday meeting, and hauled in the baskets of food. Although they had already been fasting for several days, tasting anything was considered a breach of the fast.[7] The service began by reading Exodus 12, the story of Israel's miraculous deliverance from Egypt, which was followed by a homily on the meaning of Passover. The long hours of the night were then spent reading the Scriptures, praying, and making intercession for Israel. They probably recited the Egyptian Hallel, Psalms 113–118, which were traditionally sung at the Passover supper and again at synagogue the next morning.

> From the even until cockcrowing keep awake, and assemble together in the church, watch and pray, and entreat God; reading, when you sit up all night, the Law, the Prophets, and the Psalms, until cockcrowing, and baptizing your catechumens, and reading the Gospel with fear and trembling, and speaking to the people such things as tend to their salvation: put an end to your sorrow, and beseech God that Israel may be converted, and that He will allow them a place of repentance . . .

> —*Apostolic Constitutions* 5.19

There was another dimension to the all-night vigil that was very real to the proto-Catholics. *They were watching and waiting for the Lord's return.* Jesus had warned his disciples many times during passion week to prepare for his second coming. "Watch ye therefore: for ye know not when the master of the house cometh, at evening, or at midnight, or at the cockcrowing, or in the morning: lest coming suddenly he find you sleeping."[8] The children of Israel have long had the expectation that the Messiah would appear at *Pesah*. Jewish households to this day still set an extra goblet on the Passover table, known as Elijah's cup, and fill it with wine. It symbolizes the hope that Elijah, the herald and forerunner of the Anointed One, will come that very night to announce the redemption of the world.[9]

---

7. *Apostolic Tradition* 29
8. Mark 13:35–36
9. Malachi 4:5; Matthew 17:10–13

The Passover Lectionary

An ancient lectionary for the paschal vigil has survived in the homily known as *Peri Pascha*. It has traditionally been attributed to Melito of Sardis, but that may or may not be true. The internal evidence all points to a date in the 140s. Pseudo-Melito cites Revelation but little else in the New Testament, the work is completely bereft of Paul, and there are far too many parallels and affinities with Justin Martyr not to be contemporaneous.

We learn that the primitive Easter service borrowed heavily from the Passover *Haggadah*. The *Haggadah* is a written text that gives the order of the evening supper, fulfilling the commandment in Exodus 13:8 to "tell your son" of their deliverance from bondage. The head of each Jewish household was charged with telling (*haggadah* in Hebrew) the story of the death angel and their hasty departure from Egypt. The false apostles took the traditional *Haggadah* and put a Christian spin on it.

The opening line of *Peri Pascha* indicates they began by reading Torah. "The scripture from the Hebrew Exodus having been read . . ." In the first century, the Jewish head of house would be prompted at this point by a question from the youngest child: "What mean ye by this service?"[10] This was changed in the post-Temple period to the more familiar: "How is this night different from all other nights?" In *Peri Pascha*, the proto-Catholics kicked off the discourse by asking, "What is the Pascha?"[11] The Catholic homily then goes on to address the three topics Jewish fathers were obligated by tradition to cover. "The Passover—because the Omnipresent passed over the houses of our forefathers in Egypt. The Unleavened Bread—because our forefathers were redeemed in Egypt. The bitter herbs—because the Egyptians embittered the lives of our forefathers in Egypt."[12] Their exegesis of "bitter herbs" is typical of the allegorical way the sectarians expounded Scripture:

> Bitter for you therefore is the feast of unleavened bread . . . bitter for you, Judas, whom you hired; bitter for you, Herod, whom you followed; bitter for you, Caiaphas, whom you trusted; bitter for you, the gall you prepared; bitter for you, the vinegar you produced; bitter for you, the thorns you culled. . . .
>
> —*Peri Pascha* 93

10. Exodus 12:26
11. *Peri Pascha* 46
12. Mishnah *Pesahim* 10.5

Finally, we note that there are close textual similarities between passages in the Mishnaic tractate on Passover and the Catholic homily. Rabbi Gamaliel stated, "He brought us forth from slavery to freedom, anguish to joy, mourning to festival, darkness to great light, subjugation to redemption,"[13] and pseudo-Melito wrote, "It is he that delivered us from slavery to liberty, from darkness to light, from death to life, from tyranny to eternal royalty."[14]

The pre-Pauline *Pascha* was also a commemoration of the Hebrew deliverance, albeit from a Christian perspective. It was not a celebration of the resurrection of Jesus Christ. Indeed, only about twenty lines out of the eight hundred-plus sentences in *Peri Pascha* even allude to the resurrection. For pseudo-Melito and his contemporaries, the sprinkling of the blood on the doorpost and the lamb eaten in haste were fulfilled by Christ's suffering on Calvary. "What is the Pascha? It gets its name from its characteristic: from suffer (*pathein*) comes suffering (*paschein*). Learn therefore who is the suffering one, and who shares the suffering of the suffering one."[15] The Catholics did not link Easter with the resurrection until the New Testament was assimilated into their canon several decades later.

The Season of Baptism

The false apostles designed the entire cycle of Holy Week around the initiation rites of circumcision, immersion, and sacrifice. They were consciously following an established Passover precedent that went back to the Lawgiver himself. Strangers and foreigners were circumcised prior to *Pesah* every year because it was a requirement to participate in the festival.[16]

Passover was therefore the designated season for baptism. "Let him attend to frequent fastings, and approve himself in all things, that at the end of these three months he may be baptized on the day of the festival.[17] Several days before the 14th day of Nisan, the male initiates would be circumcised, and the multi-day fast that followed doubled as a time of healing. They would then spend Passover night studying the Scriptures, old and new. "Spend the night in vigil, reading the Scriptures, and *instructing*

13. *Ibid* 10

14. *Peri Pascha* 68

15. *Ibid* 46

16. Exodus 12:43–48; Joshua 5:8–10

17. *Recognitions of Clement* 3.67, see also 3.72

them."[18] Just as Jewish proselytes were tutored in the finer points of the law before their immersion, so Catholic catechumens were instructed as they awaited baptism.

In the first century, the paschal fast would continue up until daybreak, when they would form a procession and march together to the waters of baptism. The catechumens were baptized at the crack of dawn. After being immersed, they would be given bread sprinkled with salt as a substitute for their first offering. In later years, if there were no candidates for baptism, they would end the fast at the third hour of the night.[19] They then reclined together at the table and ate the Lord's Supper, their substitute for the Passover meal.

Quartodecimans and Easter Sunday

The New Covenant *Pascha* was tied to the same calendrical point as the old festival. The Hebrew patriarchs, following their flocks around the desert, measured time by the waxing and waning of the moon. The twelve tribes made their escape from Egypt on the fourteenth day after the new moon, the phase of the lunar cycle when there is a full moon in the sky. It was the ideal time for a large population to travel at night with their flocks and herds. The ecclesiastical year began in the spring and the first month, Nisan, was defined as the lunation in which the vernal equinox occurred.

> **The *Computus*** – The formula used to compute the date of Easter is known as the *computus*. In the first century, the Christian Easter was celebrated on the same day as the Jewish Passover, 14 Nisan. Easter Sunday was an innovation of the Roman church circa AD 120, and it gradually replaced the old Quartodeciman observance. Easter is now celebrated on the first Sunday following the paschal full moon after March 21, the vernal equinox.

Moses commanded them to commemorate the passing over of the death angel on the fourteenth day of the first month. The false apostles adopted this formula for their festival, and it became the norm for centuries in the ancient assemblies of Asia Minor and Syria, the cradle of Catholicism.

The intricacies of the Hebrew calendar were not familiar to their Greek converts. How were they able to calculate the precise day? We assume that the false apostles, with their knowledge of paschal customs, made the critical determination in the first century. After these men died off, they were instructed to follow the lead of their "brethren of the circumcision,"

18. *Apostolic Tradition* 20, emphasis mine
19. *Didascalia Apostolorum* 21.19

the believing Jews. We do not know how the date was disseminated to the remote villages in Anatolia and Syria, but perhaps they sent special messengers from Israel, which was the custom of the Sanhedrin.

> It behooves you, then, our brethren, in the days of the Pascha to make inquiry with diligence and to keep your fast with all care. And you shall make a beginning when your brethren who are of the People keep the Passover. For when our Lord and Teacher ate the Passover with us, He was betrayed by Judas after that hour; and immediately we began to be sorrowful, because he was taken from us. By the number of the moon, as we count according to the reckon of the believing Hebrews, on the tenth of the moon, on the second day of the week. . .Whenever, then, the fourteenth of the Pascha falls, so keep it; for neither the month nor the day squares with the same season every year, but it is variable. When therefore that People keep the Passover, do you fast; and be careful to perform your vigil within their [feast of] unleavened bread.

> *—Didascalia Apostolorum* 21

> Do not you yourselves compute [the date], but keep it when your brethren of the circumcision do so: keep it together with them; and if they error in their computation, do not be concerned.

> *—Panarion* 6.70.10

Rome was the birthplace of Easter Sunday. Sometime in the first quarter of the second century, the Christians in Rome began to terminate the fast on the first Sunday after the paschal full moon. Irenaeus believed he could trace this convention back to Xystus (alternate spelling: Sixtus), the head of the Roman church from approximately AD 115 to AD 125.

> Among these were the presbyters before Soter, who presided over the church which thou now rulest. We mean Anicetus, and Pius, and Hyginus, and Telephorus, and Xystus. They neither observed it [the 14th of Nisan] themselves, nor did they permit those after them to do so.

> *—History of the Church* 5.24.14

Why did they make this change? We can only speculate, but it is a tremendous distance from Jerusalem to Rome, and transmitting information was slow and unreliable in the second century. The responsibility for making this vital calculation fell on the shoulders of the Roman elders, men not schooled in astronomy. Every year, in the springtime, they had to face the same bewildering and frustrating task. It was immeasurably easier just to use the first Sunday after the large and very visible Jewish community in Rome had eaten the lamb.

Rome, the mother church of the west, exported the simplified date to the children that sprang from her loins. Easter Sunday was not only planted in France, Greece, and Carthage, but also in Egypt, Judaea, Cappadocia, Edessa, and Mesopotamia. It was the only paschal observance these Catholics had ever known. The divergence in paschal customs between them and the Quartodecimans was papered over and ignored for several decades.

In AD 154, the rift was addressed in a formal way. Polycarp, the bishop of Smyrna, traveled to Rome that year to discuss the paschal question with Anicetus, the Roman bishop. Each made a case for their tradition, citing the presbyters that came before them, but they were unable to find a workable compromise.[20] Nevertheless, a spirit of toleration and conciliation prevailed for the next several decades, until Victor was elected to the bishopric in AD 189. An overbearing, arrogant man, Victor enjoyed exercising the newly assumed authority of the Roman church. He proceeded to exclude Theodotus, the champion of the adoptionists, from fellowship, and then excommunicated all of the Quartodecimans.

Eusebius has preserved details of the Paschal controversy and the correspondence which sprang from it.

> A question of no small importance arose at that time. For the parishes of all Asia, *as from an older tradition*, held that the fourteenth day of the moon, on which day the Jews were commanded to sacrifice the lamb, should be observed as the feast of the Lord's Passover. It was therefore necessary to end their fast on that day, whatever day of the week it should happen to be. But it was not the custom of the churches in the rest of the world to end it at this time, as they observed the practice which, from apostolic tradition, has prevailed to the present time, of terminating the fast on no other day than on that of the resurrection of our Savior.
>
> —*History of the Church* 5.23, emphasis mine

Polycrates of Ephesus wrote a passionate reply back to Victor on behalf of the Asian bishops. He was quite adamant about the great antiquity and correctness of 14 Nisan.

---

20. *History of the Church* 5.24

We observe the exact day; neither adding nor taking away. For in Asia also great lights have fallen asleep, which shall rise again on the day of the Lord's coming, when he shall come with glory from heaven, and shall seek out all the saints. Among these are Philip, one of the twelve apostle, who fell asleep in Hierapolis; and his two aged virgin daughters and another daughter, who lived in the Holy Spirit and now rests at Ephesus; and, moreover John, who was a both a witness and a teacher, who reclined upon the bosom of the Lord, and, being a priest, wore the sacerdotal plate. He fell asleep at Ephesus. And Polycarp in Smyrna, who was a bishop and martyr; and Thraseas, bishop and martyr from Eumenia, who fell asleep in Smyrna. Why need I mention the bishop and martyr Sagaris who fell asleep in Laodicea, or the blessed Papirius, or Melito, the eunuch who lived altogether in the Holy Spirit, and who lies in Sardis, awaiting the episcopate from heaven, when he shall rise from the dead? All these observed the fourteenth day of the Passover according to the Gospel, deviating in no respect, but following the rule of faith. And I also, Polycrates, the least of you all, do according to the tradition of my relatives, some of whom I have closely followed. For seven of my relatives were bishops, and I am the eighth. And my relatives always observed the day when the people put away the leaven.

—History of the Church 5.24

In the end, Victor was persuaded to back down, and the unity of the Great Church was restored.

The Quartodeciman churches enjoyed perfect communion with the rest of the Catholic world until the Council of Nicaea. When Constantine convened the first great council of the *Katholika Ekklesia* in AD 325, the principle item on the agenda was the standardization of Easter. The churches using the Roman rule had the votes and prevailed: "It is our duty not to have anything in common with the murderers of our Lord; and as the custom now followed by the churches of the west, of the south, of the north, and by some of those of the east, is the most acceptable, it has appeared good to all."[21] They settled on the first Sunday following the paschal full moon after the March equinox. The church at Antioch went along with the majority and, at the Antiochene Synod of AD 341, cast out those who

---

21. *Life of Constantine* 3

reckoned the festival "with the Jews."[22] The Quartodecimans now found themselves branded as heretics and put outside the camp.

The Nicene Council may have settled the Sunday Easter observance for all time, but they still could not agree on the correct *computus*, or formula for computing the date. The Roman church kept its 84-year paschal cycle and the other churches their *computus*, so Christians around the world still found themselves celebrating the resurrection on different Sundays. The deviation between the paschal feasts of Rome and Alexandria reached an embarrassing four weeks in AD 387. After several centuries of experimentation, a variant of the 19-year cycle promoted by Alexandria, the astronomical center of the ancient world, became normative. The custom then developed for the bishop of Alexandria to determine the proper date on behalf of them all, and transmit it by letter to the other bishops.

Despite all of their efforts, uniformity on observing Easter still eludes the daughters of Nicaea. After forcing an agreement on the Sunday observance, and then achieving consensus on the *computus*, the entire western calendar was recalibrated in the sixteenth century. The old Julian calendar had been getting further and further out of synch with the seasons with each passing century. In AD 1582, Pope Gregory XIII commissioned a panel of experts, and they recommended that ten days be dropped from the calendar and altered the rules for adding leap year. The Roman Catholics adopted the papal reforms, but the Greek and Russian churches did not. Thus, in 2012, as the Latin and Protestant churches were joyously celebrating the feast on April 8th, their brethren in the Orthodox rites were still struggling to maintain the paschal fast until the following Sunday.

22. *Synod of Antioch* 1

Chapter Twelve

Chronology and Mythology
Problems with the Received Tradition

What is history, but a fable agreed upon?
—NAPOLEAN BONAPARTE

IT TOOK ONE HUNDRED years and three separate steps to complete the myth of apostolic succession. First, the false apostles had to invent a legitimate connection with the twelve apostles. They did this at the very beginning by misrepresenting Paul and portraying a relationship with Peter and James which did not exist. Then, they had to bring Paul into the picture. This phase began in the middle of the second century with Marcion and ended with Polycarp's ringing endorsement. Finally, they had to close the chronological gap between step one and step two. There could not be an eighty or ninety-year hiatus, an unexplained break, in the historical record, so letters were manufactured to help fill the void. The most famous of these were written in the name of the first century bishop of Antioch, Theophorus Ignatius.

The Ignatian letters are the Piltdown Man of the patristic world. The most famous scientific hoax of the twentieth century was actually a human cranium fitted with the jawbone of an orangutan. The molars were carefully filed, the jawbone broken at the critical spot where it joined the skull, and the bones stained with chemicals to impart the impression of great antiquity. To further the deception, the Piltdown quarry where they were found was salted with the bones of extinct animals. Almost the entire British anthropological community was taken in by the fraud. The French and American scientists, to their credit, were not as gullible and remained suspicious. Nevertheless, for nearly half a century, Piltdown Man was touted as the vital missing link that confirmed the theories of Charles Darwin. How were presumably intelligent men duped so easily? Rather easily, as it turns out. It fit their preconceived ideas of what the creature should look like and advanced a theory they already believed in. They were blinded by their own ideological biases.

We find the same blindness among scholars and churchmen regarding Ignatius. Not a single, solitary scrap of information is known about the man apart from what we are told in these letters. He is believed to have been the first or second bishop of Antioch, and there may be a kernel of historical truth in this. Peter is considered the founding apostle in the pseudo-Clementine literature. Ignatius was thought for many years to have had the direct anointing of Peter, but by the fourth century, a man named Evodius had snuck in there.[1] This was done to push Ignatius' bishopric up to the turn of the first century, when this group of letters was supposedly composed. There is in fact not a single point of intersection between the received tradition about Syrian Christianity and the New Testament.

What does the Bible tell us about the church at Antioch? According to Acts 11:19–26, the Syrian church was founded by unnamed Jewish Christians who, in their enthusiasm, had witnessed to Greek-speaking natives. It would not be untenable to suggest that their names might be found among the "prophets and teachers" of Acts 13.1. "Now there were in the church that was at Antioch certain prophets and teachers; as Barnabas, Simeon that was called Niger [black], and Lucius of Cyrene, and Manaen, which had been brought up with Herod the tetrarch, and Saul." Barnabas was dispatched by the Judean leadership to sort things out, and no doubt he appointed the first elders and deacons.[2] The Antioch mission was an unqualified success: "And much people was added to the Lord."[3] Paul and Barnabas taught the Antiochenes for a full year and often resorted there on their home visits.[4]

There are three separate collections of letters attributed to Ignatius, known as the short, middle, and long recensions. The seven epistles of the middle recension are considered genuine by most Roman Catholic and Orthodox theologians, and not a few Protestants as well. These letters are addressed to six different churches and one esteemed colleague:

1. *Apostolic Constitutions* 8
2. Acts 11:22
3. *Ibid* 11:24
4. *Ibid* 11:26

- Ephesians
- Magnesians
- Trallians
- Romans
- Philadelphians
- Smyrnaeans
- The bishop of Smyrna, Polycarp

The short recension includes just three of these letters. Preserved only in Syriac, they are widely considered to be an abridgement of the middle epistles addressed to Polycarp, the Ephesians, and the Romans. On the other hand, the long version is an expansion of the "Accepted Seven," and includes six additional letters whose authenticity no one will defend. This group of forgeries was a product of the fourth century, and it reflects the doctrinal controversies of that era. Indeed, the first attested citation comes from Stephanus Gobarus in the year AD 570.

The story or scenario posited by the letters is this. The venerable bishop of Antioch has been arrested by Roman authorities and is en route to stand trial in Rome. Whenever the company would make a stop on the journey, he would dash off a pastoral letter to one of the parties above. The traditional date for his Anatolian adventure is the second half of Trajan's reign (AD 98 to AD 117), but there is no compelling reason behind it.

There is a mountain of evidence which indicates 1) the letters are ficti-tious, and 2) they belong to a later age. There are few concrete details about the trip, the geographic setting or the political landscape that would inspire confidence in the story. Instead, a sense of vagueness permeates the whole tale. The few specifics we are treated to, the names of the bishops of Ephe-sus, Magnesia, and Tralles, for instance, are never seen again in Catholic tradition. There is no independent confirmation of their existence. The one historical figure that would serve to anchor the dating, the bishop of Rome, is not greeted by name.

Then there is its uniqueness. Like an erratic boulder that has been pushed down the mountain by glaciers and deposited in an alpine meadow, the Ignatian corpus is strikingly different from the genuine documents of the period. There are no agrapha, few allusions to the Old Testament, and only three direct citations from the Hebrew Scriptures. The promi-nent place accorded to bishops is at variance with every other Christian document of the early second century. And pseudo-Ignatius refers to the *Katholika Ekklesia*, a designation which will not appear for another 50 years if the conventional chronology is adopted.

More serious are the anachronisms. It is not easy to compose something of this length without occasionally slipping up. One of the worst blunders is found in the *Epistle to the Magnesians*. In the midst of a rambling sentence, he says of Christ: "who is his eternal Word, *not proceeding forth from silence. . . .*"[5] This statement is meant to refute a signature cosmological tenet of Valentinus, who would not begin to teach for another thirty years. Another chronological lapse occurs in the *Epistle to the Philadelphians*. "If any confesses Christ Jesus the Lord, but denies the God of the law and of the prophets, saying that the Father of Christ is not the Maker of heaven and earth, he has not continued in the truth any more than his father the devil. . ."[6] This is an obvious jab at Marcion, who made the distinction between the God of the law and prophets and the Father of Jesus Christ. Marcion would also not arrive on the scene for another thirty years.

Moving ahead in the patristic record, what do we find? There is absolutely no witness to Ignatius between the time of his alleged martyrdom and the middle of the second century. The universally admired bishop of Antioch is, for some inexplicable reason, never mentioned by Papias, Hegesippus, pseudo-Barnabas, the *Shepherd of Hermas*, or Justin Martyr. The spiritual superstar who seemingly dazzled the Christian world of his day does not merit a single acknowledgement by the generation that followed.

Ignatius doesn't arrive on the patristic scene until AD 155, after an unexplained absence of nearly 50 years. Our first sighting of the man comes from the *Epistle of Polycarp to the Philippians*. This letter also has its own discrepancies. In chapter nine, Ignatius has not "ran in vain" and is "with the Lord;" but in chapter 13, he is very much alive and is writing letters. This part of chapter 13 is regarded by all as an interpolation. But the latter part of that chapter sounds to our ears like the newly minted letters are being introduced and passed around for the first time:

> The epistles of Ignatius, written by him to us, and all the rest (of his epistles) which we have by us, we have sent to you, as you requested. They are subjoined to this epistle, and by them ye may be greatly profited; for they speak of faith and patience, and all things that tend to edification in our Lord. Any more certain information

5. *Ignatius to the Magnesians* 8.2
6. *Ignatius to the Philadelphians* 6

you may have obtained respecting both Ignatius himself, and those that were with him, have the goodness to make known to us.

—Polycarp to the Philippians 13

This letter can be securely dated to AD 155 or AD 156, providing a *terminus ad quem* for the Ignatian forgeries.

A production date of AD 150 is also consistent with the internal evidence. Pseudo-Ignatius possesses only the most rudimentary knowledge of Paul. Although claims are made for a broader familiarity, all that can be said for certain is that he was familiar with 1 Corinthians. Even the passage his supporters usually trot out for a broader awareness, *Ignatius to the Ephesians* 12:2, undermines their case. "Ye are initiated into the mysteries of the Gospel with Paul, the holy, the martyred, the deservedly most happy, at whose feet may I be found, when I shall attain to God; *who in every epistle makes mention of you in Christ Jesus*" (emphasis mine). Excluding the pastoral letters, the Ephesian Christians are mentioned in one and only one epistle: 1 Corinthians. Our ghostwriter is unaware of Paul's imprisonment, no doubt because he did not have the Acts of the Apostles before him.[7] There is not a single reference to John or the Fourth Gospel, although Ignatius is addressing the same churches the son of Zebedee had walked among just decades before. In fact, if John lived until AD 98, as Catholic tradition claims, the two men would have been contemporaries for a number of years. You would reasonably expect Ignatius to be thankful for the godly influence of John and share a few anecdotes about his spiritual mentor. Such does not happen in the Ignatian world.

We have weighed the authenticity of the Ignatian letters in the balance and found them wanting. We are not the first to question their authenticity. There has always been a cloud of doubt and skepticism hanging over the good bishop of Antioch. The introductory note in the Ante-Nicene Fathers, Volume 1, puts it like this: "The epistles ascribed to Ignatius have given rise to more controversy than any other documents connected with the primitive Church." Their historicity has been endlessly debated by the experts in the field because, like the Piltdown Man, the parts seem to fit but one cannot help feeling that something is amiss.

---

7. *Ignatius to the Romans* 4 – "They were apostles, I am but a condemned man: they were free, while I am, even until now, a servant."

First Epistle of Clement

There is a second way to close the ninety-year gap: Take genuine church documents and push their dating further back in time. It is generally accepted that the letter known as *1 Clement*, sent by the Roman church to their brethren at Corinth, was written around AD 96. This presumption, however, rests on the flimsiest of foundations. The letter does not identify the author; only by tradition is it assigned to Clement, and then, taking another leap of faith, it is dated from an oblique mention of "sudden and successive" calamities. Then, for no logical reason whatsoever, these afflictions are identified with a persecution under the Emperor Domitian, which probably never happened.[8]

We know from the twin testimonies of Dionysius of Corinth and Hegesippus that *I Clement* was circulating prior to AD 170.[9] On the other hand, it could not have been published before AD 145 because of the author's familiarity with Paul. The author heartily recommends *the* epistle Paul had sent to the apostolic church at Corinth, indicating an acquaintance with I Corinthians but not 2 Corinthians.[10] He cites the Epistle to the Hebrews multiple times, and believes that Paul had journeyed to "the furthest bounds of the west," obviously picked up from Romans 15:24.[11] We conclude that *1 Clement* was written at the time when the Catholics were beginning to flirt with Paul.

How did this letter come to be identified with Clement? There are a series of clues buried in the *Shepherd of Hermas* and the *Muratorian Canon*, both from Rome, which may help uncover its true history. The first clue from the *Muratorian Canon* enables us to accurately date the *Shepherd of Hermas*. "But Hermas wrote the *Shepherd* very recently, in our times, in the city of Rome, while bishop Pius, his brother, was occupying the chair of the church of the city of Rome." Pius had the oversight of the Roman church for fourteen years, beginning AD 140, and so the *Shepherd* and *I Clement* were contemporaneous.

The second clue is from the *Shepherd of Hermas*. "You will therefore write two books, and you will send one to Clemens and the other to Grapte.

---

8. See Page 170 for a discussion on the phantom Domitiatic persecution

9. *History of the Church* 4.21, 4.23

10. *1 Clement* 47

11. It is equally obvious from this passage the author had never seen the Acts of the Apostles or he would have known that Paul did not fulfill this desire.

And Clemens will send his to foreign countries, for permission has been granted to him to do so."[12] This Clemens may have been the "Clement" of the letter which now bears his name. He was apparently the secretary who corresponded with foreign churches on behalf of the Roman church. His name was probably appended to the original letter they sent to the Corinthians and then, as the letter was copied, it remained. This otherwise unknown scribe was quickly forgotten in favor of the legendary figure of their founding myth.

The Apostolic History of the proto-Catholics

The Syriac *Teaching of the Apostles* has preserved the most complete exposition of their apostolic mythology that we possess. Although the extant book was composed late in the second century, it contains a significant amount of pre-Pauline material and legends. It provides a list of the apostles and the countries they opened up to the gospel and Paul, the one who "labored more abundantly than they all," is conspicuously absent.[13] His legacy is instead parceled out among John, Simon Peter, Andrew, and Luke. The following citation retains the original numbering scheme.

4. "Antioch, and Syria, and Cilicia, and Galatia, even to Pontus, received the apostles' ordination to the priesthood from Simon Cephas, who himself laid the foundation of the church there, and ministered there up to the time when he went up from thence to Rome on account of Simon the sorcerer, who was deluding the people of Rome with his sorceries."

5. "The city of Rome, and all Italy, and Spain, and Britain, and Gaul, together with all the rest of the countries round about them, received the apostles' ordination to the priesthood from Simon Cephas, who went up from Antioch, and he was ruler and guide there, in the church which he had built there, and in the places round about it."

6. "Ephesus, and Thessalonica, and all Asia, and all the country of the Corinthians, and all Achaia and the parts round about it, received the apostles' ordination to the priesthood from John the evangelist,

12. *Shepherd of Hermas* Vision 2, Chapter 4

13. 1 Corinthians 15:10

who had leaned upon the bosom of our Lord; who himself built a church there, and ministered in his office of Guide which he held there."

7. "Nicaea, and Nicomedia, and all the country of Bithynia, and Inner Galatia, and the regions round about it, received the apostles' ordination to the priesthood from Andrew, the brother of Simon Cephas, who was himself Guide and Ruler in the church which he had built there, and was priest and ministered there."

8. "Byzantium, and all the country of Thrace, and the parts about it as far as the great river [the Danube], the boundary which separates from the barbarians, received the apostles' ordination to the priesthood from Luke the apostle, who himself built a church there, and ministered there in his office of Ruler and Guide which he held there."

9. "Edessa, and all the countries round about which were on all sides of it, and Zoba, and Arabia, and all the north, and the regions round about it, and the south, and all the regions on the borders of Mesopotamia, received the apostles' ordination to the priesthood from Addaeus the apostle, one of the seventy-two apostles, who himself made disciples there, and built a church there, and was priest and ministered there in his office of Guide which he held there."

—Syriac *Teaching of the Apostles*

"There must be a mistake," you say, "No one could possibly get it this wrong." However, earlier in this book is another enumeration of the pioneering apostles and the places where they had labored. "Also what James had written from Jerusalem, and Simon from the city of Rome, and John from Ephesus, and Mark from Alexandria the Great, and Andrew from Phrygia, and Luke from Macedonia, and Judas Thomas from India: that the epistles of an apostle might be received and read in the churches that were in every place."

There can be no doubt: this is really what the sectarians taught and believed.

Another source of these fanciful tales was a converted Jew named Hegisippus. He had traveled throughout much of the Christian world, from Palestine to Corinth to Rome, and by talking with elders in each place, he had soaked up their oral traditions and folklore. Snippets of his five-part book entitled *Memoirs* have been preserved in Eusebius. This was his understanding of the apostolic period.

> In addition to these things the same man, while recounting the events of that period, records that the church up to that time had remained a pure and uncorrupted virgin since, if there were any that attempted to corrupt the sound teachings of salvation, they lay until then concealed in obscure darkness. But when the sacred college of apostles had suffered death in various forms, and the generation of those that had been deemed worthy to hear the inspired wisdom with their own ears had passed away, then the league of godless error took its rise as a result of the folly of heretical teachers who, because none of the apostles was still living, attempted henceforth with a bold face to proclaim, in opposition to the preaching of the truth, the 'knowledge which is falsely so-called.'

> *—History of the Church* 3.32

This would have been news to Peter, Paul, and John, who had plenty to say about the false prophets, false teachers, false apostles, deceivers, and antichrists in their midst. No one familiar with the New Testament as it stands could possible voice such an opinion.

The apostle John had the oversight of the Christian movement at the latter end of the sixties and possibly into the seventies. In his writings, he gives us first-hand information on the fracturing of the Truth during this critical period.

> Little children, it is the last time: and as ye have heard that antichrist shall come, even now there are many antichrists; whereby we know it is the last time. They went out from us, but they were not of us; for if they had been of us, they would no doubt have continued with us: but they went out, that they might be made manifest that they were not all of us.

> *—1 John 2:18–19*

John identifies the nature of the opposition in his second letter. "For many deceivers are entered into the world, who confess not that Jesus is come in the flesh." In his third epistle, John fingers one of the troublemakers by name: Diotrephes. In 2 Peter, the apostle addresses the false teachers who were bringing in "damnable heresies." Jude devotes an entire letter to the ungodly men who had "denied" the Lord and turned the "grace of God into lasciviousness."

Every time Hegesippus can be checked by an independent source, he turns out to be wrong. Dead wrong. Let us review his version of James's death. Hegisippus would have us believe that the brother of Jesus was known in all Israel, even among the priests, as a righteous man. James was therefore invited to speak to the people during Passover from the parapet of the temple. In a bizarre twist, he is asked to restrain Israel from believing in Jesus, the very thing he was giving his life to advance. When James declares the divinity of Christ, he is thrown from the heights and clubbed to death. Hegesippus places the martyrdom in AD 67, whereas the historian Josephus, who personally knew many of the players and politicians involved and could well have been living in Jerusalem at the time, said it happened the year Festus died (AD 62). The fourth century historian Eusebius gives us both accounts, but it is clear he believes Hegesippus.[14] To modern sensibilities, the Hegesippian story is nothing short of ridiculous.

There are many such nuggets buried in this stratum of tradition. Peter, who was the apostle to the circumcision in the canonical Scriptures, spent his life outside Israel in the Clementine version of events. "The excellent and approved disciple, who, as being fittest of all, was commanded to enlighten the dark part of the world, namely the west, and was enabled to accomplish this.[15] Paul, of course, did more to enlighten the west than anyone. The *Apology of Aristides*, written in the 130s, also leaves out Paul's contribution. "He had twelve disciples who, after his ascension to heaven, went forth into the provinces of the world and declared His greatness. As for instance, one of them traversed the countries about us (Greece), proclaiming the doctrine of the truth."[16] Paul, the first Christian missionary into Greece, was not one of the Twelve. It is certain the apostle John was meant, see Paragraph 6 above. The *Didascalia Apostolorum* stockpiled many of the old teachings and tales, which were later brought up-to-date by the book of Acts. "But when we had divided the whole world into twelve parts, and were gone forth among the Gentiles into all the world to preach the word, then Satan set about and stirred up the People to send after us false apostles for the undoing of the word."[17]

This brings us to a fascinating phenomenon associated with early Catholicism: *The closer you get to the apostolic period, the less they know*

---

14. *History of the Church* 2.23

15. *Clement to James* 1; see also Galatians 2:7–9

16. *Apology of Aristides* 2

17. *Didascalia Apostolorum* 23

about the New Testament. Hegesippus (and his contemporaries) were completely unaware of the false teachers and doctrinal disputes within the New Testament fellowship, believing the church had remained an "unsullied virgin," free of heresy, until the last apostle was gone. They did not know the fate of James, the leader of the Christian movement, even though it was

> **The Paradox of Proximity** – It is a historical fact that the closer you get to the apostolic period, the less the Church Fathers know about the events and characters of the New Testament. This is completely contrary to what you would expect if the *Katholika Ekklesia* actually was the successor to the apostles. The first and second century literature reveals a church full of myths and traditions completely unrelated to the New Testament record and often in direct contradiction to it.

known to the outsider Josephus. They did not realize that Peter, whom they considered the emissary to the west, had spent most of his life ministering to Jews. They did not acknowledge Paul, the one who had brought the gospel to the Gentiles, and they were ignorant of his exploits in Asia Minor and Greece. In short, the first and early second century Catholics knew almost nothing about the three main characters of the New Testament.

On top of this, there is an abrupt break between the Christians who inhabit the New Testament and those we read about in the earliest Catholic writings. There are only a couple of connecting links even claimed by the *Katholika Ekklesia*, when there should be dozens, an unbroken chain of fellowship from biblical times. The saints and young ministers of the New Testament should have become the grey-haired, old pillars of the faith. You would expect to see Christianity running into the second and third generations, as it had in Timothy's family. Paul could thus write to Timothy of "the unfeigned faith that is in thee, which dwelt first in thy grandmother Lois, and thy mother Eunice; and I am persuaded that in thee also."[18] We should find fourth and fifth generation Christians in the annals of the Church Fathers. We should know what became of Cephas and Apollos, perhaps something of the later exploits of Timothy and Titus, and we should possess the correspondence of a Silas. But no, a curtain suddenly falls with the last chapter of Revelation, and when the limelight of history begins to shine again, there is an entirely new cast of characters on the stage.

One of the key links in the chain of succession was Polycarp of Smyrna. Irenaeus stated that Polycarp had been "instructed by apostles," meaning— although he doesn't actually say it—the apostle John. This is chronologically possible only if Polycarp and John had both lived to an extreme old

18. 2 Timothy 1:5

age. The famous bishop declared he had served Christ for eighty-six years when he was burned at the stake in AD 156, and Irenaeus asserted that John "remained among them up to the times of Trajan," or AD 98.[19] How likely is it that both attained octogenarian status when very few men in the Roman Empire even made it to sixty? There is a simple explanation: They had to stretch John's life to an absurd length to make their chronology work.

We can check the Polycarp-John claim from another angle. Surely one who had been so close to John would have been intimately acquainted with his writings. Why then did Polycarp's successors refuse to accept two of John's letters, 2 and 3 John, and why so much hesitation about the book of Revelation? Eusebius, some two hundred years later, classed the minor Johannine epistles among the "disputed" and not the "accepted" books, and neither letter has ever been given a place in the Syrian Bible. And in his day (AD 325), the jury was still out on Revelation. Eusebius reported that the church was "evenly divided" on the Apocalypse, and the book did not find a settled place in the western canon until the Third Council of Carthage in AD 397.[20]

The writings under Peter's name also belie their claims to an apostolic pedigree. Peter was so deeply embedded in their earliest mythology that it took centuries to free themselves from Petrine pseudepigrapha. *The Preaching of Peter*, now an unacknowledged relic of their past, was considered sacred writ in the pre-Pauline church. The *Epistle of Peter to James* was a key member of their founding charter, and it has also been disowned. The *Muratorian Canon*, the New Testament of the Roman church circa AD 180, does not include either 1 Peter or 2 Peter, but it does express confidence in the thoroughly fraudulent *Revelation of Peter*. The other Roman works of the mid-second century, the *Shepherd of Hermas* and *I Clement*, also lack 1 and 2 Peter. If the Roman bishops actually were the heirs to St. Peter's throne, would they not possess his genuine correspondence and would they not know what was counterfeit?

The whole scenario becomes even more far-fetched when you consider that Peter may have dispatched his first epistle *from Rome*.[21] Just a few years after the Canonist wrote, 1 Peter is attested by such widely scattered authors as Irenaeus of Lyons, Tertullian of Carthage, and Clement of Alexandria. It is a different story with 2 Peter. It is simply absent from the writings of the Fathers until the beginning of the third century. Although there

19. *Martyrdom of Polycarp 9; Against Heresies* 2.22.5

20. *History of the Church* 3.25

21. 1 Peter 5:13

are indications it had been known to Clement of Alexandria (c. AD 190), Origen, his successor, was the first to reference a second Petrine epistle, and he did not believe it was from the hand of the apostle. The canonical status of 2 Peter was still unresolved as late as the fourth century.

Chapter Thirteen

Peter and Rome

For we have not followed cunningly devised fables,
when we made known unto you
the power and coming of our Lord Jesus Christ,
but were eyewitnesses of his majesty.

—2 PETER 1:16

HUNDREDS OF MILLIONS OF Christians have been taught—and fervently believe—that Peter set up the visible Kingdom of God in the city of Rome. They have pinned their faith and hope of eternal salvation on this claim. But is it true?

This myth goes all the way back to the beginning of the sect. It was manufactured by the pseudo-apostles and first broadcast to the world in the *Epistle of Clement to James.* This fraudulent work immediately sets about to establish the primacy of Peter. He was declared in the first few sentences to be "the first of the apostles," "the first to whom the Father revealed the Son," "the called and elect," and "the excellent and approved disciple." It was necessary to exalt Peter to serve as a counterweight to the canonical Paul.

> **Apostolic Succession** – The foundational myth of the *Katholika Ekklesia* is that Peter founded the church at Rome, he was the bishop for 25 years, and the succession has continued unbroken until the present. There is, however, no unambiguous evidence that Peter was ever in Rome. Indeed, the New Testament can account for his whereabouts for most of the apostolic period, and it is in or around Israel. The bishops immediately following Peter on the succession list are also sheer fiction, just a name embellished with pious legends.

We are then told that Peter had been sent to "enlighten the west" and that he had made it as far as Rome. Years have seemingly passed and multitudes of Romans have been saved. Sensing he is about to die, Peter handpicks Clement to be his successor. The scene is carefully choreographed. Peter grabs Clements' hand, stands up in the midst of the congregation, publicly endows him with the "chair of the teacher," and grants him the power to loose and bind. Clement initially declines the honor but, after hearing Peter's ringing endorsement, he reluctantly consents.

Apocryphal tales about Peter's tenure in Rome sprang up like weeds in the second century. In the *Teaching of Simon Cephas*, Peter arrives in Rome in the third year of Claudius Caesar (AD 44). It asserts that he served "in the rank of Superintendent of Rulers for 25 years," an odd turn of phrase for the first pope. Peter then has a showdown with Simon Magus in the public forum, and raises a man from the dead. The *Acts of Peter and Paul* is the first time that Paul is incorporated into the Roman lore. Paul travels to Rome in the reign of Nero Caesar (AD 54 to AD 68) and is heartily welcomed by Peter. In this version of events, it is Nero who arranges the contest with Simon the Magician. Simon flies up into the air, whereupon Peter commands the false angels to release him, and Simon falls ignominiously to his death.

The Roman succession had to be juggled around as new information became available in the middle of the second century. The *Teaching of Simon Cephas* designates Ansus, who was also called Isus, as Peter's direct successor, and the *Acts of Barsamya* concurs with an Ansus. This Ansus may have morphed into Lainus, the man whom we call Linus. Linus was one of the Roman saints who joined Paul in salutations at the end of 2 Timothy. The similarity in names was probably irresistible to someone trying to reconcile the conflicting accounts.

Two competing theories emerged out of this chaos by the end of the second century. Irenaeus, who was closely allied with the progressive wing of the movement, gives his understanding of the Roman bishopric as follows:

> The blessed apostles [Peter and Paul] then, having founded and built up the Church [of Rome], committed into the hands of Linus the office of the episcopate. Of this Linus, Paul makes mention in the epistles to Timothy. To him succeeded Anacletus; and after him, in the third place from the apostles, Clement was allotted the bishopric.

> —*Against Heresies* 3.3.3

This is the sequence currently accepted by the Vatican. Tertullian, writing from the relative backwoods of North Africa 20 years later, tells us that Clement had been directly ordained by Peter; he knew nothing of a Linus or an Anacletus.[1] Tertullian is simply restating the traditional teaching of the Church as promulgated in the *Epistle of Clement to James*.

The following chart is a sampling of the most ancient evidence of the Roman succession, along with their official position at the present. The lists have been arranged in ascending chronological order. We do not find any real consistency, which is to say, we are not on firm ground historically, until we reach the fifth name around the turn of the first century. The first four, at the very least, are suspect. They are nothing more than a name embellished with pious legends. Clement seems to wall off the historic figures from the legendary ones.

Clement to James	Teaching Simon Cephas	Hegesippus	Irenaeus	Tertullian	Hippolytus	Vatican
AD 75	AD 150	AD 160	AD 185	AD 200	AD 225	Present
Peter	Peter	Peter	Peter/ Paul	Peter	Peter	Peter
Clement	Ansus (Isus)	Linus	Linus	Clement	Linus	Linus
		Cletus	Anacletus		Clement	Anacletus
		Clemens	Clement		Cletus	Clement
			Evaristus			Evaristus

In 1947, the Vatican felt it necessary to revisit the Rock of their Succession. It exposed for all time the illusory nature of these men. Up until then, Cletus had been considered the third bishop after Peter, and Anacletus was fifth in the line of succession. After 1,900 years, though, it had finally become clear that Cletus and Anacletus were one and the same person. It had somehow escaped their attention all those years. So, poor Cletus was eliminated, his paper existence and good name rubbed out just as easily as he had been created in the first place.

1. *On Prescription* 32

The Roman Church of the New Testament

What does the Bible and classical history tell us about the church at Rome? It may have been the "strangers of Rome, Jews and proselytes," part of the crowd that had witnessed the miracle of Pentecost in AD 30, which first carried the torch of faith to Rome.[2] It was therefore Jewish from the very beginning.[3] However, by the time Paul had written to the Roman Christians in AD 57, it had become a mixed church. "For I speak to you Gentiles, inasmuch as I am the apostle of the Gentiles, I magnify mine office. . . ."[4]

Dio Cassius provides a tidbit of information from the beginning of Claudius's reign that may or may not be relevant. "When the Jews (of Rome) had again multiplied to the point where their numbers made it difficult to expel them from the city without a riot, he did not directly banish them but forbade them to gather together in accordance with their ancestral way of life."[5] The Jewish synagogues were therefore closed in AD 41, but the Christians, with their little home gatherings, were probably left unmolested.

In AD 49, Claudius Caesar expelled all of the Jews living in Rome, including Priscilla and Aquila.[6] Suetonius's account of the matter tells us that the gospel of Jesus Christ had rent the Jewish community and was causing civil disorder. "Since the Jews were continually making disturbances at the instigation of Chrestus, he expelled them from Rome."[7] In his epistle to the Romans, written AD 57, Paul boasts that their faith "was spoken of throughout the whole world."[8] He mentions two men and two women who were laboring there in the gospel.[9] Andronicus and Junio were probably the older servants of God in Italy and quite possibly the founding apostles. That they had plenty to shepherd is certain: Tacitus speaks of "an immense multitude" of Christians who were tortured in the fall of AD 64.[10]

---

2. Acts 2:10

3. Romans 4:1 "What shall we say then that Abraham our father, as pertaining to the flesh, hath found?"; 7:1 "Know ye not, brethren, (for I speak to them that know the law,) how that the law hath dominion over a man as long as he liveth?"; see also 14:2–17.

4. Romans 11:13

5. *History* 60.6

6. Acts 18:2

7. *Life of Claudius* 25.4

8. Romans 1:8

9. *Ibid* 16:7, 16:12

10. Tacitus, *Annals* 15.44

Is there *any* scriptural evidence that would place Peter in Rome? The book of Acts provides us with periodic glimpses of his whereabouts for some 20 years, and it was nowhere near Rome. After the resurrection in AD 30, Peter, along with the other apostles, stayed in Jerusalem for several years. This period is covered from the beginning of Acts until chapter seven. In chapter eight, Peter and John follow Philip's mission into Samaria in the geographic center of the country. In the ninth chapter, we find Peter in the coastal region directly west of Jerusalem. Specifically, he was in Lydda, Saron, and Joppa.[11] In the tenth chapter, Peter is led by the Spirit to Cornelius in Caesaria. All of this took place before AD 40, based on the dating benchmark we are given in Acts 11:28.[12] We learn from Acts 12 that Peter was tossed into prison in Jerusalem "about that time."

The year AD 48 again finds Peter in the holy city. From there he travels north up the coastline to meet with Paul and the young Greek church at Antioch.[13] The apostles and elders gathered in Jerusalem AD 49 to decide the Gentile issue, and Peter delivers what might be called the keynote address.[14]

We are left in the dark for most of the fifties. Some see evidence that Peter visited Corinth in 1 Corinthians, but this is straining the text. "Now this I say, that every one of you saith, I am of Paul; and I of Apollos; and I of Cephas (Peter); and I of Christ."[15] Paul was actually making the point that following Peter—or any of the apostles, for that matter—to the exclusion of unity, was a mark of division and error. In AD 56, Paul wrote to the Galatian saints, reminding them that, as Simon Peter had ministered to the Jewish believers, so he (Paul) had been sent to the Gentile world.[16]

Our best source on Simon Peter from AD 57 to AD 62 is Paul; not so much from what he says but from he does not say. Peter was apparently taking a sabbatical when Paul wrote to the Roman church AD 57. Paul addressed this epistle to "all that be in Rome, beloved of God, called to be saints;" not to the august apostle who supposedly sat on the *cathedra*. Peter is likewise missing from the main body of the letter and the extensive catalogue of names and personal salutations at its conclusion. By my count,

---

11. Acts 9:32, 9:35, 9:38
12. Claudius Caesar was proclaimed emperor in January, AD 41.
13. Galatians 2:11
14. Acts 15:7–11
15. 1 Corinthians 1:12
16. Galatians 2:7, 8

Paul greets 29 Christians who were living in Rome, many of them by name, but he never mentions Peter.

Paul subsequently spent two full years in Rome, from AD 60 to AD 62, and while imprisoned he corresponded by letter, five or six of which have been preserved in the New Testament. Once again, he never mentions Peter. As was his custom, he passes along greetings from his immediate circle, but we never see a single salutation from Peter, the supposed head of the Roman church. It seems that every time the paper trail would allow us to check on Peter, the Galilean fisherman is out of town.

Let's repeat the question: Is there any evidence from the New Testament that would place Peter at Rome? There *may* be. It is possible that Peter fled to Rome after James was martyred in AD 62. The only Biblical basis for his presence in the Eternal City is the enigmatic greeting at the end of 1 Peter. "The church that is at Babylon, elected together with you, saluteth you; and so does Marcus my son."[17] Babylon, the ancient enemy of Israel, the military power that had taken them into captivity, was often used as a euphemism for Rome, the latest world power to persecute the people of God. In Revelation 17:18, John identifies Babylon the Mother of Harlots as "that great city which reigneth over the kings of the earth." Earlier in the chapter, he makes the identification virtually certain. "The seven heads are seven mountains, on which the woman sitteth."[18] Rome has been known as the city on seven hills since time immemorial.

The little favor that Paul asks at the end of 2 Timothy adds weight to this interpretation. "Only Luke is with me. Take Mark, and bring him with thee; for he is profitable to me for the ministry."[19] So here we have Timothy bringing Mark to Rome, and a bit later, Peter is writing from "Babylon" with Mark at his side. These two letters were written within a year or two of each other, so the chronology fits.

The stories of Peter's martyrdom at Rome have no more validity than anything else rooted in the *Clementina*. Their seminal myth was preserved in the Syriac *Teaching of the Apostles*. "And Nero Caesar dispatched Simon Cephas with the sword in the city of Rome."[20] After the Gospel of John was assimilated into their canon, including the information contained in John

17. 1 Peter 5:13

18. Revelation 17:19

19. 2 Timothy 4:11

20. Syriac *Teaching of the Apostles*, final sentence

13:36 and 21:19, a more sensational death was constructed for Peter. The first appearance of the replacement myth is found in the *Teaching of Simon Cephas*. "Caesar had commanded that Simon should be crucified with his head downwards, as he himself had requested."[21] It is echoed by multiple sources later in the second century and has become the accepted tradition of the Church.[22]

All that we actually know about Peter's death is contained in just two short passages. In John 21:18, the Lord told Simon that he would need to be dressed and cared for in his old age. "Verily, verily, I say unto thee, When thou wast young, thou girdest thyself, and walkedst whither thou wouldest: but when thou shalt be old, thou shalt stretch forth thy hands, and another shall gird thee, and carry thee whither thou wouldest not." In the next verse, he says that Peter would glorify God in his death if he remained true to his calling until the end. Peter, in his second epistle, is now nearing the end of the journey and, like many elderly people, is anticipating his demise. "Knowing that shortly I must put off this my tabernacle, even as our Lord Jesus Christ hath shown me."[23] This matter-of-fact statement sounds more like a man resigned to a terminal illness than someone facing the horrors of crucifixion.

This book began by exploring a movement founded upon fraudulent documents, fashioned by false apostles to promote a counterfeit Christianity. The church which was built on that foundation has been just as adept at counterfeiting canons and commandments in the name of the twelve apostles as the founders. In the fullness of time, the popes became powerful enough to drop this fiction and issued bulls under their own "apostolic" authority. The Church of Rome has been the source of terrible spiritual blindness and bondage, but at the same time we must acknowledge that we owe her an incalculable debt. It was the institution that gathered up the precious remains of the apostolic age, preserved them in their purity, and transmitted them down the long road of history.

The teachings of Jesus have been the light of the world for almost two thousand years. Originating in the heart of the Eternal One, they are the only connection we have with our Maker; our only avenue to eternal life. His words will judge the world on the last day.

21. *Teaching of Simon Cephas* 6.3
22. *Acts of Peter and Paul*; *On Prescription* 36; *History of the Church* 3.1
23. 2 Peter 1:14

Placing the New Testament Writings
in History

THE GOSPELS, THE EPISTLES, and the Revelation were all published prior to AD 70. The destruction of the Temple that year sent shock waves reverberating through the Jewish and Christian communities. When the daily sacrifice ceased forever on August 5th, it marked the end of the old provision for sin and uncleanness. The effect upon institutional Judaism cannot be overstated. Yet, despite its importance, the New Testament is silent on the subject. True, Jesus had predicted it would happen, and his prognostications have proven accurate. But it was never fully exploited and capitalized upon by the apostles as it would have been had they been writing after the fact. It would have provided ammunition as nothing else to bolster their claim as the New Israel.

The four Gospels were all produced within a ten-year period at the end of the apostolic period. The church was responding to the false teachings which were mounting at the time. Those who had walked with Jesus and knew the story most intimately felt the need to preserve the words and deeds of the Master. The Torah-observant teachers had confused many in the fifties, and the early sixties saw the emergence of the Gnostic movement. This highlighted the need for an authoritative text, and several of the apostles and their closest companions stepped in to meet the need.

Matthew was the first to set down his recollections and understanding of events. It would have been presumptuous for someone to write an account of the life and ministry of Jesus before one of the eye-witnesses. The Gospel of Matthew was in circulation by AD 58, when the proto-Catholics broke fellowship, but not much earlier as Paul is never depicted carrying a written Gospel text or preaching from one. The tradition that Matthew was written in the Hebrew language goes back to Papias, in the early years of the second century[1] However, we note that the *Epistle of Barnabas*, a contemporary source, quotes from the Greek Gospel of Matthew. The Ebionites used Matthew exclusively, which the Catholic Fathers called "The Gospel of the Hebrews," so an early translation into Hebrew was indeed possible.

A remarkably early citation of Matthew occurs in 1 Timothy 5:18. "For the scripture saith, thou shalt not muzzle the ox that treadeth out the corn. And, The laborer is worthy of his reward." This epistle is notoriously difficult to date, but in all likelihood it was written before Paul's imprisonment in AD 58. It is highly significant that Paul labels both Deuteronomy 25:4 and Matthew 10:10 as "Scripture."

The Gospel of Mark, like Matthew, is anonymous. Marcus was the cousin of Barnabas, and both men were involved in evangelical work. His mother hosted the evening prayer meeting in Jerusalem where Peter went after being released from prison. Thirty years later Peter refers to him as a "son" because of their long association in the gospel and respective ages.[2] Along with Matthew, the Gospel of Mark was probably one of the works alluded to in the introduction of Luke's Gospel: "Forasmuch as *many* have taken in hand to set forth in order a declaration of those things which are most surely believed among us, even as they delivered them unto us, which from the beginning were eyewitnesses and ministers of the word . . . ." We are getting ahead of ourselves here, but Mark was thus compiled around AD 60.

Can we venture to guess where it was written? Mark is most closely identified with the missions in Asia, from the time he went with Paul and Barnabas until he joined Peter's greeting at the end of his first epistle. He may have brought the manuscript to Rome when he joined Paul, finished or not, giving Luke immediate access to it.[3]

The Gospel of Luke was written after Matthew and Mark, but before the Acts of the Apostles. Luke begins the Acts in this way: "The former treatise have I made, O Theophilus, of all that Jesus began both to do and teach." The former treatise, of course, was the Gospel of Luke. The Acts of the Apostles terminates rather abruptly with events which can be dated to AD 62, giving us a *terminus ad quem*. The "Beloved Physician" had accompanied Paul to Rome and possibly roomed with him during his house arrest. At first, the Gospel was proclaimed openly: "And many of the brethren in the Lord, waxing confident by my bonds, are much more bold to speak the word without

1. *History of the Church* 3.39
2. 1 Peter 5:13
3. Philemon 23

fear."[4] As Nero's emotional condition worsened and the political situation deteriorated, open public meetings came to a halt. This left Paul and Luke with time to write. Paul set down for the ages some of his finest works, the five "prison epistles," as well as his theological masterpiece, Hebrews. Luke gathered in the recollections and stories of Paul, combined it with information from other sources, and wrote his Gospel. Luke was just one of several companions Paul had the first year or two in Rome. But by the time Paul had an audience with Nero, he was the only one left. "For Demas hath forsaken me, having loved this present world, and is departed unto Thessalonica; Crescens to Galatia, Titus unto Dalmatia. Only Luke is with me."[5]

The first three Gospels are remarkably similar, giving rise to what is known as the synoptic problem. Most scholars posit a priority of one, usually the Gospel of Mark, which the others borrowed material from, along with a lost common source "Q," from the German word quelle, meaning source. But it is not necessarily to resort to plagiarism to explain the parallels. The gospel was an oral message for the first 30 years and there was, by necessity, a lot of rote memorization. As the apostles went from town to town preaching, they would tell the same parables and recount the same stories. Matthew, Mark, and Luke each put down what he knew of the common stock of apostolic teaching, which we now call "Q."

The Fourth Gospel offers up few clues about its date of composition, but the second half of the 60's is the most probable. In John 5:2, we are given a description of the Pool of Bethesda *in the present tense*. This pool, with its five covered porticoes, was buried beneath rubble from the time the Romans leveled Jerusalem until it was unearthed in the 19th century. The author of the Johannine Gospel knew very specific details that were hidden after AD 70.

The Gospel of John is significantly different from the other three. After decades of reflection, and 35 years of preaching the Good News, John had reached some conclusions about the person of Jesus Christ. To Jewish believers, he emphasized his divinity and sonship. "In the beginning was the Word, and the Word was with God, and the Word was God . . . And the Word was made flesh, and dwelt among us, (and we beheld his glory, the glory as of the only begotten of the Father), full of grace and truth."[6] To the emerging Gnostics, who were veering off in the direction of Docetism—the odd doctrine that Jesus was a spiritual apparition without

4. Philippians 1:14
5. 2 Timothy 4:10–11
6. John 1:1, 1:14

a physical body—he focused on his humanity. We thus read that Jesus got tired, thirsty, he wept, was whipped, his body pierced, and he bled.[7]

James' epistle was a product of the late forties. The "scattering" that he refers to in the opening line occurred just a few years after Jesus died.[8] According to Suetonius, the reign of Claudius Caesar (AD 41 to AD 54) was marked with successive droughts and poor harvests.[9] One of these famines hit Palestine and the neighboring territories with special severity during the procuratorship of Tiberius Alexander, AD 46 to AD 48.[10] It was the "great dearth" mentioned in Acts 11, and the Antiochene Christians were moved to send aid to the mother church. "And there stood up one of them named Agabus, and signified by the Spirit that there should be great dearth throughout all the world which came to pass in the days of Claudius Caesar. Then the disciples, every man according to his ability, determined to send relief unto the brethren which dwelt in Judaea."[11] This drought may be alluded to toward the end of the letter. "Be patient therefore, brethren, unto the coming of the Lord. Behold, the husbandman waiteth for the precious fruit of the earth, and hath long patience for it, until he receive the early and latter rain.[12]

The economic distress this produced in an agrarian society exacerbated the normal tensions between landowners and laborers. "Behold, the hire of the labourers who have reaped down your fields, which is of you kept back by fraud, crieth."[13] Inflation, resulting from the scarcity of foodstuffs, may be behind the words that "Your gold and silver is cankered [devalued], and the rust of them shall be a witness against you."[14] Finally, it may be significant that the letter contains not a trace of the gentile controversy that so dominated the council held at Jerusalem AD 49.

The two letters to the Thessalonian church are the oldest Pauline epistles extant. They hearken back to the very first missions in Europe: Philippi, Thessalonica, Athens, and Corinth. During their stay in Athens,[15] Paul decided to send Timothy to Thessalonica, and he and Sylvanus (Silas) headed

---

7. John 4:6; 4:7, 19:28; 11:35; 19:1; 19:34

8. Acts 8:1

9. *Claudius* 18:2

10. *Antiquities* 3, 20

11. Acts 11:28–29

12. James 5:7; 5:17–18

13. *Ibid* 5:4

14. *Ibid* 5:3

15. 1 Thessalonians 3:1

for Corinth.[16] That is probably when Paul wrote to tell them Timothy was coming. During their time in Corinth, Paul was called before the proconsul Gallio, which brings us to one of the most secure dating landmarks in the New Testament.[17] An inscription was uncovered in Delphi, barely 50 miles away, which declares that Gallio was the proconsul of Achaia in the twelfth year of Claudius Caesar. That is approximately AD 52 in our calendar.

The epistles to the Galatians, the Romans, and the Corinthians should all be treated together. They all address the immediate problem of the false apostles who had been following Paul. After passing through "Galatia and Phrygia," Paul spent two whole years at Ephesus.[18] He wrote to the Galatians not long after his arrival in AD 55. "I marvel that ye are *so soon* removed from him that called you into the grace of Christ unto another gospel . . . ."[19] After some time in the Asian capital, he wrote to the Corinthian church about such common pastoral concerns as unity, morality, faith, and charity. A few months later, the false apostles visited Corinth, and Paul left for Greece to head them off at the pass.[20] While en route, he fired off his second epistle from Macedonia.[21] This time, Paul vigorously defends his calling and apostleship, and refers to his detractors as "false apostles" and "deceitful workers."[22] He wrote to the Roman church after arriving in Corinth circa AD 57, perhaps while he was staying with Gaius.[23]

First Timothy may also be the product of his three month stay at Corinth.[24] We learn from the opening lines he had left Ephesus and passed through Macedonia.[25] According to Acts 16:3, Paul took Timothy into the ministry in AD 51, and he was still a young man when Paul wrote this letter. "Let no man despise thy youth; but be thou an example of the believers, in word, in conversation, in charity, in spirit, in faith, in purity. Till I come, give attendance to reading to exhortation, to doctrine."[26] He wrote almost

16. *Ibid* 3:2-3
17. Acts 18:11-17
18. Acts 19:1–10
19. Galatians 1:6, emphasis mine
20. Acts 20:1
21. 2 Corinthians 7:5
22. 2 Corinthians 11:1-31
23. Romans 16:1, 16:23
24. Acts 20:1–3
25. 1 Timothy 1:3
26. *Ibid* 4:12–13

the identical words to Titus and to the Corinthian church.[27] Because Paul left Timothy behind in Ephesus, with all of its challenges, he now passes along lots of practical advice. This letter is full of instructions on choosing elders, suggestions on how a young minister should treat an older presbyter, and counsel on dealing with the latest problem in the church, the circumcising teachers.[28]

Titus was contemporaneous with 1 Timothy. It is easy to get thrown off the trail by the language of Titus 1:5: "For this cause *left* I thee in Crete, that thou shouldest set in order the things that are wanting, and ordain elders in every city, as I had appointed thee." This seems to imply that Paul had been there with him. However, another rendering is that Titus had been *left* behind—and dispatched to Crete—instead of going with the other apostles to Jerusalem. Titus may have been expecting he would be among those delivering the contribution to the poor and needy.[29]

When Paul left Ephesus, he had planned to meet Titus in Troas, the chief port from Asia to Macedonia.[30] However, they ended up connecting on the Macedonian side.[31] That is probably when he dispatched Titus to Crete. Titus was charged in this letter with setting things in order, ordaining elders, and above all, purging the churches of the Circumcisers.[32] Paul provides Timothy with pretty much the same list of qualifications for elders and deacons, but we can be sure he did that with all of his younger companions. Finally, we note there is no hint in this epistle that Paul is—or has ever been—in prison.

Paul's correspondence to the Philippians, Colossians, Ephesians, Philemon, and 2 Timothy are known as the prison epistles. They were all written from Rome while Paul was waiting to appear before Nero, in the period from AD 60 to AD 63.

---

27. Titus 2:5 "Let no man despise thee." and 1 Corinthians 16:11 "Let no man therefore despise him."

28. *Ibid* 1:5–10

29. The men who accompanied Paul to Jerusalem are listed in Acts 20:4. Titus was not one of their number. "And there accompanied him into Asia Sopater of Berea; and of the Thessalonians, Aristarchus and Secundus; and Gaius of Derbe, and Timothy; and of Asia, Tychicus and Trophimus."

30. 2 Corinthians 2:12-13

31. *Ibid* 7:5-7

32. Titus 1:10-15

Philippians speaks of Caesar's court[33] and Caesar's household.[34] It was written early in Paul's Roman imprisonment when they still had the liberty to preach openly. "And many of the brethren in the Lord, waxing confident by my bonds, are much more bold to speak the word without fear." Three of the letters—Ephesians, Colossians, and Philemon—were delivered by the same messengers, so we know they were contemporary. Second Timothy also makes reference to Rome,[35] but it was written a year or two later. By this time Nero's mental state had deteriorated, and Paul's situation had taken a turn for the worse. Paul's letter carrier, Tychicus, had left for Ephesus,[36] and Demas, who had been in Rome when Colossians was written, had forsaken him and was headed for Thessalonica.[37]

A severe earthquake hit the lower Lycus Valley in the early sixties. The historian Tacitus lumps it in with events from the seventh year of Nero's reign,[38] or approximately AD 61.[39] He specifically said that Laodicea was toppled, but the fifth century Orosius includes the neighboring cities of Colossae and Hierapolis as well.[40] Paul's epistle to the Colossians makes no mention of the calamity, so he was either not aware of it or it had not yet happened. Laodicea was subsequently rebuilt, but Colossae remained in ruins and slid into obscurity. In AD 69, when John received the vision on Patmos, there was no longer a church in Colossae, but there was a gathering of the saints at Laodicea.[41]

We should probably count Hebrews among the captivity epistles. Timothy had joined Paul in salutations at the beginning of the Philippian and Colossian letters, but we now learn that Timothy has been set at liberty and may be leaving.[42] If it is indeed this simple, then Paul wrote Hebrews after the Colossians/Ephesians/Philemon trio, but before 2 Timothy. Paul wrote this letter anonymously because he was such a controversial figure in Israel. Nevertheless, he did not go out of his way to hide his identity,

33. Philippians 1:13

34. *Ibid* 4.22

35. 2 Timothy 1:16-17

36. *Ibid* 4:12

37. Colossians 4:14; 2 Timothy 4:10

38. AD 54 to AD 68

39. Annals 14.27

40. Orosius, *History Against the Pagans* 7.7.12

41. Revelation 3:14

42. Hebrews 13:23

and it may be easily surmised. Hebrews 2:3 tells us the author was not an eye-witness; in 13:24, we learn that he was in Italy; in 10:34, he had been in prison; and in 13:23, he was a close associate of Timothy. Paul depicts Jesus Christ to his Jewish audience as the eternal high priest of our faith, the fulfillment of the Law and Prophets.

First Peter was most likely written in AD 63 or early AD 64, shortly before Rome went up in flames. James had been brutally murdered by the Sanhedrin in AD 62, and Israel was not a safe place for a Christian leader like Peter. With Paul under house arrest, Peter may have gone to Rome to help out. He wrote this letter to assure the saints in Asia Minor, the product of Paul's ministry, of the surety of their faith. The situation was tense and, although open hostility had not yet broken out, he repeatedly admonishes them to be extra diligent to obey the civil authorities and not to make themselves a target.[43] Tacitus tells us that the Christians were "a class hated for their abominations," "a most mischievous superstition," and "evil."[44] It was thus easy for Nero to fix the blame on such a despised minority, but we should remember that these sentiments existed before the fire. No doubt they were shared by the Greek populace in Asia Minor and had been since Paul had the run-in with the Ephesian silversmiths.[45]

First and Second Peter, Jude, and the three Johannine epistles all address the proto-Gnostic doctrine which was spreading in the middle sixties. These teachers may have been emboldened by the prolonged leadership vacuum in Asia due to the imprisonment of Paul, the Neronian terror, and the war in the Holy Land. Paul's letter to the Colossians provides our first glimpse of the heresy, and it was written AD 61 or AD 62. This epistle almost reads like a Gnostic dictionary with its lexicon of principalities, thrones, dominions, wisdom, mysteries, fullness, angels, and, above all, knowledge (or gnosis). A few years later, according to John the apostle, the heresy had taken on a more definite shape. "Hereby know ye the Spirit of God: Every spirit that confesseth that Jesus Christ is come in the flesh is of God."[46] John, who could personally vouch that Jesus had come in the flesh and taken the nature of Abraham, was warning of the Christological error of docetism. Peter and Jude both speak of this doctrine as "denying the Lord."[47]

---

43. 1 Peter 2:12–15, 3:16–17, 4:14–16
44. Tacitus, *Annals* 15.44
45. Acts 19:23–41
46. 1 John 4:2
47. 2 Peter 2:1; Jude 4

The Book of Revelation

The book of Revelation, and the date it was written, is so intrinsically linked with speculation on the post-apostolic church that it is worth the time to examine the facts. The information which can be uncovered is devastating to Catholic tradition.

There is no substance to the tradition that John had been exiled to Patmos by the Romans. You will search in vain for any reference in classical history to Patmos as a place of punishment. The island of Giardos, close to the Greek mainland, was the most common penal colony in antiquity. Because it is deficient in water, a sentence to this island was considered extremely harsh.[48] The Roman poet Juvenal twice mentions Giardos in connection with exile, and in more recent times, Seventh Day Adventists and political prisoners have been banished there.

Tacitus wrote several volumes on Roman history from the late 90's until his death in AD 117. He was thus as contemporary with the alleged Johannine exile date of AD 95 as one could hope to find. He mentions three islands as places where the Romans exiled dissidents and criminals. One was the aforementioned Giardos, and the other two were the remote Cyclades islands of Amorgos and Donoussa.[49] Curiously, both are fairly close to Patmos. It is safe to conclude that, outside of Catholic tradition, Patmos was not used as a Roman penal colony.

Then there is the date. Churchmen from the time of Irenaeus (c. AD 185) have placed John's tenure on the isle of Patmos "toward the end of Domitian's reign" in an alleged Roman pogrom of Christians.[50] That is the basis for the AD 95 date found in most Bible commentaries. However, there is a huge problem with what is commonly called the Second Great Persecution: it didn't happen. That there was a political reign of terror in the latter half of Domitian's reign is well documented. But outside of the well-known execution of Flavius Clemens for "adopting Jewish customs," there is no evidence that religion played a role.

Suetonius, who was living in Rome during the latter part of Domitian's reign, nowhere mentions Christians in connection with the period. He faithfully records Nero's treatment of those following what he considered a "malignant superstition," but his list of victims of Domitian's tyrannical cruelty

48. *Satires* 1.73, 10.170

49. *Annals* 3.68, 4.30

50. *Against Heresies* 5.30

does not include Christians.[51] Pliny, a member of the senate who also resided in the capital at this time, later wrote that he never had anything to do with the trial of Christians.[52] We do not read of the alleged Domitianic persecution in the works of the Fathers until the end of the second century.

A more plausible date for John's vision is between the death of Nero in AD 68 and the fall of Jerusalem in AD 70. This squares nicely with the series of clues given in Revelation 17:9–10. "And here is the mind which hath wisdom. The seven heads are seven mountains on which the woman sitteth. And there are seven kings: five are fallen, and one is, and the other is not yet come; and when he cometh, he must continue a short space." The first part tells us in plain language what was meant by the "Mother of Harlots." Rome has long been known as the City on Seven Hills. Then, if we begin the count with Augustus, who was the first *imperator* (or king) of the Roman Empire following the Republic, the fifth emperor, the last one "fallen," would be Nero. He fell by his own sword on June 9, AD 68. The king "now reigning" would therefore be Galba, and the one "not yet come" who would "continue a short space" would be Otho, who sat on the throne from January to April of AD 69.

We also notice that the instructions from the angel to measure the temple were given in the *present* tense, which strongly suggests it was still standing.[53] Despite the best intentions and efforts of Titus to spare the Sanctuary, it was accidentally set afire in August of AD 70.

Revelation makes several references to those who worshipped the emperor and his statue, and some have been reluctant to place the beginning of the Imperial cult this early. But that is to miss the point. As the angel told John at the beginning of the book and at the end, he was revealing "things which must shortly come to pass" and "things which must shortly be done."[54] John had witnessed the early stages of emperor worship in Asia Minor, where it had been a feature of life since Augustan times, and he was warning the saints that the trial of their faith was going to intensify.[55] It was not long in coming. Vespasian, who assumed the purple in November, AD 69, issued an edict condemning to death all who refused to worship his image.

---

51. *Nero 16*

52. *Pliny Letter No. 96*

53. Revelation 11:1–2

54. *Ibid* 1:1, 22:6

55. *Ibid* 13:15, 15:2, 16:2, 19:20, 20:4

By the use of highly symbolic imagery, the book of Revelation describes the horrific conditions for the Christians in the second half of the sixties. Nero initiated a bloody pogrom in AD 64, blaming the torching of Rome in the early hours of June 19 on the much maligned new sect. His meeting with Paul may have been fresh in his mind. The fire blazed for nine days, razing three entire districts of Rome to the ground, severely damaging another seven, and leaving only four unscathed. The Roman historian Tacitus describes the horror of that summer:

> Therefore, to scotch the rumor (that he had started the fire), Nero substituted as culprits, and punished with the utmost refinements of cruelty, a class of men loathed for their vices, whom the crowd styled Christians. Christus, the founder of the name, had undergone the death penalty in the reign of Tiberius by sentence of the procurator Pontius Pilatus, and the pernicious superstition was checked for a moment, only to break out once more, not merely in Judaea, the home of the disease, but in the capital itself, where all things horrible or shameful in the world collect and find a vogue. First, then, the confessed members of the sect were arrested; next, on their disclosures, vast multitudes were convicted, not so much on the count of arson as for hatred of the human race. And derision accompanied their end: they were covered with wild beasts' skins and torn to death by dogs; or they were fastened on crosses, and when daylight failed, were burned to serve as lamps by night. Nero offered his gardens for the spectacle, and gave an exhibition in his circus, mixing with the crowd in the habit of a charioteer, or mounted on his car. Hence, in spite of a guilt which had earned the most exemplary punishment, there arose a sentiment of pity due to the impression that they were being sacrificed not for the welfare of the state but to the ferocity of a single man.

> —*Annals* 15.44

A second source, Suetonius, also bears witness to the suffering of the saints under Nero. "Punishments were also inflicted on the Christians, a sect professing a new and malignant religious belief."[56]

What had begun in the capital quickly spilled over into the provinces. Peter, writing to the saints in Asia Minor four or five years before, encouraged them to endure the "fiery ordeal" and the "trial of their faith" that had come upon them. It seemed to be social harassment and verbal abuse—the actions of local magistrates—more than anything. "Having a good

56. *Nero* 16

conscience; that, whereas they speak evil of you, as of evildoers, they may be ashamed that falsely accuse your good conversation in Christ.... If ye be reproached for the name of Christ, happy are ye for the spirit of glory and of God resteth upon you."[57] However, it escalated quickly after Nero turned the spotlight on them. A couple of years later, Antipas was martyred at Pergamum and the apostle John was forced into hiding on Patmos "for the word of God and the testimony of Jesus Christ."[58] Imperial Rome was indeed "drunken with the blood of the saints and with the martyrs of Jesus."[59]

At the eastern end of the empire, the political turmoil in Palestine finally boiled over into outright rebellion. In AD 67, Nero's hand-picked general, Vespasian, attacked Judaea from the north. By AD 69, the country had been reduced to rubble and the Roman armies encircled the Holy City. The end was eminent. The words of Revelation 6:6 ("A measure of wheat for a penny, and three measures of barley for a penny; and see thou hurt not the oil and the wine") are echoed almost exactly by Josephus when he described the final stages of the siege. "Many clandestinely bartered their possessions for a single measure of wheat, if they were rich, or barley, if they were poor;" and later he tells of the sacred wine and oil being distributed to the multitude and consumed.[60]

The Year of the Four Emperors, AD 69, was an unprecedented period of civil war, with foreign troops actually spilling blood in the streets of Rome. The world as they knew it was going up in flames. The Four Horsemen were galloping through the empire, and it seemed as if the fulfillment of all things was nigh at hand.

57. 1 Peter 3:16, 4:14
58. Revelation 1:9
59. *Ibid* 17:6
60. *Wars of the Jews* 5.10.2, 5.13.6

The Earliest Patristic Witnesses to the New Testament Books

Book	Approx. Date	Earliest Attestation	Approx. Date	Second Citation	Approx. Date
Matthew	58	*Didache*	90	*Ep Barnabas*	132
Mark	58 to 60	Papias	130	Justin Martyr	150
Luke	60 to 62	Basilides	130	Marcion	140
John	circa 65	Basilides	130	Justin Martyr	150
Acts	63	*Polycarp to Philippians*	155	Marcion, *On the Resurrection*	155
Romans	57	Basilides	130	Marcion	140
1 Corinthians	56	Basilides	130	Marcion	140
2 Corinthians	57	Basilides	130	Marcion	140
Galatians	56	Marcion	140	Polycarp	155
Ephesians	61	Basilides	130	Marcion	140
Philippians	60	Marcion	140	Polycarp	155
Colossians	61	Marcion	140	Valentinus	140
1 Thessalonians	52	Marcion	140	Polycarp	155
2 Thessalonians	52	Marcion	140	Polycarp	155

Book	Approx. Date	Earliest Attestation	Approx. Date	Second Citation	Approx. Date
1 Timothy	57	Polycarp	155	*To Autocylus*	170
2 Timothy	63	Polycarp	155	*Mur Canon*	180
Titus	57	Tatian	160	Irenaeus	185
Philemon	61	Marcion	140	*Mur Canon*	180
Hebrews	circa 62	*Shepherd*	145	*I Clement*	150
James	circa 47	*Shepherd*	145	*I Clement* (?)	150
1 Peter	circa 63	Papias	130	*2 Clement*	145–150
2 Peter	circa 64	Origen	220	Hippolytus	230
1 John	circa 65	Papias	130	Polycarp	155
2 John	65+	*Mur Canon*	180	Irenaeus	185
3 John	65+	Origen	220	Dionysius of Alexandria	255
Jude	65+	*Mur Canon*	180	Irenaeus	185
Revelation	69	Papias	130	*Dialogue/ Trypho*	145

The entire Ignatian corpus is considered fraudulent, as discussed in chapter twelve. The original core of seven letters was forged very close to AD 150, and they have not been included in the above list. We have also placed 1 Clement in the middle of the second century instead of its traditional date at the end of the first century.

Dating the Patristic Literature

A Tentative Timeline

	Name or Author	Chronological Markers of Significance
70–90	*The Epistle of Peter to James*	Peter instructs the elders to give the books of his sermons only to the *circumcised,* an indication of authenticity and great antiquity.
	Epistle of Clement to James	Peter endows Clement with the "chair of the teacher." Clement had been asked to compile a book of Peter's sermons and send it to James. He now sets out to publish the *Preaching of Peter,* the precursor to the *Recognitions* and *Homilies of Clement.*
	The Preaching of Peter	This book is introduced to the sectarians in *The Epistle of Peter to James* and *The Epistle of Clement to James.*
	The Didache	Speaks of apostles (i.e., false apostles) in the present tense, so it was written within the first generation. There is an allusion to the Jewish dietary laws, but none to circumcision.
120–140	Papias of Hierapolis	Knew the Gospel of Mark and possibly Revelation.
	The Epistle of Barnabas	Chapter 16 refers to the Hadrianic decree of AD130 to erect a Roman temple in Jerusalem; sprinkled throughout with agrapha.
	The Apology of Aristides	Addressed to Caesar Titus Hadrianus Antoninus, emperor from AD 117 to AD 138.

	Name or Author	Chronological Markers of Significance
140–150	The Shepherd of Hermas	The Muratorian Canon states explicitly that the Shepherd was written when Pius had the oversight of the Roman church; in addition, Vision 2.4 is similar to 2 Clement 14.
	2 Clement	Contains numerous agrapha and two citations of 1 Corinthians 2:9 without attribution. 2 Clement 4.5 and 1 Apology 16:11 both employ the phrase "workers of righteousness."
	Peri Pascha	Pre-Pauline; Passover referred to as a "mystery" as it is in Justin's Dialogue 40
	Dialogue with Trypho the Jew	Written after Bar Kokhba Rebellion, contains a loose paraphrase of Romans 3:12–17.
	First Apology of Justin	Bar Kokhba Revolt is "lately raged" and Marcion is "still alive," no knowledge of Paul, expresses doctrine of the Real Presence
	Second Apology of Justin	Expounds Simon Magus myth and contains Johannine language.
150–155	1 Clement	Single mention of Paul, cites 1 Corinthians 2:9; compare chapter 23 with 2 Clement 11. Numerous agrapha.
	Seven Letters of Pseudo-Ignatius	Paul is acknowledged by name, 1 Corinthians is cited, author also knew epistles to Romans and Ephesians. Refers to Ekklesia Katholika and expresses doctrine of the Real Presence in several epistles (Ignatius to Romans 7; Smyrnaeans 7, Ephesians 20).
155–160	Polycarp to the Philippians	Paul is lavishly endorsed and referred to by name four times. He is freely quoted, including: 1 Corinthians, Romans, Ephesians, Philippians, 1 and 2 Timothy, 1 and 2 Thessalonians and Galatians. Also cites 1 Peter, 1 John, Acts, and Tobit.
	The Martyrdom of Polycarp	Cites 1 Corinthians 2:9, is familiar with the epistle to the Romans, and refers to Ekklesia Katholika.

	Name or Author	Chronological Markers of Significance
170–180	*Gospel of Barnabas* (pre-Islam)	Paul is mentioned by name and disparaged; all of the canonical gospels are used, including John. The sectarians circumcised, kept the dietary laws, and washed before prayer. "Barnabas" is one of the Twelve, contrary to Acts 4:36, showing they did not accept the Acts of the Apostles. The strident adoptionist tone tells us it was a controversial issue.
	The Epistle of the Apostles	This document dates itself in chapter 17. It was initially written around AD 150 and redacted AD 180. The later interpolation, chapters 31 to 33, consists of a "prophesy" of a man named Saul, indicating a familiarity with Acts.
	Muratorian Canon	The Pauline corpus and Acts are fully accepted and the fragment refers to the *Ekklesia Katholika*. The Canonist omits 1 Peter while just a few years later, the epistle is cited by Irenaeus, Tertullian, and Clement of Alexandria.
	Syriac *Teaching of the Apostles*	The book is a lame attempt to integrate the old proto-Catholic mythology of the apostolic period with the history presented in Acts. Paul is known, but his history is subtly distorted. The Church went on to accept the canonical Acts, even in conservative Syria. A production late in the second century is indicated.

Epistle of Peter to James

Peter to James, the lord and bishop of the holy Church, under the Father of all, through Jesus Christ, wishes peace always:

1. Knowing, my brother, your eager desire after that which is for the advantage of us all, I beg and beseech you not to communicate to any one of the Gentiles the books of my preachings which I sent to you, nor to any one of our own tribe before trial; but if anyone has been proved and found worthy, then to commit them to him, after the manner in which Moses delivered *his books* to the Seventy who succeeded to his chair. Wherefore also the fruit of that caution appears even till now. For his countrymen keep the same rule of monarchy and polity everywhere, being unable in any way to think otherwise, or to be led out of the way of the much-indicating Scriptures. For, according to the rule delivered to them, they endeavor to correct the discordances of the Scriptures, if any one, haply not knowing the traditions, is confounded at the various utterances of the prophets. Wherefore they charge no one to teach, unless he has first learned how the Scriptures must be used. And thus they have amongst them one God, one law, one hope.

2. In order, therefore, that the like may also happen to those among us as to these Seventy, give the books of my preachings to our brethren, with the like mystery of initiation, that they may indoctrinate those who wish to take part in teaching; for if it be not so done, our word of truth will be rent into many opinions. And this I know, not as being a prophet, but as already seeing the beginning of this very evil. For some from among the Gentiles have rejected my legal preaching, attaching themselves to certain lawless and trifling preaching of the man who is my enemy. And these things some have attempted while I am still alive, to transform my

words by certain various interpretations, in order to the dissolution of the law; as though I also myself were of such a mind, but did not freely proclaim it, which God forbid! For such a thing were to act in opposition to the law of God which was spoken by Moses, and was borne witness to by our Lord in respect of its eternal continuance; for thus he spoke: "The heavens and the earth shall pass away, but one jot or one tittle shall in no wise pass from the law." And this He has said, that all things might come to pass. But these men, professing, I know not how, to know my mind, undertake to explain my words, which they have heard of me, more intelligently than I who spoke them, telling their catechumens that this is my meaning, which indeed I never thought of. But if, while I am still alive, they dare thus to misrepresent me, how much more will those who shall come after me dare to do so!

3. Therefore, that no such thing may happen, for this end I have prayed and besought you not to communicate the books of my preaching which I have sent you to any one, whether of our own nation or of another nation, before trial; but if any one, having been tested, has been found worthy, then to hand them over to him, according to the initiation of Moses, by which he delivered *his books* to the Seventy who succeeded to his chair; in order that thus they may keep the faith, and everywhere deliver the rule of truth, explaining all things after our tradition; lest being themselves dragged down by ignorance, being drawn into error by conjectures after their mind, they bring others into the like pit of destruction.

Now the things that seemed good to me, I have fairly pointed out to you; and what seems good to you, do you, my lord, becomingly perform. Farewell.

The Response

4. Therefore James, having read the epistle, sent for the elders; and having read it to them, said: "Our Peter has strictly and becomingly charged us concerning the establishing of the truth, that we should not communicate the books of his preachings, which have been sent to us, to any one at random, but to one who is good and religious, and who wishes to teach, and who is circumcised, and faithful. And these are not all to be committed to him at once; that, if he be found injudicious in the first, the others may not be entrusted to him. "Wherefore let him be proved not less than six

years. And then according to the initiation of Moses, he *that is to deliver the books* should bring him to a river or a fountain, which is living water, where the regeneration of the righteous takes place, and should make him, not swear—for that is not lawful—but to stand by the water and adjure, as we ourselves, when we were regenerated, were made to do for the sake of not sinning.

5. "And let him say: 'I take to witness heaven, earth, water, in which all things are comprehended, and in addition to all these, that, air also which pervades all things, and without which I cannot breathe, that I shall always be obedient to him who gives me the books of the preachings; and those same books which he may give me, I shall not communicate to any one in any way, either by writing them, or giving them in writing, or giving them to a writer, either myself or by another, or through any other initiation, or trick, or method, or by keeping them carelessly, or placing them before *any one,* or granting him permission *to see them,* or in any way or manner whatsoever communicating them to another; unless I shall ascertain one to be worthy, as I myself have been judged, or even more so, and that after a probation of not less than six years; but to one who is religious and good, chosen to teach, as I have received them, so I will commit them, doing these things also according to the will of my bishop.

6. "'But otherwise, though he were my son or my brother, or my friend, or otherwise in any way pertaining to me by kindred, if he be unworthy, that I will not vouchsafe the favor to him, as is not meet; and I shall neither be terrified by plot nor mollified by gifts. But if even it should ever seem to me that the books of the preachings given to me are not true, I shall not so communicate them, but shall give them back. And when I go abroad, I shall carry them with me, whatever of them I happen to possess. But if I be not minded to carry them about with me, I shall not suffer them to be in my house, but shall deposit them with my bishop, having the same faith, and setting out from the same persons *as myself.* But if it befall me to be sick, and in expectation of death, and if I be childless, I shall act in the same manner. But if I die having a son who is not worthy, or not yet capable, I shall act in the same manner. For I shall deposit them with my bishop, in order that if my son, when he grows up, be worthy of the trust, he may give them to him as his father's bequest, according to the terms of this engagement.

7. "'And that I shall thus do, I again call to witness heaven, earth, water, in which all things are enveloped, and in addition to all these, the all-pervading air, without which I cannot breathe,

that I shall always be obedient to him who gives me these books of the preachings, and shall observe in all things as I have engaged, or even something more. To me, therefore, keeping this covenant, there shall be a part with the holy ones; but to me doing anything contrary to what I have covenanted, may the universe be hostile to me, and the all-pervading ether, and the God who is over all, to whom none is superior and none is greater. But if even I should come to the acknowledgment of another God, I now swear by him also, be he or be he not, that I shall not do otherwise. And in addition to all these things, if I shall lie, I shall be accursed living and dying, and shall be punished with everlasting punishment.' "And after this, let him partake of bread and salt with him who commits them to him."

8. James having thus spoken, the elders were in an agony of terror. Therefore James, perceiving that they were greatly afraid, said: "Hear me, brethren and fellow-servants. If we should give the books to all indiscriminately, and they should be corrupted by any daring men, or be perverted by interpretations, as you have heard that some have already done, it will remain even for those who really seek the truth, always to wander in error. Wherefore it is better that they should be with us, and that we should communicate them with all the fore-mentioned care to those who wish to live piously, and to save others. But if any one, after taking this adjuration, shall act otherwise, he shall with good reason incur eternal punishment. For why should not he who is the cause of the destruction of others not be destroyed himself?"

The elders, therefore, being pleased with the sentiments of James exclaimed, "Blessed be He who, as foreseeing all things, has graciously appointed thee as our bishop; "and when they had said this, we all rose up, and prayed to the Father and God of all, to whom be glory forever. Amen.[1]

1. Roberts, Alexander and James Donaldson, *The Ante-Nicene Fathers: Translations of the Writings of the Fathers to AD 325*. Volume VIII. Grand Rapids: Wm. B. Eerdmans, 1991. p. 215–7.

Epistle of Clement to James

Clement to James, the lord, and the bishop of bishops, who rules Jerusalem, the holy church of the Hebrews, and the churches everywhere excellently rounded by the providence of God, with the elders and deacons, and the rest of the brethren, peace be always.

1. Be it known to you, my lord, that Simon, who, for the sake of the true faith, and the most sure foundation of his doctrine, was set apart to be the foundation of the Church, and for this end was by Jesus Himself, with His truthful mouth, named Peter, the first-fruits of our Lord, the first of the apostles; to whom first the Father revealed the Son; whom the Christ, with good reason, blessed; the called, and elect, and associate at table and in the journeyings *of Christ;* the excellent and approved disciple, who, as being fittest of all, was commanded to enlighten the darker part of the world, namely the West, and was enabled to accomplish it—and to what extent do I lengthen my discourse, not wishing to indicate what is sad, which yet of necessity, though reluctantly, I must tell you—he himself, by reason of his immense love towards men, having come as far as Rome, clearly and publicly testifying, in opposition to the wicked one who withstood him, that there is to be a good King over all the world, while saving men by his God-inspired doctrine, himself, by violence, exchanged this present existence for life.

2. But about that time, when he was about to die, the brethren being assembled together, he suddenly seized my hand, and rose up, and said in presence of the church: "Hear me, brethren and fellow-servants. Since, as I have been taught by the Lord and Teacher Jesus Christ, whose apostle I am, the day of my death is approaching, I lay hands upon this Clement as your bishop; and to him

I entrust my chair of discourse, even to him who has journeyed with me from the beginning to the end, and thus has heard all my homilies—who, in a word, having had a share in all my trials, has been found steadfast in the faith; whom I have found, above all others, pious, philanthropic, pure, learned, chaste, good, upright, large-hearted, and striving generously to bear the ingratitude of some of the catechumens.

"Wherefore I communicate to him the power of binding and loosing, so that with respect to everything which he shall ordain in the earth, it shall be decreed in the heavens. For he shall bind what ought to be bound, and loose what ought to be loosed, as knowing the role of the Church. Therefore hear him, as knowing that he who grieves the president of the truth, sins against Christ, and offends the Father of all. Wherefore he shall not live; and therefore it becomes him who presides to hold the place of a physician, and not to cherish the rage of an irrational beast."

3. While he thus spoke, I knelt to him, and entreated him, declining the honor and the authority of the chair. But he answered: "Concerning this matter do not ask me; for it has seemed to me to be good that thus it be, and all the more if you decline it. For this chair has not need of a presumptuous man, ambitious of occupying it, but of one pious in conduct and deeply skilled in the word *of God*.

"But show me a better *than yourself*, who has travelled more with me, and has heard more of my discourses, and has learned better the regulations of the Church, and I shall not force you to do well against your will. But it will not be in your power to show me your superior; for you are the choice first-fruits of the multitudes saved through me. However, consider this further, that if you do not undertake the administration of the Church, through fear of the danger of sin, you may be sure that you sin more, when you have it in your power to help the godly, who are, as it were, at sea and in danger, and will not do so, providing only for your own interest, and not for the common advantage of all. But that it behooves you altogether to undertake the danger, while I do not cease to ask it of you for the help of all, you well understand. The sooner, therefore, you consent, so much the sooner will you relieve me from anxiety."

4. "But I myself also, O Clement, know the griefs and anxieties, and dangers and reproaches, that are appointed you from the uninstructed multitudes; and these you will be able to bear nobly, looking to the great reward of patience bestowed on you by God. But also consider this fairly with me: When has Christ need of

your aid? Now, when the wicked one has sworn war against His bride; or in the time to come, when He shall reign victorious, having no need of further help? Is it not evident to anyone who has even the least understanding, that it is now? "Therefore with all good-will hasten in the time of the present necessity to do battle on the side of this good King, whose character it is to give great rewards after victory. Therefore take the oversight gladly; and all the more in good time, because you have learned from me the administration of the Church, for the safety of the brethren who have taken refuge with us."

5. "However, I wish, in the presence of all, to remind you, for the sake of all, of the things belonging to the administration. It becomes you, living without reproach, with the greatest earnestness to shake off all the cares of life, being neither a surety, nor an advocate, nor involved in any other secular business. For Christ does not wish to appoint you either a judge or an arbitrator in business, or negotiator of the secular affairs of the present life, lest, being confined to the present cares of men, you should not have leisure by the word of truth to separate the good among men from the bad.

"But let the disciples perform these offices to one another, and not withdraw *you* from the discourses which are able to save. For as it is wicked for you to undertake secular cares, and to omit the doing of what you have been commanded to do, so it is sin for every layman, if they do not stand by one another even in secular necessities. And if all do not understand to take order that you be without care in respect of the things in which you ought to be, let them learn it from the deacons; that you may have the care of the Church always, in order both to your administering it well, and to your holding forth the words of truth."

6. "Now, if you were occupied with secular cares, you should deceive both yourself and your hearers. For not being able, on account of occupation, to point out the things that are advantageous, both you should be punished, as not having taught what was profitable, and they, not having learned, should perish by reason of ignorance. "Wherefore do you indeed preside over them without occupation, so as to send forth seasonably the words that are able to save them; and so let them listen to you, knowing that whatever the ambassador of the truth shall bind upon earth is bound also in heaven, and what he shall loose is loosed. But you shall bind what ought to be bound, and loose what ought to be loosed. And these, and such like, are the things that relate to you as president."

7. "And with respect to the presbyters, take these *instructions*. Above all things, let them join the young betimes in marriage, anticipating the entanglements of youthful lusts. But neither let them neglect the marriage of those who are already old; for lust is vigorous even in some old men.

"Lest, therefore, fornication find a place among you, and bring upon you a very pestilence, take precaution, and search, lest at any time the fire of adultery be secretly kindled among you. For adultery is a very terrible thing, even such that it holds the second place in respect of punishment, the first being assigned to those who are in error, even although they be chaste. "Wherefore do you, as elders of the Church, exercise the spouse of Christ to chastity (by the spouse I mean the body of the Church); for if she be apprehended to be chaste by her royal Bridegroom, she shall obtain the greatest honor; and you, as wedding guests, shall receive great commendation. But if she be caught having sinned, she herself indeed shall be cast out; and you shall suffer punishment, if at any time her sin has been through your negligence."

8. "Wherefore above all things be careful about chastity; for fornication has been marked out as a bitter thing in the estimation of God. But there are many forms of fornication, as also Clement himself will explain to you. "The first is adultery, that a man should not enjoy his own wife alone, or a woman not enjoy her own husband alone. If anyone be chaste, he is able also to be philanthropic, on account of which he shall obtain eternal mercy. For as adultery is a great evil, so philanthropy is the greatest good.

"Wherefore love all your brethren with grave and compassionate eyes, performing to orphans the part of parents, to widows that of husbands, affording them sustenance with all kindliness, arranging marriages for those who are in their prime, and for those who are without a profession, the means of necessary support through employment; giving work to the artificer, and alms to the incapable."

9. "But I know that ye will do these things if you fix love into your minds; and for its entrance there is one only fit means, viz., the common partaking of food. Wherefore see to it that ye be frequently one another's guests, as ye are able, that you may not fail of it. For it is the cause of well-doing, and well-doing of salvation. "Therefore all of you present your provisions in common to all your brethren in God, knowing that, giving temporal things, you shall receive eternal things. Much more feed the hungry, and give drink to the thirsty, and clothing to the naked; visit the sick; showing yourselves to those who are in prison, help them as ye are able,

and receive strangers into your houses with all alacrity. However, not to speak in detail, philanthropy will teach you to do everything that is good, as misanthropy suggests ill-doing to those who will not be saved."

10. "Let the brethren who have causes to be settled not be judged by the secular authorities; but let them by all means be reconciled by the elders of the church, yielding ready obedience to them. Moreover, also, flee avarice, inasmuch as it is able, under pretext of temporal gain, to deprive you of eternal blessings. "Carefully keep your balances, your measures, your weights, and the things belonging to your traffic, just. Be faithful with respect to your trusts. "Moreover, you will persevere in doing these things, and things similar to these, until the end, if you have in your hearts an ineradicable remembrance of the judgment that is from God. For who would sin, being persuaded that at the end of life there is a judgment appointed of the righteous God, who only now is long-suffering and good,3 that the good may in future enjoy forever unspeakable blessings; but the sinners being found as evil, shall obtain an eternity of unspeakable punishment. And, indeed, that these things are so, it would be reasonable to doubt, were it not that the Prophet of the truth has said and sworn that it shall be."

11. "Wherefore, being disciples of the true Prophet, laying aside double-mindedness, from which comes ill-doing, eagerly undertake well-doing. But if any of you doubt concerning the things which I have said are to be, let him confess it without shame, if he cares for his own soul, and he shall be satisfied by the president. But if he has believed rightly, let his conversation be with confidence, as fleeing from the great fire of condemnation, and entering into the eternal good kingdom of God."

12. "Moreover let the deacons of the church, going about with intelligence, be as eyes to the bishop, carefully inquiring into the doings of each member of the church, *ascertaining* who is about to sin, in order that, being arrested with admonition by the president, he may haply not accomplish the sin. "Let them check the disorderly, that they may not desist from assembling to hear the discourses, so that they may be able to counteract by the word of truth those anxieties that fall upon the heart from every side, by means of worldly casualties and evil communications; for if they long remain fallow, they become fuel for the fire.

"And let them learn who are suffering under bodily disease, and let them bring them to the notice of the multitude who do not know of them, that they may visit them, and supply their wants according to the judgment of the president. Yea, though they do this without his knowledge, they do nothing amiss. These things, then, and things like to these, let the deacons attend to."

13. "Let the catechists instruct, being first instructed; for it is a work relating to the souls of men. For the teacher of the word must accommodate himself to the various judgments of the learners. The catechists must therefore be learned, and unblameable, of much experience, and approved, as you will know that Clement is, who is to be your instructor after me. For it were too much for me now to go into details. However, if ye be of one mind, you shall be able to reach the haven of rest, where is the peaceful city of the great King."

14. "For the whole business of the Church is like unto a great ship, bearing through a violent storm men who are of many places, and who desire to inhabit the city of the good kingdom. Let, therefore, God be your shipmaster; and let the pilot be likened to Christ, the mate4 to the bishop, and the sailors to the deacons, the midshipmen to the catechists, the multitude of the brethren to the passengers, the world to the sea; the foul winds to temptations, persecutions, and dangers; and all manner of afflictions to the waves; the land winds and their squalls to the discourses of deceivers and false prophets; the promontories and rugged rocks to the judges in high places threatening terrible things; the meetings of two seas, and the wild places, to unreasonable men and those who doubt of the promises of truth. "Let hypocrites be regarded as like to pirates. Moreover, account the strong whirlpool, and the Tartarean Charybdis, and murderous wrecks, and deadly founderings, to be nought but sins. In order, therefore, that, sailing with a fair wind, you may safely reach the haven of the hoped-for city, pray so as to be heard. But prayers become audible by good deeds."

15. "Let therefore the passengers remain quiet, sitting in their own places, lest by disorder they occasion rolling or careening. Let the midshipmen give heed to the fare. Let the deacons neglect nothing with which they are entrusted; let the presbyters, like sailors, studiously arrange what is needful for each one. Let the bishop, as the mate, wakefully ponder the words of the pilot alone. Let Christ, even the Saviour, be loved as the pilot, and alone believed in the matters of which He speaks; and let all pray to God for a prosperous voyage. "Let those sailing expect every tribulation, as traveling over a great and troubled sea, the world: sometimes, indeed, disheartened, persecuted, dispersed, hungry, thirsty, naked, hemmed in; and, again, sometimes united, congregated, at rest; but also sea-sick, giddy, vomiting, that is, confessing sins, like disease-producing bile—I mean the sins proceeding from bitterness,

and the evils accumulated from disorderly lusts, by the confession of which, as by vomiting, you are relieved of your disease, attaining healthful safety by means of carefulness.

16. "But know all of you that the bishop labors more than you all; because each of you suffers his own affliction, but he his own and that of every one. Wherefore, O Clement, preside as a helper to every one according to your ability, being careful of the cares of all. Whence I know that in your undertaking the administration, I do not confer, but receive, a favor.

"But take courage and bear it generously, as knowing that God will recompense you when you enter the haven of rest, the greatest of blessings, a reward that cannot be taken from you, in proportion as you have undertaken more labor for the safety of all. So that, if many of the brethren should hate you on account of your lofty righteousness, their hatred shall nothing hurt you, but the love of the righteous God shall greatly benefit you. Therefore endeavor to shake off the praise that arises from injustice, and to attain the profitable praise that is from Christ on account of righteous administration."

17. Having said this, and more than this, he looked again upon the multitude, and said: "And you also, my beloved brethren and fellow-servants, be subject to the president of the truth in all things, knowing this, that he who grieves him has not received Christ, with whose chair he has been entrusted; and he who has not received Christ shall be regarded as having despised the Father; wherefore he shall be cast out of the good kingdom.

"On this account, endeavor to come to all the assemblies, lest as deserters you incur the charge of sin through the disheartening of your captain. Wherefore all of you think before all else of the things that relate to him, knowing this, that the wicked one, being the more hostile on account of every one of you, wars against him alone. Do you therefore strive to live in affection towards him, and in kindliness towards one another, and to obey him, in order that both he may be comforted and you may be saved."

18. "But some things also you ought of yourselves to consider, on account of his not being able to speak openly by reason of the plots. Such as: if he be hostile to any one, do not wait for his speaking; and do not take part with that man, but prudently follow the bishop's will, being enemies to those to whom he is an enemy, and not conversing with those with whom he does not converse, in order that every one, desiring to have you all as his friends, may be reconciled to him and be saved, listening to his discourse.

"But if any one remain a friend of those to whom he is an enemy, and speak to those with whom he does not converse, he also himself is one of those who would waste the church. For, being with you in body, but not with you in judgment, he is against you; and is much worse than the open enemies from without, since with seeming friendship he disperses those who are within."

19. Having thus spoken, he laid his hands upon me in the presence of all, and compelled me to sit in his own chair. And when I was seated, he immediately said to me: "I entreat you, in the presence of all the brethren here, that whensoever I depart from this life, as depart I must, you send to James the brother of the Lord a brief account of your reasonings from your boyhood, and how from the beginning until now you have journeyed with me, hearing the discourses preached by me in every city, and *seeing* my deeds. And then at the end you will not fail to inform him of the manner of my death, as I said before. "For that event will not grieve him very much, when he knows that I piously went through what it behooved me to suffer. And he will get the greatest comfort when he learns, that not an unlearned man, or one ignorant of life-giving words, or not knowing the rule of the Church, shall be entrusted with the chair of the teacher after me. For the discourse of a deceiver destroys the souls of the multitudes who hear."

20. Whence I, my lord James, having promised as I was ordered, have not failed to write in books by chapters the greater part of his discourses in every city, which have been already written to you, and sent by himself, as for a token; and thus I despatched them to you, inscribing them "*Clement's Epitome of the Popular Sermons of Peter.*" However, I shall begin to set them forth, as I was ordered.[1]

1. Roberts, Alexander and James Donaldson, *The Ante-Nicene Fathers: Translations of the Writings of the Fathers to AD 325.* Volume VIII. Grand Rapids: Wm. B. Eerdmans, 1991. p. 218–22.

The Didache

The Lord's Teaching Through the Twelve Apostles to the Nations

1. There are two ways, one of life and one of death, but a great difference between the two ways. The way of life, then, is this: First, you shall love God who made you; second, love your neighbor as yourself, and do not do to another what you would not want done to you. And of these sayings the teaching is this: Bless those who curse you, and pray for your enemies, and fast for those who persecute you. For what reward is there for loving those who love you? Do not the Gentiles do the same? But love those who hate you, and you shall not have an enemy. Abstain from fleshly and worldly lusts. If someone strikes your right cheek, turn to him the other also, and you shall be perfect. If someone impresses you for one mile, go with him two. If someone takes your cloak, give him also your coat. If someone takes from you what is yours, ask it not back, for indeed you are not able. Give to everyone who asks you, and ask it not back; for the Father wills that to all should be given of our own blessings (free gifts). Happy is he who gives according to the commandment, for he is guiltless. Woe to him who receives; for if one receives who has need, he is guiltless; but he who receives not having need shall pay the penalty, why he received and for what. And coming into confinement, he shall be examined concerning the things which he has done, and he shall not escape from there until he pays back the last penny. And also concerning this, it has been said, Let your alms sweat in your hands, until you know to whom you should give.

2. And the second commandment of the Teaching; You shall not commit murder, you shall not commit adultery, you shall not commit pederasty, you shall not commit fornication, you shall not steal, you shall not practice magic, you shall not practice

witchcraft, you shall not murder a child by abortion nor kill that which is born. You shall not covet the things of your neighbor, you shall not swear, you shall not bear false witness, you shall not speak evil, you shall bear no grudge. You shall not be double-minded nor double-tongued, for to be double-tongued is a snare of death. Your speech shall not be false, nor empty, but fulfilled by deed. You shall not be covetous, nor rapacious, nor a hypocrite, nor evil disposed, nor haughty. You shall not take evil counsel against your neighbor. You shall not hate any man; but some you shall reprove, and concerning some you shall pray, and some you shall love more than your own life.

3. My child, flee from every evil thing, and from every likeness of it. Be not prone to anger, for anger leads to murder. Be neither jealous, nor quarrelsome, nor of hot temper, for out of all these murders are engendered. My child, be not a lustful one. for lust leads to fornication. Be neither a filthy talker, nor of lofty eye, for out of all these adulteries are engendered. My child, be not an observer of omens, since it leads to idolatry. Be neither an enchanter, nor an astrologer, nor a purifier, nor be willing to look at these things, for out of all these idolatry is engendered. My child, be not a liar, since a lie leads to theft. Be neither money-loving, nor vainglorious, for out of all these thefts are engendered. My child, be not a murmurer, since it leads the way to blasphemy. Be neither self-willed nor evil-minded, for out of all these blasphemies are engendered. Rather, be meek, since the meek shall inherit the earth. Be long-suffering and pitiful and guileless and gentle and good and always trembling at the words which you have heard. You shall not exalt yourself, nor give over-confidence to your soul. Your soul shall not be joined with lofty ones, but with just and lowly ones shall it have its intercourse. Accept whatever happens to you as good, knowing that apart from God nothing comes to pass.

4. My child, remember night and day him who speaks the word of God to you, and honor him as you do the Lord. For wherever the lordly rule is uttered, there is the Lord. And seek out day by day the faces of the saints, in order that you may rest upon their words. Do not long for division, but rather bring those who contend to peace. Judge righteously, and do not respect persons in reproving for transgressions. You shall not be undecided whether or not it shall be. Be not a stretcher forth of the hands to receive and a drawer of them back to give. If you have anything, through your hands you shall give ransom for your sins. Do not hesitate to give, nor complain when you give; for you shall know who is the good repayer of the hire. Do not turn away from him who is

in want; rather, share all things with your brother, and do not say that they are your own. For if you are partakers in that which is immortal, how much more in things which are mortal? Do not remove your hand from your son or daughter; rather, teach them the fear of God from their youth. Do not enjoin anything in your bitterness upon your bondman or maidservant, who hope in the same God, lest ever they shall fear not God who is over both; for he comes not to call according to the outward appearance, but to them whom the Spirit has prepared. And you bondmen shall be subject to your masters as to a type of God, in modesty and fear. You shall hate all hypocrisy and everything which is not pleasing to the Lord. Do not in any way forsake the commandments of the Lord; but keep what you have received, neither adding thereto nor taking away therefrom. In the church you shall acknowledge your transgressions, and you shall not come near for your prayer with an evil conscience. This is the way of life.

5. And the way of death is this: First of all it is evil and accursed: murders, adultery, lust, fornication, thefts, idolatries, magic arts, witchcrafts, rape, false witness, hypocrisy, double-heartedness, deceit, haughtiness, depravity, self-will, greediness, filthy talking, jealousy, over-confidence, loftiness, boastfulness; persecutors of the good, hating truth, loving a lie, not knowing a reward for righteousness, not cleaving to good nor to righteous judgment, watching not for that which is good, but for that which is evil; from whom meekness and endurance are far, loving vanities, pursuing revenge, not pitying a poor man, not laboring for the afflicted, not knowing Him Who made them, murderers of children, destroyers of the handiwork of God, turning away from him who is in want, afflicting him who is distressed, advocates of the rich, lawless judges of the poor, utter sinners. Be delivered, children, from all these.

6. See that no one causes you to err from this way of the Teaching, since apart from God it teaches you. For if you are able to bear the entire yoke of the Lord, you will be perfect; but if you are not able to do this, do what you are able. And concerning food, bear what you are able; but against that which is sacrificed to idols be exceedingly careful; for it is the service of dead gods.

7. And concerning baptism, baptize this way: Having first said all these things, baptize into the name of the Father, and of the Son, and of the Holy Spirit, in living water. But if you have no living water, baptize into other water; and if you cannot do so in cold water, do so in warm. But if you have neither, pour out water three times upon the head into the name of Father and Son and

Holy Spirit. But before the baptism let the baptizer fast, and the baptized, and whoever else can; but you shall order the baptized to fast one or two days before.

8. But let not your fasts be with the hypocrites, for they fast on the second and fifth day of the week. Rather, fast on the fourth day and the Preparation [Friday]. Do not pray like the hypocrites, but rather as the Lord commanded in His Gospel, like this: Our Father who art in heaven, hallowed be Thy name. Thy kingdom come. Thy will be done on earth, as it is in heaven. Give us today our daily (needful) bread, and forgive us our debt as we also forgive our debtors. And bring us not into temptation, but deliver us from the evil one (or, evil); for Thine is the power and the glory forever. Pray this three times each day.

9. Now concerning the Eucharist, give thanks this way. First, concerning the cup: We thank thee, our Father, for the holy vine of David Thy servant, which You madest known to us through Jesus Thy Servant; to Thee be the glory forever. And concerning the broken bread: We thank Thee, our Father, for the life and knowledge which You madest known to us through Jesus Thy Servant; to Thee be the glory forever. Even as this broken bread was scattered over the hills, and was gathered together and became one, so let Thy Church be gathered together from the ends of the earth into Thy kingdom; for Thine is the glory and the power through Jesus Christ forever. But let no one eat or drink of your Eucharist, unless they have been baptized into the name of the Lord; for concerning this also the Lord has said, "Give not that which is holy to the dogs."

10. But after you are filled, give thanks this way: We thank Thee, holy Father, for Thy holy name which You didst cause to tabernacle in our hearts, and for the knowledge and faith and immortality, which You modest known to us through Jesus Thy Servant; to Thee be the glory forever. Thou, Master almighty, didst create all things for Thy name's sake; You gavest food and drink to men for enjoyment, that they might give thanks to Thee; but to us You didst freely give spiritual food and drink and life eternal through Thy Servant. Before all things we thank Thee that You are mighty; to Thee be the glory forever. Remember, Lord, Thy Church, to deliver it from all evil and to make it perfect in Thy love, and gather it from the four winds, sanctified for Thy kingdom which Thou have prepared for it; for Thine is the power and the glory forever. Let grace come, and let this world pass away. Hosanna to the God (Son) of David! If anyone is holy, let him come; if any one is not so, let him repent. Maranatha. Amen. But permit the prophets to make Thanksgiving as much as they desire.

11. Whosoever, therefore, comes and teaches you all these things that have been said before, receive him. But if the teacher himself turns and teaches another doctrine to the destruction of this, hear him not. But if he teaches so as to increase righteousness and the knowledge of the Lord, receive him as the Lord. But concerning the apostles and prophets, act according to the decree of the Gospel. Let every apostle who comes to you be received as the Lord. But he shall not remain more than one day; or two days, if there's a need. But if he remains three days, he is a false prophet. And when the apostle goes away, let him take nothing but bread until he lodges. If he asks for money, he is a false prophet. And every prophet who speaks in the Spirit you shall neither try nor judge; for every sin shall be forgiven, but this sin shall not be forgiven. But not everyone who speaks in the Spirit is a prophet; but only if he holds the ways of the Lord. Therefore from their ways shall the false prophet and the prophet be known. And every prophet who orders a meal in the Spirit does not eat it, unless he is indeed a false prophet. And every prophet who teaches the truth, but does not do what he teaches, is a false prophet. And every prophet, proved true, working unto the mystery of the Church in the world, yet not teaching others to do what he himself does, shall not be judged among you, for with God he has his judgment; for so did also the ancient prophets. But whoever says in the Spirit, Give me money, or something else, you shall not listen to him. But if he tells you to give for others' sake who are in need, let no one judge him.

12. But receive everyone who comes in the name of the Lord, and prove and know him afterward; for you shall have understanding right and left. If he who comes is a wayfarer, assist him as far as you are able; but he shall not remain with you more than two or three days, if need be. But if he wants to stay with you, and is an artisan, let him work and eat. But if he has no trade, according to your understanding, see to it that, as a Christian, he shall not live with you idle. But if he wills not to do, he is a Christ-monger. Watch that you keep away from such.

13. But every true prophet who wants to live among you is worthy of his support. So also a true teacher is himself worthy, as the workman, of his support. Every first-fruit, therefore, of the products of wine-press and threshing-floor, of oxen and of sheep, you shall take and give to the prophets, for they are your high priests. But if you have no prophet, give it to the poor. If you make a batch of dough, take the first-fruit and give according to the commandment. So also when you open a jar of wine or of oil, take the first-fruit and give it to the prophets; and of money (silver) and

clothing and every possession, take the first-fruit, as it may seem good to you, and give according to the commandment.

14. But every Lord's day gather yourselves together, and break bread, and give thanksgiving after having confessed your transgressions, that your sacrifice may be pure. But let no one who is at odds with his fellow come together with you, until they be reconciled, that your sacrifice may not be profaned. For this is that which was spoken by the Lord: "In every place and time offer to me a pure sacrifice; for I am a great King, says the Lord, and my name is wonderful among the nations."

15. Appoint, therefore, for yourselves, bishops and deacons worthy of the Lord, men meek, and not lovers of money, and truthful and proved; for they also render to you the service of prophets and teachers. Therefore do not despise them, for they are your honored ones, together with the prophets and teachers. And reprove one another, not in anger, but in peace, as you have it in the Gospel. But to anyone that acts amiss against another, let no one speak, nor let him hear anything from you until he repents. But your prayers and alms and all your deeds so do, as you have it in the Gospel of our Lord.

16. Watch for your life's sake. Let not your lamps be quenched, nor your loins unloosed; but be ready, for you know not the hour in which our Lord will come. But come together often, seeking the things which are befitting to your souls: for the whole time of your faith will not profit you, if you are not made perfect in the last time. For in the last days false prophets and corrupters shall be multiplied, and the sheep shall be turned into wolves, and love shall be turned into hate; for when lawlessness increases, they shall hate and persecute and betray one another, and then shall appear the world-deceiver as Son of God, and shall do signs and wonders, and the earth shall be delivered into his hands, and he shall do iniquitous things which have never yet come to pass since the beginning. Then shall the creation of men come into the fire of trial, and many shall be made to stumble and shall perish; but those who endure in their faith shall be saved from under the curse itself. And then shall appear the signs of the truth: first, the sign of an outspreading in heaven, then the sign of the sound of the trumpet. And third, the resurrection of the dead—yet not of all, but as it is said: "The Lord shall come and all His saints with Him." Then shall the world see the Lord coming upon the clouds of heaven.[1]

1. Roberts, Alexander and James Donaldson, *The Ante-Nicene Fathers: Translations of the Writings of the Fathers to AD 325.* Volume VII. Grand Rapids: Wm. B. Eerdmans, 1991. p. 377–382.

Bibliography
Cited Works and Suggested Reading

Amidon, Philip R., *The Panarion of St. Epiphanius, Bishop of Salamis: Selected Passages*. London: Oxford University Press, 1990.

Bauer, Walter, *Orthodoxy and Heresy in Earliest Christianity*. Philadelphia: Fortress, 1971.

Bradshaw, Paul F., Maxwell E. Johnson, and L. Edward Phillips, *The Apostolic Tradition*. Minneapolis: Fortress, 2002.

Connolly, R. Hugh, *Didascalia Apostolorum*. Oxford: Clarendon Press, 1929. http://www.bombaxo.com/didascalia.html, January 22, 2008.

Daube, David, *The New Testament and Rabbinic Judaism*. Peabody, Massachusetts: Hendrickson, 1990.

Dix, Gregory, *The Shape of the Liturgy*. New York: Seabury, 1983.

Dix, Gregory, *Apostolike Paradosis: The Treatise on the Apostolic Tradition of St. Hippolytus of Rome*, 2nd ed. London: SPCK, 1968; reprint Ridgefield, Conn.: Morehouse, 1992.

deSilva, David A, *Introducing the Apocrypha: Message, Context, and Significance*. Grand Rapids, Michigan: Baker, 2002.

Di Sante, Carmine, *Jewish Prayer: The Origins of the Christian Liturgy*, translated by Matthew J. O'Connell New Jersey: Paulist, 1991.

Donin, Rabbi Hayim Halevy, *To Be a Jew*. New York: Basic, 1991.

Donin, Rabbi Hayim Halevy, *To Pray as a Jew*. New York: Basic, 2001.

Gavin, F, *The Jewish Antecedents of the Christian Sacraments*. Whitefish, Mon.: Kessinger,2007.

Grant, Robert M., *The Formation of the New Testament*. New York: Harper and Row, 1965.

Hahneman, Geoffrey Mark, *The Muratorian Fragment and the Development of the Canon*. New York: Oxford University Press: 1992.

Hall, Stuart George, editor, *Melito of Sardis—Peri Pascha*. Oxford: Clarendon Press, 1979.

Harris, Horton, *The Tubingen School*. Oxford: Clarendon Press, 1975.

Harnack, Adolf, *Marcion: The Gospel of the Alien God*. Jamestown, New York: Labyrinth, 1990.

Hertling, Ludwig, S.J. and Engelbert Kirschbaum,, S.J., *The Roman Catacombs and their Martyrs*, translated by M. Joseph Costelloe and S. J. Darton Milwaukee, Wis.: Bruce, 1975.

Hopkins, Clark, *The Discovery of Dura-Europos*. New Haven: Yale University Press, 1979.

Idelsohn, A. Z., *Jewish Liturgy and its Development*. New York: Dover Publications, 1995.

Jaenen, Cornelius J., *The Apostles' Doctrine and Fellowship*. Brooklyn, New York: Legas Publishing, 2003.

James, Montague Rhode, *The Apocryphal New Testament*. Oxford: Clarendon Press, 1924.

Jeremias, Joachim, *The Eucharistic Words of Jesus*. Philadelphia: Fortress, 1977.

Josephus, Flavius, *The Complete Works of Josephus*, translated by William Whiston Grand Rapids: Kregel, 1991.

Klein, Isaac, *A Guide to Jewish Religious Practice*. New York: KTAV, 1992.

Metzger, Bruce M., *The Canon of the New Testament*. Oxford: Clarendon Press, 1987.

Neusner, Jacob, *The Mishnah: A New Translation*. New Haven: Yale University Press, 1988.

Neusner, Jacob, *The Tosefta: Translated from the Hebrew*, volumes I & II Peabody, Massachusetts: Hendrickson, 2002.

Niederwimmer, Kurt, *The Didache: A Commentary*, translated by Linda Maloney Minneapolis: Fortress, 1998.

Oesterley, W.O.E., *The Jewish Background of the Christian Liturgy*. Oxford: Clarendon Press, 1925.

Osiek, Caroline, *Shepherd of Hermas: A Commentary*. Minneapolis: Fortress, 1999.

Petuchowski, Jakob J., Editor, *Contributions to the Scientific Study of Jewish Liturgy*. New York: KTAV, 1970.

Ragg, Lonsdale and Laura Ragg, *The Gospel of Barnabas* London: 1907. http://www.sacred-texts.com/isl/gbar/index.htm, June 1, 2008.

Ramsay, William M. *The Cities and Bishoprics of Phrygia Volume 1, Part 2*. London, Oxford at the Clarendon Press, 1897

Roberts, Alexander and James Donaldson, *The Ante-Nicene Fathers. Translations of the Writings of the Fathers to AD 325*. Grand Rapids: Wm. B. Eerdmans, 1991.

Robinson, John A. T., *Redating the New Testament*. Philadelphia: Westminster, 1976.

Rutgers, L.V., *Subterranean Rome*. Leuven: Peeters, 2000.

Schaff, Philip, *The Nicene and Post-Nicene Fathers*. Grand Rapids: Wm. B. Eerdmans, 1989.

Schaff, Philip and Henry Wace, *The Nicene and Post-Nicene Fathers*. Grand Rapids: Wm. B. Eerdmans, 1991.

Schoedel, William R., *Ignatius of Antioch: A Commentary on the Letters of Ignatius of Antioch*. Philadelphia: Fortress, 1985.

Sheppard, A. R. R. *R.E.C.A.M. Notes and Studies No. 6: Jews, Christians and Heretics in Acmonia and Eumeneia. Anatolian Studies. Vol. 29, 1979, pp. 169–180*. Published by British Institute at Ankara. http://www.tor.org/stable/3642737

Steinsaltz, Adin, *A Guide to Jewish Prayer*. New York: Schocken, 2000.

Stevenson, J., *The Catacombs: Rediscovered Monuments of early Christianity*. Hampshire, Eng.: Thames and Hudson Ltd., 1978.

Suetonius Tranquillus, Gaius, *The Twelve Caesars*, translated by Robert Graves Whitefriars: London, 1970.

Van Voorst, Robert E., *The Ascents of James*. Atlanta: Scholars, 1989.

Williams, Frank, *The Panarion of Epiphanius of Salamis*. New York: E. J. Brill, 1994.

Index

Call-out box subjects and pages are bolded